Halfway Home

The Story of a Father and Son Hiking the Pacific
Crest Trail

Donald L Reavis
Quentin T Reavis

www.DonaldLReavis.com

Copyright ©2015 – Donald L Reavis

ISBN -978-1-942845-27-0

Acknowledgements

Very seldom is an extraordinary accomplishment achieved without the help of others. Writing this book has been no different. First I would like to thank Sharla, who has been my biggest supporter. She continues to be my trail angel long after the journey's end.

I would like to thank my hiking partner Family Man, for his constant input into the contents of *Halfway Home*. His journals, pictures, and excellent memory earned him the position of co-author.

To our editors Aurora Commentz and Doddie Messick we will forever be grateful. Thank you for taking the time out of your busy schedules to edit our adventure. You continue to amaze me the way you refine a manuscript.

Table of Contents

Half Way Home
The story of a father and son hiking the
Pacific Crest Trail
2013

Prologue

Lightning flashed, and for a brief moment it illuminated the jagged mountain above the trail. I sat there on a cold rock looking around with each flash not knowing when I might spot the cougar we were sure we had seen about a half mile back. Another flash and thunder rolled up the valley. *Where is Family Man?* We had missed the last spring and the next reliable water was 15 miles ahead. Family Man had left me with the backpacks twenty minutes earlier to return the estimated 300 yards back down the trail to find the spring.

"Where is Family Man?" I muttered again. It could have been a deer, but the methodical movements of the eyes were different from the many deer we had seen over the last 2619 miles. My thoughts returned to the beginning of the trail where our journey had started five months before. As I thought about what had transpired since we had left the Mexican border, I started softly singing, "O Lord my God/ When I in awesome wonder/ Consider all the worlds Thy Hands have made." The lightning strikes were getting closer now and all I could do was turn to the One who had seen us safely through this far and with much greater volume sing out, "I see the stars, I hear the rolling thunder/ Thy power throughout the universe displayed."

Quentin hiking in Yosemite National Park 2008

Chapter One - The Origin of a Dream

My earliest encounter with the Pacific Crest Trail came through a friend who had hiked the trail from the Mexican border through the High Sierras. He did this thirty plus years ago and twenty years before the official completion of the trail. As Mark Renicker showed us pictures of his adventures, I never even gave much thought to adding it to my bucket list. I do recall how I thought he had accomplished a great thing, and am still of that opinion today.

Thirty years later our family found ourselves tucked away in the little southern California mountain town of Wrightwood only a mile and a half, as the crow flies, from the trail. The trail was one of those things that just existed without interfering in my life. Every May we were reminded of this wayfaring life as the grubby looking hikers made their way into Wrightwood for resupply. They would congregate in front of the post office. Considering they looked homeless and in definite need of a shower, we kept our distance. Eventually it became obvious that this judgmental attitude towards hiker trash did not wear off on my son Quentin. In his teenage years, Quentin and his friends would spend their days up on the mountain and were always friendly to the hikers. It did not take long before the prospect of spending half a year in the wilderness intrigued him, and a dream was born.

Quentin's love for the wilderness drew him to Yosemite for his intern work after graduation from culinary school. Immersion into this environment only intensified his dream. He loved his work and loved the mountains. His days off were spent in riotous living on the edge of disaster, climbing rocks that he felt needed to be climbed. So it was a mixed blessing when he told us he and a friend were going to go backpacking into the backcountry. With my minimal knowledge of this backcountry, all I could think about was mountain lions, bears, and psycho maniacs. I was sure he would get lost in this vast wilderness. How would we deal with his loss? How would his dad handle the crisis? I have been told that I may be a little over controlling, and I was not sure how I would fix this challenge if he did come up missing. Nevertheless, he never asked if he could take this weekend jaunt, so I could always blame his disappearance on his own stupidity. I really struggled with God during the few days Quentin was off the grid. The situation was so far out of my control that I had to let God in. All I could do was resign myself to the inadequacy of my abilities.

Quentin and Steve returned safely from their sixty mile hike with pictures and stories of a beautiful country and an experience of endurance. There was excitement in his voice as he talked about the days of pushing on down the trail while experiencing the panorama of nature with every step. Like a drug addict strung out on coke, Quentin knew these days out on the trail only intensified the burn for more.

Meanwhile I was busy eating cheeseburgers and fries to maintain the incredible healthy body I had grown into. I still had no intentions of hiking any trail, let alone a long one. Sharla, my wife and best friend, has always loved hiking the trails around Wrightwood and tried many times to get me to join her. I avoided such strenuous activities by making excuses whenever possible.

7

This all changed when the doctor advised I either lose weight or take the chance of becoming a diabetic. He was even crazy enough to use the term obese. We knew a lifestyle change was necessary so we purchased a treadmill and started walking. Working our way up from twenty minutes the first day to being able to do seven miles in two hours gave me confidence that weight loss was possible. Returning to Wrightwood after a year in Florida, I had walked over six hundred miles on the treadmill and lost thirty-five pounds. My attitude about hiking trails was changing as I acquired the desire to do my walking outdoors instead of going nowhere on a machine. It was about this time when Quentin hit me up with the idea of a father/son PCT hiking team. Apprehensive about completing such an undertaking, I finally agreed to hike from the Mexican border to Wrightwood with him. Once he had broken down my resistance, he intensified his resolve to achieve his dream.

Mount Whitney

Chapter Two - Physical, Emotional and Financial

Now that you know how a dream of this magnitude is conceived and allowed to foster in one's life, we will attempt to share the road from dream to reality. This is not intended to be a "how to" book, enough of those already exist. We will only cover a few things to give you a little background of what we went through. There are three factors we had to consider before an undertaking of this magnitude was possible: physical conditioning, emotional preparedness, and finances.

To say we properly prepared ourselves for the physical demands of the PCT would be stretching it at best. We spent hours on the treadmill, which kept the legs in motion and toughened the feet. Sharla shared my newfound love of backpacking and joined in on the training. After doing a few day trips around the local mountains we decided to tackle the 90 miles of trail from Big Bear to Wrightwood. I took a couple of days off work and on June 29, 2011, our daughter dropped us off at the trail above Big Bear. You could tell by the size of our backpacks we were amateurs. My pack weighed in at close to 55 pounds and Sharla's oversized load with the bear canister weighed 45 pounds. It was only due to our inexperience that we took a bear canister on this part of the trail. When we shared with people the adventure on which we were about to embark, which at that time we considered extreme, everyone had an opinion and offered a lot of professional advice. So not only did we carry the bear canister for the food, we both carried pepper spray canisters clipped to our chest. I really believe that if a bear had spotted us on the trail, it would most likely have died laughing after telling the other bears about the two overloaded hikers stumbling down the trail.

On the third day of that hike it got hot. Really hot! Like, who is crazy enough to go hiking over the 4th of July weekend hot? When we passed the Deep Creek Hot Springs, we witnessed a naturalist dancing in the sand next to the springs, and any desire we had of resting there quickly vanished. After cooling off in the river at a less populated spot, we continued on down the trail. In the early afternoon the temperature rose to well over a hundred degrees and, with the sun beating off the granite, we were cooking. We stopped to rest in what little shade we could find and were fairly sure we were close to having a heat stroke. Our water was as hot as we were, and we decided it was time to get off the trail. When we came out of the valley we had cell service and called our friends to bail us out. We returned in June of 2012 to the base of Deep Creek and finished the trail up to Wrightwood. Finishing this segment raised our trail experience to a hundred miles.

Once we had taken up hiking, Mount Whitney showed up on our radar. Just a little blip at first, but the desire continued to grow until we won the lottery for a single day permit. On July 10, 2011 at 2:30 in the morning Sharla and I along with Quentin, his wife, Brittany, and two others started up the tallest mountain in the contiguous United States. Above 13,000 feet, altitude sickness became very real to the point two of our party were not able to go on. To start back down was one of the toughest decisions I have ever had to make. The emotions of accepting failure after exerting this much energy were overwhelming. Three of us turned around while the others continued to climb. Only two made it to the top.

We learned a valuable lesson on this failed attempt and started laying plans for another try at the summit. Six weeks later, Sharla and I returned to Whitney Portals where we attained a last minute permit. That afternoon we climbed to Lone Pine Lake, just over 10,000 feet, where we stopped for the night. The next day we climbed to 12,000 feet and set up camp. These short days were necessary to allow our bodies to acclimate to the altitude. On the third morning, we woke up at 4:00 a.m. With the help of headlamps we started up the switchbacks to the crest. The stars were extremely bright and the Milky Way flooded the sky. From a thousand feet above the camp we could see a line of headlamps as other climbers inched their way up the mountain. We made it to the crest at the same time the sun popped above the horizon bringing definition to the jagged snow splattered peaks beyond. Climbing the rugged granite trail from the crest to the summit on that cold August morning, we felt the effect caused by the lack of oxygen. We summited Mount Whitney at 8:20 a.m. where we found three guys smoking weed. I don't know if it was the altitude or the excitement of the accomplishment, but it was difficult to even sign the register. The 14,497 foot mountain had been conquered giving way to greater challenges.

It had been Sharla's plan to join us for a good part of the PCT, but her real interest was the High Sierras via the John Muir Trail (JMT). We came to an agreement that Sharla and I would hike the JMT in 2012, and then the girls would be our support for the PCT in 2013. On the afternoon of July 30th after picking up our permits at Lone Pine, Sharla and I left Whitney Portals during a thunderstorm with heavy packs and climbed to Lone Pine Lake. Repeating what we had done the year before we took a couple of days to acclimate. On the third day we crossed over the crest at 13,700 feet. Spread out in front of us were mountains of solid granite for as far as the eye could see. Below we could see the crystal clear waters of Hitchcock and Guitar lakes. Beyond Guitar Lake another lake was visible, aptly named Timberline Lake. On down the valley, behind the jagged granite peaks, was where we planned to spend the night.

11

The step over the crest to start the descent into the unknown was taken with excitement and apprehension. I had lain awake many nights contemplating this very moment. We had seen this vast valley beyond the crest. The interior with miles upon miles of immaculate landscape only seen in pictures by most, also brought the dangers of isolation. For the next two weeks we would not be able to hear from our family. Though our friends and family might argue, we had weighed this aspect of the adventure and had come to grips with the consequences of being off the grid. When we stepped down off the crest we no longer had communication with the outside world.

Making it down to Crabtree Meadows that evening, we found we were not alone even this deep into the mountains. We could hear people hollering over on the other side of the stream and two other hikers were camped just a couple hundred yards away from our tent. A mule team came out of the ranger station the next morning and headed up the trail which we had descended. We met a number of southbound JMT hikers including a 75 year old lady hiking solo. She had told her 80 year old husband that she wanted to hike the trail before she got too old. We found out later she made it all the way up Mount Whitney. A family from Michigan was making this their summer vacation.

We climbed over Big Horn Plateau and, after spending a night along Tyndall Creek, started the climb to Forester Pass. By now we realized we were going to be blessed with thunderstorms each afternoon. This day was no exception. We waited by the lake at the bottom of the switchbacks for one storm to play out. One lightning strike on the ridge left a crashing echo bouncing off the granite walls. Finally it moved on, and we started the climb to the pass. As we climbed, another dark and menacing cloud rolled over the ridge to the southwest and the thunder gave way to hail. Wrapped in our ponchos we hunkered down somewhat beneath a boulder as half inch diameter hail plummeted around us. This was not our idea of a pleasant afternoon.

When we crossed over Forester Pass at 13,200 feet, we were again treated to an awesome view of the valley beyond. Water trickled out from beneath what little snow was left on the mountain joining the springs that were coming out of the rocks. With every step, we descended towards the valley where the streams came together to make Bubbs Creek. More of a river than a creek, the water tumbled over the rocks rushing to get to the valley below. We followed the river through Vidette Meadows, and where Bubbs Creek turned left and headed for the Pacific, we turned right climbing towards Charlotte Lake. Over the next few days we climbed over Glen, Pinchot, and Mather passes. We strolled along the bubbling streams, walked around the reflecting lakes, and descended the Golden Staircase. We walked along the swampy meadows as we headed up towards Muir Pass. It was there that we stopped along the Middle Fork of Kings Canyon for a lunch of noodles.

As we sat there next to the river discussing the climb that lay ahead, it became clear to me that Sharla was discouraged. We had been dreaming of a long warm shower and real food we could indulge in at the Vermillion Valley Resort on Edison Lake in a few days. Sadly, we had just run into a south bounder who advised that the ferry had stopped running due to the low water in the lake. So our dream of a nice warm shower, clean clothes and real food was ripped from our grasp. Along with being out of communications with our family while our daughter was in Russia on a mission trip, that news was more than Sharla could handle. I knew what I had to do. I had to give her an out. It really didn't matter to me, as I would be passing this way again. It was decided we would exit over Bishop Pass. The climb over Bishop Pass was not an easy one as it was our sixth high altitude pass. We spent our last night in the wilderness along a lake in Dusy Basin. We were tired and hungry as we walked into South Lake the next afternoon. Even though we didn't make it to Yosemite, we left the trail with a sense of accomplishment. We now had the confidence that we could survive in the wilderness and enough experience to plan a PCT thru hike.

Training for the emotional stress of the trail is no less crucial than the physical training. During our little jaunt over the High Sierras, Sharla and I were introduced to the mental aspect of backpacking. Not really knowing how to prepare ourselves for this emotional upheaval, we started reading in preparation for the PCT. Besides trail journals, which in my opinion are the most accurate depictions of trail life, we read numerous trail related books. The compiled experiences of numerous PCT thru hikers brought us to the conclusion that an emotional bubble would need to be built. This bubble was built through continuous study of the trail, gaining knowledge every day. Another tool we used in gaining knowledge was Google Earth™. Google Earth™ is a virtual interactive globe on to which we could install the map of the PCT. For months up to the departure date we studied the three dimensional trail from one end to the other. Just a note here for the armchair hikers, it's a lot easier to hike Google Earth™ than the real thing. At the beginning of the trail it is necessary to push through a considerable amount of pain as the walls of the emotional bubble are still very thin and can easily be popped.

Many of you may be asking why we would not be relying on God to carry us through this time of emotional challenges. At this point in our planning, we had only asked the Creator for revelation on the sanity of the hike not for emotional support. As we will share later in this book, as our self-reliance deteriorated, our reliance on God strengthened.

Financial responsibility becomes an issue when you're removing yourself from society for any length of time. We will not get into how to handle your personal finances. PCT thru hiking tends to promote the "disappear and ignore method" which does not settle well in real life. Fortunately, we were able to manage most of our finances online with a majority of those through automatic payment. It is still a difficult thing to let go when you exit the grid, but about six weeks into the hike the cares of the outside world start to disappear giving way to a clearer perception of God's creation and the things that really matter.

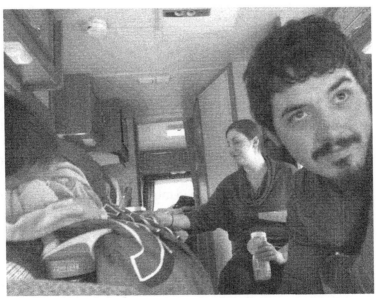
In the RV on the way to Campo

Chapter Three – Heading South

Saturday night was filled with anticipation as we continued to pack and repack our backpacks. Large totes were filled with what looked like obnoxious amounts of instant mashed potatoes, tuna, beef jerky, energy bars, candy and numerous other food items we felt were necessary. Two additional totes, called swap boxes, were placed in the back of the car. These totes were filled with items we would switch out each time we met the support team, based on the needs of the next section. Sleep did not come easily that night. Adrenaline was high and the fear of failure permeated our thoughts. Sunday morning arrived, and we were filled with the excitement of two race horses waiting for the gates to open. We attended what would be our last church service for a few weeks. Trying to keep our mind on the sermon, when we were on the brink of such an adventure, was almost impossible. Our friends wished us well, and we believed their sincerity, even though the looks in their eyes were filled with doubt.

The Southern Terminus of the Pacific Crest Trail is located just outside of Campo, California, and 180 miles south of Wrightwood. When we rolled out of Wrightwood the GPS arrival time showed 2:41 p.m. We were finally on our way. The RV, while organized, was definitely filled to capacity with the four adults, our two grandsons, Hunter and Sawyer, and two dogs (one of which was big enough to pull the caravan), clothes packed in totes, children's toys, a playpen, food, and water.

Campo is one of those out of the way small village places you won't find in a tourist brochure. There are a couple of things to see including a railroad museum. It has a population of around 2600, half of which were border patrol agents and the other half was there to give us directions to the starting point. Being brave and mighty adventurers, we were not interested in their directions. That is until we couldn't for the likes of us find the starting point to the trail which spanned the country. After wandering around the streets of Campo for a half hour in an RV with a car tagging along, we finally succumbed to asking directions. That worked very well and we drove down the gravel road to a ten foot wall that stretched east and west as far as we could see. There were plenty of our finest border patrol agents there to welcome us. We took some time taking pictures of everyone at the seven foot monument to document the beginning our insanity.

First full day on the trail

Chapter Four – Campo to Mount Laguna

April 7ᵗʰ
Day 1 – 2.3 Miles
Total 2.3 Miles

Amidst the scurrying of border agents, we left the southern terminus and were finally on the trail we had so long pursued. Walking north back down the hill we left behind the ten foot corrugated iron wall which separates our country from our southern neighbors. I walked alone through the shrubs that lined the four foot wide trail. Quentin was out ahead with his family who had chosen to walk the beginning of the trail with him. Quentin used this time to walk hand in hand with his son and convey to Brittany his appreciation for her support in this awesome journey. It didn't take long before the cool air conditioning prevailed over the hot loose sand of the trail and his family returned to the RV. Shortly after passing the one mile marker we came to a group of houses. No trail, no signs, no idea. Just two confused hikers standing there looking at the map and the gps. A well worn trail led to the back of a house, but the map showed to follow the road. We were standing there contemplating our next move when a gentleman stuck his head above the fence and told us to follow the road. We passed the post office and headed back into the brush and down to Highway 94. As we arrived at the road we met a couple of hikers going south, one of which had been without water for the last ten miles. We gave the dehydrated hikers some water and listened to their stories, taking note of what not to do.

Back in the RV with the car in tow we headed on up to Lake Morena where we set up camp. Located on Cottonwood Creek, the Lake Morena dam was built in the late 1800s to supply fresh water for the city of San Diego. For the next two nights this campground would be home to the support team and a place for us to stop in for the night.

Sharla, Quentin and Hunter enjoyed the evening exploring the area and found some boulders to climb. The smile on Hunter's face was priceless as he experienced his first rock climbing. We were soon to realize that first time experiences like these were what this journey was all about.

We had to have a campfire to set the ambiance to our first night on the trail. We located firewood and hotdogs at a small grocery store. This ended up being the only campfire we lit over the next five months. We watched the boys play as the sunset closed out this first day.

April 8th
Day 2 – 17.7 Miles
Total 20 Miles

The sun was not yet up when we crawled out of bed on our second day. The wind had picked up over the night causing the RV to rock like a dingy on the ocean and the clatter of the awning was most annoying. Quentin had already taken his dog, Whiskey, for a walk and was anxious to get on the trail. The sunshine of yesterday had been replaced with low clouds and light rain. What a way to start a long hike. To experience wet feet and soggy pants so early on the trail was not encouraging.

Sharla dropped us off at Highway 94 where we met another hiker. Lucy, a young lady from Seattle, had started at the monument at first light. Heading north, we soon crossed railroad tracks and a couple of streams. We continued to climb higher into the hills, making good time even though the rain was like ice pellets hitting our face. Stopping for a short breakfast break, we were overtaken by Tom, a hiker we had met the day before at the monument. Tom decided not to pass us since he wanted to take a break as well. During this encounter, Whiskey was in no mood to be friendly. Quentin did a good job of calming down the Labrador retriever.

As we rounded a hill overlooking the valley to the east we came across another hiker we named "Jeremiah Johnson." This hiker looked more like a mountain man than any hiker I have ever seen. We spotted Jeremiah Johnson standing tall and strong against the wind as he enjoyed the view of the valley where some bulls were fighting. An interesting gentleman, I must say, with things hanging all over his pack he must have acquired at the last trading post. The weight of his pack had to be approaching 80 pounds.

Tom caught up with us after lunch. Considering Whiskey had already met Tom we were not too concerned. At about five paces Whiskey became violent and decided this guy was a stranger. Fortunately, Tom was ready and stopped him with his trekking poles. You could tell it scared him though as he became a little irate telling Quentin that if Whiskey did that again he would "put the hurt on him." Not blaming Tom, we defused the situation and let him move ahead out of sight before the leash came off of the dog whose new trail name was "Killer."

Two miles later we came upon a dirt road where the PCT appeared to have ended. Tom was standing fifty yards to the left studying his maps, so it became leash time again for Whiskey. Tom came back down the road and apologized for his previous outburst. Quentin and Tom spent the next few minutes studying their maps and came to the conclusion we were to head south. Six tenths of a mile later we found the trail leading down a steep hill to Hauser Creek. We found the creek dry as a bone and an empty gallon water container sitting next to a sign post. Crossing the dry creek bed we climbed fifteen hundred feet to a fairly level hike across the top.

The cold mist continued as Lake Morena came into view. The sight of the campground down below brought excitement to the tired hikers anxious to be with their family. Just then a vulture flew a few feet in front as a reminder to always enjoy the moment and the beauty that's all around. Our first full day was complete and we were ready for a hot shower and warm, dry clothes.

April 9th
Day 3 – 22.6 Miles
Total 42.6 Miles

We were up at 5:45 for a six o'clock departure time. Making use of the restroom before departure, we found Jeremiah Johnson had made the shower area his hotel for the night. It sounded like he had arrived only moments earlier. Tom was outside his tent finishing breakfast when we walked by. Lucy, the girl we had met yesterday, was buried deep inside her tent.

The first six miles were fairly flat with only a few small hills. Under Buckman Spring Road, we crossed Cottonwood Creek and rested to cool our feet. While sitting there, Quentin noticed a bum dressed in camouflage tucked up under the bridge. With this being only day three, we were still green horns and were a little concerned.

A short time later we crossed underneath Interstate 8 along Kitchen Creek. Leaving the sounds of the highway behind us, we started a long drudging climb up to five thousand feet. The day was sunny and warm with a few scattered clouds giving us only moments of shade. Our feet woke up to the realization that this was not just a weekend walk in the park. They complained like a baby with diaper rash as blisters started to form. Halfway through the day we came across a sign warning of unexploded military ordinance in the area. We found out that there had been a helicopter crash some years back and not all the weapons were recovered.

Our plans for the day were to meet the girls at the Burnt Ranch campground. When we arrived we found it was still closed for the winter. The girls had already found that out and went on to a picnic area a mile down the trail. A mile may not seem far, but after you have already hiked over 21 miles another mile seems forever. A half hour later we arrived at the RV and went looking for the restaurant at Mount Laguna only to find it closed as well. We found a place to camp for the night at the Laguna Campground, a very primitive place without hookups.

It was only the third night and tensions were already running high. We had two little boys, their mother, and grandma out of their routine and in an uncomfortable cramped environment. Quentin and I came to the realization that it's not a good idea to arrive at the RV tired and grumpy. It would be better for everyone if we spent the night on the trail. It became evident that while we were dealing with physical and mental challenges, they were dealing with emotional and logistical challenges.

Chapter Five - Mount Laguna to Scissor Crossing

April 10th
Day 4 – 16.4 Miles
Total 59 Miles

We started the day by driving the RV up to the Stagecoach Trail RV Park just east of Scissor Crossing. After loading up our backpacks for a night on the trail, we headed to the town of Julian where we picked up six one gallon jugs of water and a couple of deli sandwiches and Gatorade. Driving back along Sunrise Highway we dropped the water off where the trail came close to the road. We positioned five of the gallons next to the trail for other hikers and hid one in the bushes for ourselves. Leaving Mount Laguna in the early afternoon, we had pine trees for shade before descending back into the sagebrush and manzanita. A trail runner passed us going north, and an hour later we met her going the other direction. I'm sure she was out there trolling for mountain lions. Our only strange encounter of the day was couple of guys drinking beer and playing with their radio controlled dune buggies deep in the woods.

Around 7:00 p.m. we came across Tom setting up his tent in a picnic area close to the road. We exchanged greetings and continued on back up the hill to the ridge. Around 8:45 it became necessary to put on our head lamps. Our goal was to make it to the water cache we had planted earlier in the day. Time seemed to stand still even if we weren't. Slowly we etched the miles away, up and down hills, nothing but twenty feet of the trail in front of us to see. The cold wind reminded us that we were still at a higher altitude and the sore feet reminded us of what we were doing. At 10:30 the gallon jugs of water came into view. About a gallon and a half had been taken. We dug ours out of the bushes and added it to the rest after resupplying our hydration systems. Hooking the empty jugs to Quentin's pack we continued on looking for that perfect camping spot. Finally, a mile later we found an acceptable place to roll out our sleeping bags under the stars and said good night an hour before midnight. It was tough sleeping on a slope in the sand and rocks. During the night we kept sliding down the hill off of our sleeping pads. Quentin would wake up to find Whiskey occupying his vacated pad.

April 11th
Day 5 – 17.5 Miles
Total 76.5 Miles

The sun introduced us to our fifth day. Breakfast could wait until things warmed up a bit, which didn't take long. An hour into the day we stopped for oatmeal and attempted to use the French press to make coffee. The coffee ended up looking and tasting like colored mud. The wind continued to blow as we headed generally downhill. The rocky trail was hard on our feet and slowed us down. By noon our original Scissor Crossing estimated time of arrival started slipping. Unable to establish communications with the girls for our revised pickup time, we sent out a Spot message in hopes that they would pick it up on the Internet. The Spot is a satellite based GPS device that we used to send out messages. It can also be used in case of emergency to assist search and rescue in locating an injured hiker.

We met a few more hikers. Jack from San Diego had hiked a part of the trail last year and is again attempting a thru hike. We asked if he was going to Canada and his response was, "I don't know." He told us that so much is involved in hiking the trail that you need to be flexible in your plans. It was his advice that we kept with us for the remainder of the summer. When people would ask where we were going we would only give them the next town. The next 20 to 30 miles is a lot easier to comprehend than to think about climbing and descending thousands of hills and walking all the way across the country.

We met up with Ray Pan from Pennsylvania, a rather portly fellow out for a walk trying to lose some weight. He passed us up like he was in a hurry, and we continued to leapfrog throughout the afternoon. We had just finished filling up our water at the Rodriquez Spur fire tank when Ray Pan came walking up the fire road. He had missed the trail marker and headed down the wrong trail. He was not a happy hiker as this screw up added three miles to his trail experience. We pointed at the trail marker just up the dirt road a bit. It became hilarious how he started mumbling to Quentin about how stupid it was to put the marker there. We walked with him for a short distance until the trail was again well marked. Later on Sea King, a wine sommelier from Colorado, passed us while trying to catch Ray Pan.

As the hot sun moved into the western sky the trail seemed to freeze in time. We would start a decent into the valley only to find another hill to climb. We would turn towards the north only to go around a hill and find another valley heading back south. We could see the road, but the trail would not go there. It wanted to destroy us. Following the northern slope of Granite Mountain, it lived up to its name as the granite stones dug into our feet and twisted our ankles. *Is this really for me? Do I really want to destroy my life here in the wilderness?* This hike is not for the weak. It is not for those who spend their lives sitting in a recliner. *"You must move on,"* I told myself as we continued taking steps, even when the end seemed so far away. The heat caused the sweat to flow down my back. The pain of throbbing feet drove up through my ankles and into my knees. The psychological aspects of the trail were already playing with our emotions, yet we had just begun.

We arrived at the desert floor shortly after 6:00 p.m. and started the two mile hike to the road and the pickup point. All too early I consumed the remainder of my water as I walked across the hot desert sand amongst the sagebrush. I tried to keep Quentin and Whiskey in my sight as the trail was not too defined in some places. As my throat became parched, the struggle to take even another step became real. The telephone poles were visible, yet they never seemed to get closer. Just as this defeated mentality was about to come in for the kill, I heard a voice behind me holler, "Is that my friend Don?" I looked around to see Tom high tailing it down the trail. He said he had spotted us from up on the mountain and had pushed it to catch up. His smile and excitement alone seemed to lift my spirits enough to push on to the road. At the fence I slid under the barbed wire, but Quentin decided to go on up to the gate a half mile away. Having been out of water for the last mile, I had no intention of walking another step today. Cell service was scratchy at best, and we had trouble communicating the pickup spot, which caused Sharla a little anxiety. Five minutes later she arrived and we drove down to the gate for Quentin.

Back at the campground we met a couple of new hikers. Turtle Back and Yazi had spent the day at the campground and planned to leave the next morning. While chatting with them, Yazi said he was sure he had met me before and wondered if I was a trail angel. We then realized he had been to our home in Wrightwood in 2011. There is some twisted humor to this story. Yazi had come up to the house to check his email. He had a video camera with a case that needed a bigger hole for a microphone. I loaned him my drill and asked if he wanted help. He declined the offer and went outside. A few minutes later he came back in with a sheepish look on his face. He had forgotten to take the camera out of the case and had drilled right through it. Turtle Back could not stop laughing when Yazi told the story. This was when Turtle Back gave me the trail name of Stagecoach. Considering we had the RV following us along the trail and were staying at the Stagecoach Trail RV Park, it was appropriate.

Most hikers have trail names. Before Stagecoach Trail RV Park we had only encountered novice hikers like ourselves who had not yet been given trail names. While you do not give yourself a trail name, you have the right to accept or decline the one someone lays on you. As we move further north you will find very few real names mentioned in this book. Why a trail name and not your given name? I always thought it was easier to remember than an individual's real name. Having completed the trail, it is now my opinion a trail name is a hiker's identity through a transformational experience.

April 12ᵗʰ
Day 6 – 0 Miles
Total 76.5 Miles

With 76 miles behind us it was time to take a day to rest our blistered feet and reflect on how things were going. We soaked our feet in water with Epsom salt and went over plans for the next section up to Paradise Café. After running Turtle Back and Yazi up to the trail head, Sharla and I went to Julian for breakfast at an awesome café. We also picked up some groceries. Later that day Quentin and Brittany made a trip into town for their alone time, leaving the boys with Grandma and Grandpa. Shortly after dark we had our packs ready for a two day trip in the San Felipe Wilderness Area.

Chapter Six – Scissor Crossing to Warner Springs

April 13th
Day 7 – 23.5 Miles
Total 100 Miles

Quentin woke me up as he was rummaging around the RV. We knew it would be a hot and dry climb out of Scissor Crossing, and we wanted to get an early start. Sharla dropped me off at the fence so I could do the half mile necessary to catch up with Quentin. With a cup of coffee in hand, I crawled under the barbed wire fence and hiked down to the gate. Quentin was waiting where the trail crossed the road, and we headed north arriving at the bridge at 7:00 a.m. We signed the register and started to climb the switchbacks leaving the lower desert floor behind us. The mountains gave us shade early on as we zigzagged back and forth on the grueling climb. It only took an hour to make it to the assumed top. As always with the PCT, the assumed top is an imaginary thing. With the switchbacks now behind us, we headed north on a track that paralleled San Felipe Road. For ten miles we were blessed with what we called "Land of Purgatory." Scorched by fire, it appeared we were the only living creatures along the trail. We did spot a couple out ahead while climbing the switchbacks. We never caught them, but we heard later they were extremely unprepared for the terrain and had to head cross country down to the road after running out of water. We spent a lot of time under our Chrome Dome umbrellas for shade as the heat became unbearable. Halfway through Purgatory we came across another young couple from Orange County who were section hiking.

Around two in the afternoon we cleared the burn area and made a run for the 3rd Gate Water Cache. Exhausted, we stopped short of the cache for an hour to rest and let the mountain cool down. While sitting in the shade the young couple we had met earlier along with two other hikers came by. A few minutes later two southbound hikers advised us that the water cache was just around the corner. Sure enough, only a hundred yards away we crossed 3rd Gate where a sign pointed to the water down the side trail. I found a place in the shade and watched our packs while Quentin ran down to the cache and brought back a gallon of water. We thought we would make it to Barrel Springs by the end of the day, but that was still 10 miles away and it was almost 5:00 p.m.

As we continued north the terrain was getting better, but we again questioned the PCT designers and their idea of a good trail. Blisters were again causing a lot of discomfort and demanded attention. As the sun was setting we could see the clouds billowing over the mountains to the north. We took off our sunglasses and put on head lamps. As the stars and the moon took the place of the disappearing sun, the chilly wind began to intensify, driving away the heat of the day. Around and around the hills we walked, again with only the light from our headlamps illuminating the way. We moved north ever so slowly as the dark clouds took away our moon and then the stars. Around 9:00 p.m. the ominous clouds sent out wisps of fog to engulf the trail. By 10:00 p.m. we had no idea which way we were headed, but we did come across Billy Goat's Cave. Quentin thought about getting inside the old mining cave, but the spiders changed his mind. It is rumored that the legendary hiker Billy Goat sleeps here when hiking this section.

The GPS showed 2 ½ miles to Barrel Springs. That is a long way to walk when it's late at night and cold damp wind is chipping away at your confidence. We had already hiked over 22 miles and the body was rejecting any form of encouragement from the hiker's desire to reach this goal. Trudging along we finally came across a mosaic of rocks making out the numbers 100. Verification with the GPS confirmed we had hiked a hundred miles of trail over the last week. There wasn't any celebration, just an acknowledgement of tired feet and long days. It was decided that we would not even attempt to make Barrel Springs but would look for the next flat spot to sleep. An hour before midnight found us in a dry stream bed rolling out our mats and sleeping bags. The fog was still drifting over us as we fell into a fitful sleep after a long day in hostile terrain. My body, still producing energy, created an overheated sleeping bag. My spirit was dampened by throbbing feet and ankles complaining of abuse.

April 14th
Day 8 – 9.5 Miles
Total 109.5 Miles

With a hundred miles behind us and Warner Springs the goal for the day, we were up around 6:00 a.m. The heavy mist that hung over our camp gave us the deep desire to stay in our damp cocoons. Knowing "The trail will not walk itself," our motto for the next few months, we started the process of preparing for another day. Starting down a fog-shrouded, bone-chilling trail, we begged for the sun to burn away the dampness which seemed to yearn for our demise. As can be expected, the sun did not disappoint us, and by the time we made our way down into Barrel Springs the sky had cleared.

As we walked into Barrel Springs we were greeted by Tom getting into his morning routine. We found Turtle Back and Yazi camping there as well. We picked up a couple of liters of water at the trough and headed on towards Warner Springs. We thought maybe we could get there around the time the girls were expected to arrive in the afternoon. The terrain changed as we crossed meadows and streams. Small hills would pop up just to remind us that the PCT was still a challenge. We stopped frequently to rest and eat something just to maintain our strength. Coming over a hill around mid-morning we saw a rock formation out in the meadow about a half mile away. Arriving here was a dream come true as we recalled all the pictures of Eagle Rock from the journals we had read. We stopped for some pictures and met a half dozen day hikers. On across the meadow we went, sharing the trail with a herd of cows. Before noon we looked at the map, and it became apparent that we would be getting into Warner Springs Community Center by 1:00 p.m. A couple miles out, we descended into a valley which follows a stream all the way to Warner Springs. It was a relaxing walk with the sound of the water and the coolness of the shade. We met a couple on horses who encouraged us to visit the community center, that good things awaited us there.

Each year the Warner Springs Community Center, staffed with volunteers, becomes a haven for PCT hikers. For five bucks they washed and dried our dirty stinky clothes. The cheeseburgers (and I use plural here because we each had more than one) had just enough fat in them to satisfy our cravings. A freezer harboring ice cream was discovered and relieved of its burden. On the back side of the Center a couple of shower enclosures washed away the last 25 miles of dirt. The cold breeze whipping through the shower stalls was somewhat, I guess I could use the word, "refreshing." Once we were all cleaned up they brought out hot foot baths with Epsom salt to soak our feet. What a great group of volunteers! They are a great example of our responsibility in life to help our fellow man.

Tom was at the center when we arrived and Yazi and Turtle Back showed up later. By the time the girls arrived, our clothes were washed and our stomachs were full. The girls enjoyed a burger as well and we introduced them to some of our fellow hikers. It was here that Quentin received his trail name of Family Man by Jefe, a seasoned hiker, who was impressed by

Quentin's family traveling alongside him. Early in the evening we drove out to Lake Henshaw and hooked up the RV.

April 15th
Day 9 – 5.5 Miles
Total 115 Miles

Rain splattered against the window as I came out of my deep sleep, so I rolled over and returned to a hypnopompic state. The vivid picture of a winding, dusty trail kept calling out to me as the dark threatening clouds tumbled overhead. Finally, I arrived at a level of consciousness where reality cleared the cobwebs of insanity from my mind. We took our time getting around and went over to the diner for breakfast. After breakfast we opened the awning on the RV and worked under it to stay out of the rain. We got our packs ready for the 42 mile section up to Paradise Café then sat around waiting for the sun to shine. By two in the afternoon the skies appeared to be lightening up and we gave the ladies a choice. We could either leave this evening or they could take us to the trail around four in the morning for an early departure. After a brief huddle the unanimous decision sentenced us to a hard night on the ground. It was not that they didn't want our company. They knew that if we got up at 4:00 a.m. we would wake up the boys.

Chapter Seven – Warner Springs to Paradise Café

It was spitting rain when Brittany took us up to the Warner Springs Community Center where we grabbed a cup of coffee and thanked them for their hospitality. Whiskey was excited to be back on the trail as we headed out across the meadows. It didn't take long before the hound decided he needed a ground squirrel for dinner and ran all over the meadow trying to catch one. He was wearing booties to keep his feet protected and lost one as he leaped through the grass. It blended in so well with the cow patties that we were unable to find it. Passing through a dry creek bottom we walked into a private campground. A tire swing hanging from a large scrub oak tree was too tempting for Family Man. He played on the swing for a few minutes before we crossed under Highway 79 and started the climb along Aqua Caliente Creek. We crossed the creek a few times before arriving at a nice sandy camp site just before the sun went down. Turtle Back and Yazi were already there and in their bags. It had been a short day but we were back on the trail and would get an early start in the morning.

April 16th
Day 10 – 17 Miles

Routines create stability. A lack of routine can negatively affect our emotion. We had only been on the trail nine days, but the ups and downs of our emotions mirrored the dusty trail. Another day brought with it aspirations of a distant goal. It's easy at the beginning of the day to make these kinds of predictions only to be faced with a disappointing reality when the numbers start to slip. We taped up our feet, loaded up our packs, and headed up the hills. The morning haze gave way to partly cloudy skies as we struggled to maintain a positive attitude in those desert mountains. As we topped a ridge, a cold arctic wind hit us and we quickly switched to winter gear. The clouds hung tightly against the mountain tops with their tentacles reaching down to the trail. Out ahead we could see frost laden manzanita bushes on a mountain top. Fortunately, the sun did warm things up enough to melt off this ice before we topped the ridge and started down towards Mike's Place.

A remote homestead, just off the trail, Mike's Place is an oasis for PCT hikers. Mike is part of the Herrera family of Casa Herrera, a manufacturer of flour tortilla and flatbread machinery. From what his caretaker told us, Mike's family has no interest in spending time at the cabin so Mike just comes up there himself to get away and loves to entertain and help hikers. We arrived at this remote homestead in the middle of the afternoon, and the place appeared vacant. We signed the register, took off our shoes, and made ourselves at home taping the blisters on our feet. Soon we heard a noise, and the caretaker came out rubbing his eyes like we had awoken him from his afternoon slumber. He welcomed us and showed us where the filtered water was. The oranges that he offered were accepted with eagerness and rapidly consumed.

We visited with the caretaker for about an hour before thanking him for the hospitality and excusing ourselves. It was another slow, long climb, the kind that makes you want to quit. Topping this hill we found some camp sites, but strong winds discouraged any thoughts of an early night. Descending into the next valley we met a couple coming up the other way. As with most of the south bounders we met, they were on their way to the annual PCT kickoff held the last weekend in April. The man looked a lot like a Billy Goat, and the woman looked very prim and proper. They were headed up to the top, planning to camp at the place we had rejected due to the winds. Quentin encouraged them to try for Mike's Place as the storm clouds were again threatening. These same clouds pushed us lower into the valley with intent to make it to a camp site some four miles out ahead. A couple miles later Whiskey had enough for the day, and he whined enough that we stopped at a sandy creek bed which offered some protection from the cold wind.

We met Cloud Walker while we were taking one of our much deserved breaks, and he was headed south to the PCT Kickoff. He told us he worked for the forest department up at Carson Pass in the summer and was taking a toilet paper survey. He wanted to know if we buried, burned, or carried out our used TP. We looked at each other like this may be a trick question and explained we buried ours. The look on his face told us our answer was not to his liking. He reached into his backpack and pulled out a Ziploc bag of slightly discolored toilet paper. We were a little taken aback by what this transparent bag revealed. Sitting there biting our tongues we listened to Cloud Walker while he shared his vision of a day when everyone would carry out their used toilet paper. I can think of better ways to educate hikers in the methods of "leave no trace" other than showing them brown TP in a plastic bag. We were still chuckling about the Ziploc bag from our sleeping bags as the temperature continued to drop into the low 30's.

*April 17*th
Day 11 – 19.7 Miles
Total 151.7 Miles

Cold morning! It was a really cold morning. Family Man's alarm woke us up at 4:30. I did not want to get out of my sleeping bag and, thankfully, he didn't either. We had 20 miles to the highway and knew that it would be a long day. It became evident that Whiskey was not a long distance hiker and needed encouraging frequently. Family Man was becoming constantly hungry eating his lunch at 9:30 a.m. and his second lunch at 11:00 a.m. I seemed to have lost my appetite on the trail, which I contribute to the amount of fat I had to burn. The cold winds and dusty trail led to scratchy throats and runny noses. We discovered that sucking on hard candy kept our throats moist and reduced the amount of water we required. Somehow we had the idea that we would be mostly descending on this day. That was a joke. We did as much up and down hill as any other day. We really felt that the PCT planning team did it on purpose. Another trail motto rapidly became, "Expect the worst trail conditions and enjoy whatever you get," or "Where there is a hill, the trail goes over it."

Three hours into the day we came to a dirt road leading down to the Tule Spring water tank. The valley showed signs of water by the bright green trees that followed the ravine. I moaned all the way down the dirt road to the spring fed water tank 3/10 of a mile off the trail, knowing we would have to climb back up this steep hill. It was a great place to fill up our water bottles and take a break before climbing back up the fire road to the trail. We came across a Guzzler cistern. A Guzzler cistern is thought to help wildlife in water deprived areas. The concrete platform funneled into a covered, open ended tank. This one had very little water and was scummy at best. Fortunately we did not need water that desperately and moved on to where some awesome folks had stocked a cache with about eighty gallons of water, welcoming the PCT Class of 2013. We only took a liter each to get us through the nine miles left to the highway.

As we climbed out of a valley four miles from Highway 74, we spotted a hiker out ahead of us. Late in the afternoon we rounded Lookout Mountain and crossed the highway. The girls were not expecting us until 6:00 p.m. and were playing with the boys at Lake Hemet. The hiker we had spotted earlier was still in the parking lot and gave us a ride down to Paradise Café where the RV was already parked. We all enjoyed a great burger at the café before driving the RV over the mountain to the KOA at Banning. This would be the new base camp for the support team while we hiked the section through the San Jacinto Wilderness Area.

Chapter Eight – Paradise Café to Interstate 10

April 18th
Day 12 – 5.67 Miles
Total 157.37 Miles

The morning was spent getting our packs ready for an afternoon departure. Sharla and I went for groceries and breakfast at the IHOP. We had some awesome playtime with the grandsons while their parents went for lunch at a Thai restaurant. The Banning KOA was a great place for the girls to stay with its playground and cold swimming pool. Around mid afternoon Sharla drove us back to the trail. This section started with a descent for a couple of miles before a strong climb. We moved out of the manzanita bushes and into the pine trees. There were some scraggly oak trees that also gave us periodic shade. With only five and half miles behind us, the sun set below the mountains and we set up camp at Pamlico Canyon. Family Man was dealing with a really nasty rash on his legs. We didn't have any medication for a rash so I handed him the antifungal foot cream. In his words, "I headed down the fire road to use the facilities and fix my rash problem. Lathering up both hands with the cool ointment, I rubbed it into my raw thighs. Instead of soothing relief, instant burning pain had me prancing around like a prospector who had just sat down on his hot camp stove." All I heard was someone screaming, "Stagecoach!" I guess that was the wrong prescription. He was not a happy camper for awhile. We found out later that the Neosporin we were carrying was a much better match.

April 19th
Day 13 – 14.63 Miles
Total 172 Miles

Out of the tent at 6:15 we faced another cold mountain morning. The sun was shooting rays of warmth through the leaves as we taped up our feet and started down the trail. We did wait for the temperature to rise a little before stopping for breakfast. After a warm cup of oatmeal, we were ready to take on the grueling climb towards Tahquitz Peak. The climb seemed to never end as we moved higher into the mountains. On our first break we ate our apples, which were our heaviest food items and always a treat in the wilderness.

Passing by Palm View Peak we were able to get a great view of Palm Desert. In the late afternoon we met Tracks, a thru hiker from Florida, camping at the Apache Trail junction where he had descended to the spring for water. We decided we had enough water to make it to Tahquitz Creek and moved on up the mountain. Our plans were to make it to the creek by nightfall. The climb worsened, and as we slowed down, the creek became no longer an option. By the time we reached Antsell Rock we were so tired we called it a day and set up camp on the ridge. The wind was blowing so strongly that we had to find rocks to help hold things down. We had concerns about our water supply as we still had five miles before the next available water. To conserve water we left the stove packed up and ate cold food for dinner.

The section from Highway 74 to Interstate 10 is 58 miles and some of the toughest climbing to that point. We had decided to make this three night section using Family Man's two man tent, leaving my tent in the RV. We felt that reducing our weight even two pounds would help. The first night was okay, and we found that being in the same tent expedited our morning departures. It seemed that when we were safe in our own little cocoons we tended not to want to get out. Further testing revealed that the second night was not as glamorous. Two days of hiking leaves a hiker with a certain odor that is really raunchy. Three days of hiking makes a person have trouble handling their own stench. Separate tents or cowboy camping was a must for the rest of the summer.

Soon after we had fallen asleep we were awoken by someone asking if we were still awake. Irony at its best I must say. It was another hiker letting us know he would be camping on the other side of the rocks, so as not to alarm us.

April 20th
Day 14 – 17.3 Miles
Total 189.3 Miles

It was a beautiful Saturday morning when we crawled out of the tent to a sunrise coming up over Palm Desert. We started off with another 1200 foot climb, which seemed to set the stage for the day. If a mountain was in front of us we had to climb it. We stopped for a nutrition break as we topped a ridge. While we were resting, Gavin, the hiker who had spent the night on the ridge, passed us. Getting back on the trail, we continued our climb over a few more hills until descending into Tahquitz Creek. Having hiked twenty-five miles without a resupply of water, the sight of the small stream making its way down the ravine was a blessing for sore eyes. Chris from Allen Town, PA was there along with Gavin from New York. We took about an hour, while Family Man fixed soup for lunch and I filtered four liters of water.

Back on the trail, we headed for our next water stop at the North Fork of the San Jacinto River. This is the day we found out that the trail designers were really a strange, sadistic group of individuals. We also understand why they call it the Pacific Crest Trail and not the Pacific Coast Trail. We climbed to just over 9,100 feet then back down to 8,000. The trail did this roller coaster navigation several times. Five miles out of Tahquitz Creek we came to Strawberry Cienaga, a marshy side of the mountain where a person could get water if needed. By the middle of the afternoon we made it to the Strawberry Junction Camp where someone was kind enough to put an outhouse. It smelled like one but was much appreciated.

We arrived at the North Fork of the San Jacinto River in time for an early dinner. I filled our water containers as Family Man fixed a dinner of rice and chicken along with raspberry crunch for dessert. An awesome stream flowing out of the snow packs made the air about 20 degrees cooler. Putting on beanies and gloves we had the impression it was only going to get colder. While we were eating dinner, a young, shirtless hiker came up and filled his 20 ounce Gatorade bottle with water. He drank it down and refilled it, introduced himself, and headed on down the trail. Frenchy was the trail name for this energetic hiker from France. He was to become a legend on the PCT that year, but you'll have to wait for that story.

Only a couple hundred yards from where the stream made its way down the snow packed ravine, things warmed up and we changed back to warm weather hiking gear. A gradual descent took us to Fuller Ridge where we found a lot of snow on the shady side. The snow packs slowed us down and daylight ran out a half hour short of our goal. Not wanting to cross the snow at night, we started looking for a flat place to camp, finding it in an open meadow as daylight was fading. It was getting right down cold when we crawled into our sleeping bags. Turning on the GPS we found that we were still 7/10 of a mile short of the goal and still in the 'no camping zone'. We thought about it for a couple of seconds and decided we weren't camping, only sleeping.

*April 21**st*
Day 15 – 20.2 Miles
Total 209.5 Miles

Good morning from the icebox of Fuller Ridge. As the sun woke us up we found ourselves in a tent covered with ice. Condensation had frozen the fabric of the tent and had to be broken off. I had hung my shirt on a bush to dry and found it stiff as a board. Needless to say, I didn't wear it this morning.

Today we would be making the greatest single day continuous altitude change of our entire trip. Starting out at 8700 feet on Fuller Ridge we would descend to 1331 feet at Interstate 10. When every step is down it drops the weight of your body and your load hard onto your feet. It doesn't take long before your feet begin to heat up and you feel the blisters coming on. The temperature continued to climb as we reached lower altitudes. The shade of the pine trees gave way to manzanita and some other thorny bushes which badly needed trimming. Family Man's legs were looking like they had been in a fight with an alley cat. He started having second thoughts about how cool his shorts were. As this mountain landscape gave way to desert flora we passed the 200 mile marker. The sun was hot when we made it down to the desert floor and the water fountain four miles from the interstate.

The Desert Water Company had installed a life saving water fountain in the middle of the desert. We spent some time at the fountain drinking warm water and chatting with a lady named Hikes Alone. She was waiting for the sun to sink before she started the climb up San Jacinto. With only four miles to a shower and good food we headed out across the desert to Interstate 10. The first part was on a steep downhill paved road that tried to kill us. Having walked the last fifty miles on trails, we cringed as the pavement really did damage to our already energy deprived bodies. We passed the small community of Snow Creek and left the pavement.

The last two and one half miles were across sand, which felt like quicksand to exhausted hikers. There was a lot of helicopter activity going on when we passed a staging area for a power line company. We took a break while one landed and then took off again. A mile from the highway we entered a wash and the trail became difficult to follow. We had to go from signpost to signpost wading through ever deepening sand. Reaching the bridges over a railroad and the interstate, we crossed under with little fan fare. On the other side we took off our packs and sat beside the road until Sharla arrived. Our metabolism was raging from two weeks of hiking, so after a shower and clean clothes, we consumed a vast amount of pizza and drank way too much soda. We were happy to be back with our family and looked forward to a day of rest the next day. The schedule was about to change however, as a medical break loomed in our future and would temporarily take us off the trail.

April 22nd- 25th
Day 16-19 – 0 Miles
Total 209.5 Miles

> *Monday morning and things are tight and hectic in the RV. It's become a zero day to let the feet rest, and the KOA has been accommodating in letting us stay another night. We spent the day soaking our feet and picking up some much needed items. A red streak is working its way up my left foot from a blister on my little toe. Not too concerned, I spent the day working on the trail journal and getting some much needed rest. Sharla was nice enough to post a picture of the red streak on Facebook, and by mid afternoon the comments started rolling in.*

It was the consensus of all the "professionals" on social media that a doctor visit was necessary. So, after peer pressure became obnoxiously overbearing, I agreed to go in for a medical evaluation. Early evening found Sharla and Stagecoach at the Morena Valley Kaiser where we found out they only had an emergency room and that we needed to go on over to the Riverside facility. On the way back out to the car I got a call from my father who had already received a briefing on the situation and was calling to give me a verbal whipping. He was satisfied to find we had it under control. After a few hours of waiting, the doctor confirmed it was an infection and had the nurse shoot me in the rear with some antibiotics. After she prescribed a round of oral antibiotics, she had the audacity to ask when we were going back out on the trail. She was not happy with my answer and shot down the idea of us continuing toward Big Bear the following day. With doctor's orders of at least three days rest, we returned to Banning with the news. We spent the evening revising plans and came to the consensus that we would take the RV to Wrightwood, and Sharla would bring us back to the trail in three days.

Back in Wrightwood we decided to pay it forward by taking some water up on the Lone Pine Climb. With fifty gallons of bottled water in the back of the old pickup truck, we drove up the bumpy fire road to the trail. Arriving at the trail we found four hikers resting in the shade. The three young ones helped unload the truck while an older hiker introduced himself as Lodgepole and asked if his son Maverick could unload his for him so he could rest his aching feet. We excused him and thanked the hikers for their help. They had been sitting there concerned about their water condition. The long hot climb had taken more than they expected, and we arrived as if an answer to their prayers. Over the next two days the only interruption from resting came when we took another fifty gallons up to the water cache.

Chapter Nine – Interstate 10 to Big Bear

April 26th
Day 20 – 11 Miles
Total 220.5 Miles

On April 26th as the herd was celebrating the PCT kickoff at Lake Morena, Sharla was taking us back to the trail. After the normal dismal goodbyes, Family Man and Stagecoach left Interstate 10 shortly after noon and walked the short distance to Ziggy and the Bear's. Ziggy and the Bear run an oasis in the desert where they have opened up their back yard to PCT hikers. Walking into their fenced in back yard we encountered Ray Pan and Jugs sitting around a table with our host. We had no more than settled in when Sea King, also known as Timber, arrived and joined our group. Cold sodas and candy bars were in the coolers and soon were in our stomachs. Fresh fruit also was on the menu as was an occasional glance at the thermometer. We wanted to get out of this vortex, but the thermometer was stuck on 120 degrees. Now we knew that it was due to the thermometer's location in the sun, but the psychological impact deterred our departure. Ziggy encouraged us to stay until the sun gave way to a cooler evening. The suction of the vortex kept its grip on us until cheeseburgers arrived at dinner time. As we were packing up to leave, Just Lora arrived; later her trail name was changed to Ice Axe. As the sun reached out to the mountains we headed down the trail. Our plans were to make it to the White Water River eleven miles away.

We struggled against a lackadaisical attitude from a day in the shade. Up the mountain we went, past the Mesa Wind Farms. A continuous climb took us towards a saddle that looked like a wall against the setting sun. Finally after a few switchbacks we rested on top looking into the valley beyond. Darkness enclosed around us as we sat down on the ridge and thought back through the day's events and the trail ahead. With head lamps aglow we started a descent towards White Water River, walking ever so briskly into the night. On the three mile descent, Family Man found two snakes, a frog, and a black widow. He felt it was necessary to catch each one. Thankfully the snakes were not venomous, and he only aggravated the black widow. Sometime after 9:00 p.m. as we reached the valley floor, the full moon appeared from below the mountains. The moon acted as a giant mirror reflecting the sun's intense rays and illuminated the trail enough for us to extinguish our lights for the next two miles. Family Man shared that snakes come out at night during a full moon. This comment caused ol' Stagecoach to imagine every stick was a snake. At the river crossing we found a nice sandy beach which made a perfect camping spot. Before midnight we were drifting off to sleep with the sound of babbling water making its way down the valley.

April 27th
Day 21 – 15 Miles
Total 235.5 Miles

A large rock shaded us from the morning sun causing a late start. Crossing the stream, we started up towards a ridge. By mid-morning we were again experiencing temperatures approaching one hundred. On top of the ridge we picked up cell service and checked in with the girls. We received a message from my doctor that they had prescribed the wrong antibiotics, and I needed to get on the right ones as soon as possible. That was great news from the middle of nowhere. We were finding out that long distance hiking plans are fluid. The plan to make a quick stop in Big Bear for supplies and move on was changed to an overnighter with the girls.

Shortly after noon we arrived at Mission Creek where we found Ray Pan and Sea King resting in the shade of a large oak tree. The shade and cool stream was an invitation we could not turn down. A nap in the shade during the heat of the day looked like a smart move. Over the next two hours we were joined by Kiwi Legs, a young couple, a young man named Moses, and an older couple who found a tree just south of our group. The vortex tightened its grip, and before long we changed our plans to leave when the sun hit the mountains. An hour before we planned to take off, an overweight hiker with his shirt unbuttoned rumbled into our space and collapsed three feet from our pack. He peeled off his shoes as he cursed a line that would make a sailor blush and lit up a joint. Looking at this hiker in disgust, I suddenly realized this was not our first meeting.

Two years earlier I had been working on our front porch in Wrightwood when Slim, (yep, that's his trail name), came walking up the street. He was grubby and covered with dirt. He asked where the Methodist church was and when I told him five blocks down the hill, he moaned and asked if he could sit down. My thoughts remained mine as I told him, "Sure," so he sat down in the middle of the road and peeled off his shoes. I got him a drink, but due to a bathroom remodel project, I could not offer him a shower. Not wanting to leave him stranded, I drove him down to the Methodist Church and dropped him off. That, my friend, had been my introduction to hiker stench. Now back to 2013.

What had been planned as a 5 p.m. departure became an immediate departure as we packed up our stuff and walked out into the hot afternoon sun and into peace and quiet once again. It was our first encounter on this trip with Slim, who says he hikes the trail every year, even though he started at Interstate 10 instead of the border. It was not to be our last. We stopped just a mile up the trail where we crossed the stream at a beautiful three foot waterfall with a concaved rock to sit back in and enjoy the sound of the water. Five minutes into our peaceful meditation who else but Slim comes galloping around the corner and flops down on the other side of the stream. Off comes his shoes as he curses the mountain and the trail, declaring his need to soak his feet. Again we are driven from the vortex of the cool stream.

Continuing to gain altitude, we followed the valley along Mission Creek. It cooled down once the sun descended behind the mountains. Shortly after putting on our headlamps we came across Kiwi Legs setting up camp on a little plateau above the stream. Kiwi, a daughter of missionaries from New Zealand and the wife of a pastor, had hiked from Sierra City to Canada in 2012 and was trying to finish the trail this year. She told us she had lost the trail out ahead in the marsh. She had returned to the high ground for the night figuring she would cross in the daylight tomorrow. We pushed through the marsh with Family Man doing an excellent job finding the trail and jumping across a fairly wide creek. There was no way Stagecoach could jump like that. I would have ended up taking a bath. We found a log downstream about twenty feet. It was sketchy in the dark, but with shaky knees I made my way across, and we were soon up on dry land once again. A mile or so later we came across the remains of a hawk with feathers spread over a four foot area. It looked like it had been torn apart by some animal. Family Man grabbed a couple of feathers for his hat. Late into the night we came to the final crossing of Mission Creek where we made camp on the somewhat sandy creek bed.

April 28th
Day 22 – 20 Miles
Total 255.5 Miles

The little stream along which we slept was only four to six inches wide but gave enough water to fill our hydro packs and water bottles. As I was sitting there in the sand pumping water, I got bit on the leg by what I think was a spider. Two little holes and it swelled up, getting rock hard and about the size of a quarter. We were eating beef stew for breakfast when a hiker we called Grandpa came by and wished us well as he continued up the hill. An hour later we passed Grandpa as he was methodically climbing the switchbacks. He was slow but consistent, unlike ol' Stagecoach who needed to take a break every so often. It felt good to get to the higher altitudes away from the heat of the desert. At lunch time we came to Forest Flats Junction and the small stream that flowed through it. As we sat there getting water, we were joined by a number of our new found hiker friends, and you guessed it, Slim. He came crashing into the clearing and lit a fire in his wood powered cook stove. Smoke went everywhere, and I was sure we were going to be a statistic. We quickly departed the scene to be ahead of the pending fire and continued climbing to a ridge which we followed for a few miles.

Arriving at Coon Creek Cabin in the early evening we fixed dinner on the front porch of this rustic cabin and chased away some massive ants. The restroom was usable but nasty, and the trashcans were useful in unloading a couple of pounds out of our packs. I left Coon Creek Cabin ahead of Family Man. Shortly thereafter I heard a huffing, thudding sound coming up behind me. I turned thinking Family Man was being a little overexerting, but I was greeted by Slim puffing up the hill. He barreled by me for about 20 yards and plopped down in the shade on the trail. He then carried on about how he had passed everyone. I kind of shrugged my shoulders as Family Man arrived, thinking that everyone should hike his own hike, and we moved on hoping this would be our final encounter. Trudging up a fairly steep grade I spotted Family Man out ahead talking to someone under a bush. Robocop, a retired police officer who appeared to be suffering from some kind of ailment, was lying there telling Family Man about his problems. I kept going and later thought we should have given him some of our water, even though we were low ourselves. I shared that concern with Family Man when he caught up, and he said he tried but Robocop declined. I noticed Family Man was not carrying his trekking poles. He was not real thrilled the quarter of a mile back down the mountain to pick up the walking sticks.

Water was hard to come by as we climbed higher towards Onyx Summit and the water cache we had heard was there. As we passed some animal cages, we came across Moses and the young couple we started calling "The Children of Israel." The animal cages are in a wildlife sanctuary east of Big Bear and gave us a glimpse of a couple of bears, a panther, and a wolf or two. It was nice to see some wildlife but a blessing that we were separated by commercial grade wire mesh.

A dry throat creates a craving for carbonated beverages, and as we climbed the summit we talked about how great it would be to be sipping on an ice cold soda. Just as it was getting dark, we arrived at the water cache. Along with the much needed water we discovered a trail angel had left three twelve packs of soda. Dropping our packs, we grabbed a Mountain Dew and quickly consumed the moist calories it offered. The stars shined strongly and the lights of the valley danced between the branches. Not satisfied, we became greedy and had a Pepsi as well. Donning our packs, we headed on up the hill to another promised cache a mile away. We figured we would camp there for the night next to a water source. On the way Family Man could only talk about how a couch would make him a happy man. Amazingly, as we came around the corner there was the water cache along with a couch. Sitting on the raggedy, weather beaten couch in the middle of nowhere, we became acutely aware of the truth of the "Ask and it shall be given you" phrase. Though by no means charismatic in nature, our faith was starting to grow.

We sat there for a half hour looking out over Big Bear Valley talking about our experiences over the last three weeks and how much we felt blessed. Family Man wanted to sleep on the couch, but we had a problem. The couch was home to numerous bugs, and the two caffeine rich sodas we had consumed had us wide awake. Back into the night we went and hiked for another 2 ½ miles, finally setting up our tents in a narrow dry creek bed just before midnight.

April 29th
Day 23 – 10.5 Miles
Total 266 Miles

We woke to a chilly morning in the creek bed and didn't take long to tape up our blistered feet and pack the tents. We had only 10 ½ miles to Big Bear and the girls were going to meet us. We thought the trail would be easy that day but found that was not the case. A rocky downhill and a couple of mountains to cross attempted to damper our spirit. About an hour and a half from the trail head I called Papa Smurf, a trail angel in Big Bear, for a ride to Nature Inn and he was glad to accommodate. Family Man and I had been talking all morning about how good a cold root beer sounded, and sure enough as we approached Highway 18, a cooler waited by the side of the trail, courtesy of Motel 6. It was full of cold sodas, and you guessed it, two cold root beers. Thank you Motel 6, for not only leaving the light on, but also for your generosity as well.

Papa Smurf arrived twenty minutes later and, as promised, delivered us to the inn. The girls showed up ten minutes later, and we enjoyed the evening together. I was able to feed Sawyer ice cream and rock him to sleep on the porch swing. We packed our bags and prepared for the hike down Deep Creek.

Chapter Ten – Big Bear to Wrightwood

April 30th
Day 24 – 19.5 Miles
Total 285.5 Miles

     Leaving Big Bear before noon, we moved rapidly along the trail at around 2.5 mph. We were energized by the half day off and time with the family. Soon we caught up with Rambling Man, whom we had met at the hotel, and we hiked a short distance together before he stopped to rest. We loved the views of Big Bear Lake but wasted little time with breaks. Late into the evening we moved down into Holcomb Valley and along Holcomb Creek. The trail was some of the best we had experienced, and we made good time for starting so late in the day.

     It was dark when we arrived at Little Bear Springs Campground. We knew we were close when we came to the open air outhouse. It has four walls and no roof. Sharla and I had come across this abnormality two years before, and it hadn't changed. I sat alone in the dark as Family Man experienced this well thought out privy. Two hundred yards later we came to the stream and decided to cowboy camp for the night. Family Man had the bright idea that real cowboy camping meant a person was to lean up against a tree. He was in for a surprise come morning to find the tree had burned some time ago, and his pack was coated with charcoal.

May 1ˢᵗ
Day 25 – 22.3 Miles
Total 307.8 Miles

An early morning breakfast of mashed potatoes and Spam did much to curb the hunger of the long day ahead. As we were packing up and taping our feet, Tracks showed up for water, clarifying the coughing sounds we had heard earlier. He was camping just two hundred yards away, which was out of sight the night before. We followed Holcomb Creek and crossed over it a few times before we moved up into the hills towards Deep Creek. Four miles can sometimes seem forever, but the climbing was mild, and by one o'clock we were soaking our feet under the bridge in the cool waters of Deep Creek.

While sitting there enjoying the refreshing water, Kiwi Legs showed up excited to finally catch up with us. She had heard from Rambling Man that we were out ahead. Leaving the water, we headed down Deep Creek and soon Kiwi Legs caught up with us again. Family Man kept up with her for about five miles as Stagecoach lagged behind. I caught up with them at 5:00 p.m. when Kiwi Legs stopped to eat dinner. We decided not to stop as we wanted to get to the hot springs before dark. We pushed hard and arrived at the beach beside the warm water as the sun was setting. Kiwi Legs showed up five minutes later. What an interesting place. The hot springs is noted on the maps as a clothing optional hot spring. We were concerned as to what we would find. There was one hiker there doing the skinny dipping thing, but he soon left. A couple of twenty something hippies came up and asked if we had ever been to the springs before. They then proceeded to welcome us to the hot springs in a "see the unicorn" type of way. We peeled off our shoes and soaked our feet in the 104 degree muddy water letting the pain drift away.

One of the hippies with a towel wrapped around his waist asked if we had any alcohol. We looked at him like he was crazy. He went on to explain that he was not asking about the drinking kind but the type you use in backpacking cook stoves. It seems he wanted to put on some kind of fire show. We were happy to tell him all we had was butane. The forest lived to burn another day. Kiwi took off for a spot on down the trail not wanting to be close to what could become a party place. We set up camp in the sand as it got dark. We spent a half hour soaking away the pain in another pool which was only 99 degrees as the stars lit up the clear night sky.

May 2nd
Day 26 – 21.2 Miles
Total 329 Miles

Thanks to the sun coming up over the mountains we got an early start. The hot springs had healed our aching bones and feet, and the soft sand accommodated a good night's sleep. We packed up and headed north along the never ending ravines and ridges that follow Deep Creek to the desert. We did not see anything of Kiwi Legs, but the registers showed she was moving rapidly ahead. We forded the river at the bottom and moved through a brushy area before arriving at Highway 173. At the road a small sign advised that a water cache was a short distance ahead. Finding water on a hot dry trail is like a gold miner finding a nugget. We cherished every drop we found and appreciated the trail angels who were willing to give of their time and money to help the PCT hikers. Two liters later we headed on toward the Silverwood Recreation Area with a renewed drive.

Off in the distance we could see the dam that held the lake at bay, and even though it looked like only five miles we knew how deceiving that was. Back into the valley we went descending all the way only to climb back out on the other side. Finally we arrived at the spillway and crossed over the bridge along Highway 173. After the bridge we moved back into a wooded area where we came upon a cooler loaded with bananas, oranges, cantaloupe, boiled eggs and ice water. What a treat on a hot afternoon. Again we indulged in the gifts of trail angels before moving up and over the mountains where we were greeted by Silverwood Lake. It was a long way around the lake, but we kept a strong pace and found ourselves at the overpass with time to spare. While waiting in the shade of the bridge, we shared our space with millions of ants, each of us trying to avoid the other. Sharla picked us up at 6:00 p.m., and we returned to Wrightwood for a shower and clean clothes.

May 3rd
Day 27 – 18 Miles
Total 347 Miles

The next morning we stopped by McDonald's for breakfast on the way back to Silverwood Lake in an attempt to pack on some extra calories. We arrived at the drop off point with light packs and plenty of energy for this mild eighteen mile day. Moving rapidly up through the hills we found little reason to rest. One hour into the day we found we had progressed 3.74 miles and had made it over the ridge. Knowing that this kind of speed would not last, we continued to push ourselves to the limit. A couple of hours into the day we passed Grandpa. The trail was well kept and our feet felt good as we continued to maintain a rapid pace. Later in the morning we met Wall-e who later passed us moving so fast he dusted us out. The funny thing about Wall-e was his comment about how fast we were. He asked how old I was, and when I told him he said, "No wonder you're fast, as young as you are." Yet he was ten years older and going a lot faster. About four miles from Interstate 15 we came to the cliffs where we could see the Friday afternoon traffic headed for Las Vegas. What a different life we were living from the occupants in the string of vehicles racing for the desert casinos. The trail followed along the ridge as it started the descent down to Crowder Canyon. We walked across some broken up pavement which looked like an old road that had come up through the canyon a long time ago. A half mile of narrow canyon opened up at the freeway where old abutments were all that remained of a bridge from yesteryear.

It was the top of the day as we walked up the road to McDonald's. The breakfast we had eaten earlier had long ago burned off. We met a hiker named Keymaster on his way back to the trail. When we walked into the crowded fast food restaurant, we discovered what it was like to be the less-than-desirable type. Every eye in the room turned to watch as these two bums took the final table and released the burden of their backpacks onto the floor and chair beside them. After they realized we were not going to put the hurt on them with our trekking poles, they went back to their consumption of fatty food and sugar laced drinks. We joined them in the gluttonous devouring of beef and potatoes and rehydrated with lots of soda. With only five more miles to go for the day, we stumbled out into the sunshine. Stopping by the gas station we picked up a gallon of water and a mango slurpy. Sitting on the grass, just like we had seen many other thru hikers do in years gone by, we filled our hydro packs and rested.

Back on the trail, we walked under the long tunnel where the fast moving traffic passed overhead. A small stream dumped into a ditch on the west side, and we walked through the tick laden brush and past an old homestead. A train rumbled over the railroad bridge as we passed under it as well. A half mile later we went through a large culvert where a cool breeze convinced us to stay awhile and cool down. It only took ten minutes before the urge to complete the day's adventure drove us onward. A 1,200 foot climb was a little tiring in the heat, but from experience we knew it could be conquered by taking one step after the other. We moved rapidly and soon topped the hills and enjoyed the view of Swarthout Road below. Arriving at the Swarthout cache in the early afternoon we found Keymaster and Detour sitting in the shade sipping on an energy drink. Our ride showed up, and we headed home for a night of luxury.

May 4th

Day 28 – 22.5 Miles
Total 369.5 Miles

The sun was not yet up when our ride dropped us off at Swarthout Canyon. We call the climb from Swarthout Canyon Road up to Blue Ridge "The Lone Pine Climb." Our friend, Catie Adams, joined us for this grueling 7,200 feet up and 3,300 feet down, 23 mile day. Catie had planned on joining us for a week in the beginning, but due to illness she had not been able to. It was a cool morning, and even after the sun came up it remained somewhat bearable. We arrived at the water cache by mid-morning and calculated we would make Highway 2 early in the afternoon. After resting for twenty minutes we continued with the climb up to Blue Ridge at 8300 feet. Standing on Blue Ridge we were able to see into the valley. Finally, after 363 miles, we could see Wrightwood. The day was not over as we continued west and found an additional five to six hundred feet of mountains to climb. Our muscles began to ache and our feet began to say things they shouldn't, but we continued on. It became another slow motion afternoon as the miles inched by. Finally arriving at the ski resorts, we knew the end of our day was near. One last hill stood in the way, which we found was normal on this trail of struggle. The trail was rugged, and the grade was steep. Our love for the trail designers waned as we fought against the ankle twisting stones that littered the trail. Winding down the final hill we came upon the trail head at Highway 2 where Sharla waited to take us home. Arriving back into Wrightwood we stopped at Mountain Hardware and signed the trail register.

May 5th
Day 29 – 4.5 Miles
Total 374 Miles

Sunday morning, May 5th could only mean it was time to go to church. Sunday afternoon was cold and blustery as Brittany and Whiskey joined us for an afternoon hike. We ticked

56

off the four and a half miles crossing up through Grassy Meadows Camp Ground and down into Vincent Gap. Coming back down to the highway we were faced with Mount Baden Powell. The cloud enshrouded mountain and its 2,700 foot climb was calling our name.

May 6th
Day 30 – 0 Miles
Total 374 Miles

The next morning we woke up to constant rain and temperatures in the mid-forties. After a look at the forecast we decided it was not a good day to climb a mountain. Home is a great place to take a zero, and we all took advantage of this rainy day. The girls went to town for some adult time while we watched the boys and planned the next section. The rain stopped in the afternoon, but the clouds still rolled over the mountains. I went to the library and printed off our Canadian entrance permit applications and on the way back ran into a few of our hiking friends at Mile High Pizza. Later Family Man and I joined the ragtag group. Rambling Man, Sea King (Timber), Jugs, Delaware Dave, Tracks, Forrest, and another young couple we had seen in Warner Springs were sitting around the picnic tables gorging on pizza and doing what hiker trash do.

Chapter Eleven – Wrightwood to Acton KOA

May 7th
Day 31 – 20 Miles
Total 394 Miles

The clouds were still rolling in over the mountains, which were now white with ice and snow. The vortex was again tightening its grip, and we knew we had to break free. From the start we had known that this would be the toughest of all places to leave. Now with the inclement weather and hard climb ahead, the desire for comfort and warmth battled our will. We started the day delivering nine hikers up to Lightning Ridge before Sharla took us up to Vincent Gap. Family Man had attitude about the amount of time it took. He was anxious to get on the trail and put Mount Baden Powell behind us. His snide comments about "Guess we will get to Canada next year" became his motto any time things seemed to be going too slow for his liking. The lesson we learned from this shuttle operation was not to offer a ride until they have their packs on and are standing there ready to go.

We made it to the trail just before noon. The clouds still hung heavy over the mountain as we strapped on full packs weighing thirty-seven pounds. Even though I had climbed this mountain three other times, this was the first time with a full pack, and it was a workout. The first half mile is steep, and our legs were soft from the rest over the last two days. Soon we got into rain and put on our ponchos which caused me to sweat like a sauna, and soon I could feel my down jacket getting wet from the inside out. The higher we climbed the colder it got. Eventually we got into ice and snow. We could tell by footprints in the snow that someone was just a short distance ahead, and about halfway up the climb we caught up with Keymaster. Reaching the spur that leads up to the summit, we decided not to take it. We had been on top of Baden-Powell before. The trees were covered with ice and snow which was starting to melt.

From Baden-Powell we headed west along the ridge as the wind bit right through our ponchos. We had no choice but to continue, hoping the trail would soon take us to a lower altitude. It finally did, and as we descended, the ice started falling from the trees in loud crashes. This concerned us as it sounded like we were in a war zone with bombs dropping all around us. By the grace of God we didn't get hit, and by late afternoon we left the ice and snow, making our way back to Highway 2 at Islip Saddle.

Highway 2 runs from just east of Wrightwood across the San Gabriel Mountains before dropping its way down into the Los Angeles Basin. The PCT crosses this highway nine times through this section. In the winter time, the road is closed across the mountains due to the extreme weather conditions at the higher altitudes. It had been our plans to return home each night while hiking this section, but we were too early and the road was still closed. We sat at a picnic table and fixed dinner before heading up Mount Williamson. The clouds had broken up giving us a little reprieve from the foggy atmosphere. Our goal was to get over this mountain before dark, so we ate in a hurry and headed up the mountain for another climb. Our next crossing of Highway 2 was west of the tunnels. We wasted no time crossing the road, and were treated with another climb of only two to three hundred feet before we descended back down to the highway again close to Eagles Roost. On our maps we observed that the trail was closed to protect the endangered Mountain Yellow-Legged frog. This species of frog, which used to be in abundance in these parts, has all but disappeared. We assumed that they must live on the PCT between Highway 2 and Buckhorn Campground. The alternate was to walk the highway for 2.7 miles to the campground. The positive side to the road still being in hibernation was that we didn't need to worry about traffic.

Darkness was rapidly approaching as we came upon a building which we believed was owned by either the highway department or the forest service. Walking around the building, looking around for a water spigot, we found a dumpster full of broken up concrete covered with plastic. A dip in the plastic had made a reservoir with some fresh rain water there for the taking. With a resupply of water we headed down the highway in the dark. A couple of times rogue clouds swept over us running chills through our bones. By the time we reached the road leading down into the campground the sky was clear and full of brightly shining stars.

Buckhorn Camp was closed but, considering we were on foot, the gates were more of a nuisance than a blockade. We hiked down the exit and came upon campsite Number Thirteen. Not being superstitious, we were happy to find a level place to camp which had running water and a bear box. The restrooms were still locked so we left a surprise deep in the woods for some future gold miner.

May 8th
Day 32 – 25 Miles
Total 419 Miles

Another day brought some sunshine and higher temperatures. We decided to have a hot breakfast as water was readily available. Looking around we confirmed our suspicions that we were alone in the park. From the campground we had two choices as far as routes go. We could take the road around to where the PCT returned to Highway 2 which was about 1 ½ miles or we could take Burkhart Trail down to Cooper Canyon and join the PCT back up to the highway. We did what was right, adding about 3 miles to our hike and headed down Burkhart Trail. We were glad we did as it was a beautiful hike and followed a stream up Cooper Canyon for about a mile. It was a long climb back up to Highway 2. Upon arrival at the highway we rested and ate our lunch. Soon along came Grandpa hiking down the road. I guess some take the trail and others like walking on pavement. We moved on down the trail and soon passed the four hundred mile marker. At Camp Glenwood we caught up with Grandpa getting water out of a tap. A sign said to filter it, and being the upstanding citizens that we are, we did.

By mid afternoon we were down in the Station Fire burn area where the poodle-dog bush intensified and the brush was thick. This fire has historical significance to us as it was burning the day Family Man and Brittany got married. A detour took us off the trail and put us on a fire road. We made our way down to the Mill Creek Ranger Station. Along the way we came across Grandpa's tent and assumed he was inside. A short time later we stopped, fixed dinner of beef stroganoff, and got out our head lamps. Family Man started having problems with his right knee and believed it was from a slip he had the day before up on Baden-Powell. The knee problem slowed us down, and it wasn't until around eleven when we stumbled into the campground just below the ranger station. The camp ground was littered with poodle-dog bush. Shining our lights around looking for a clear spot, we found Jugs sound asleep. It was close to midnight before we crawled inside our bags.

May 9th
Day 33 – 25 Miles

The sound of cars flying down Angeles Forest Highway woke us up at 4:30. We knew the highway was close by, but did not realize it was only thirty feet away. This road is a secondary road but is heavily traveled by commuters from Palmdale to the Burbank area. We finally gave up on getting any more sleep and packed up our bags. We had to hike back up to the ranger station to get water before heading west. Crossing the Angeles Forest Highway and starting a climb up the trail, we came across a cooler filled with soda, beer, wine, water, and a couple of oranges. We took only a Diet Pepsi and a Dr. Pepper for a mid morning break and continued up the mountain. The day was hot, and as always, the climb was long. We reached a shady spot at the top of one hill and consumed our earlier find. We passed through more burned out area and started thinking all of the southern California mountains must have burned at some time or another. The clouds started building up in the early afternoon, and they were calling for thunderstorms in the early evening.

We passed by Messenger Flats where a hiker from France (yep, that's right it was Frenchy) had accidently started a fire the previous week which burned five acres. He had lit a fire in a fire ring to fix his dinner and was sure it was out. During the night he was awakened by the flames flaring up around him. He ended up losing some of his equipment but, fortunately no one was hurt. His trail name was changed to French Toast.

By early evening a thunderstorm was making its presence known behind us as we arrived at North Fork Ranger Station. A couple of five gallon containers of water were sitting on a picnic table courtesy of Ranger Todd. We ate our dinner of mashed potatoes laced with Spam and rested our feet. A large thunderstorm was building over Palmdale and moving south. Looking at the track on the weather radar it looked like it was going east of us. We still had eight miles to go to get to the KOA at Acton, so we each took two liters of water and started down the slope. As the thunderstorm was dissipating, it threw a little rain our way requiring a couple of miles in the ponchos. By the time we turned the corner and headed west again it had pretty much cleared off, and we sat down to enjoy a few minutes of the multicolored sunset.

The trail got easier, and we picked up our speed for a short period until Family Man's knee started acting up again. In an act that would make a duct tape enthusiast proud, we taped up his knee on the outside of his thermals. "Why over the thermals?" you may ask. Well, we had pulled enough duct tape off of our toes to know that hair comes with it. Enough said about that. With his knee taped up, Family Man was on the move again. We followed a gentle downhill slope with good trail and picked up the speed to the point we were almost running. It was getting darker, yet we didn't want to interrupt the pace by stopping and putting on our headlamps.

Around ten we caught our first glimpse of the highway and the KOA, but it did its best to elude us. The trail would take us just above the campground, then to the south around and over another mountain. Family Man was again dragging his right foot managing to kick as many rocks as possible. Kicking rocks on the trail is a sign of exhaustion. After a long day your legs turn to rubber which results in dragging your feet. Add this fatigue to a knee that shoots pain all the way up and down your leg with every step, and you have a recipe for disaster. In my compassionate fatherly way, I would chuckle and call him "Black Toe Joe" each time he would kick one of these immovable objects. All of a sudden the end of a trekking pole whizzed by my face and disappeared into the darkness. It seems ol' Family Man had lost his temper and took it out on his high grade collapsible aluminum walking stick. The price a person pays for losing his temper at night in the wilderness is fifteen minutes digging in the bushes.

Coming around a corner two eyes reflected back at us from up in the bushes. This unknown creature had eyes about six inches apart and was only about forty yards away. It just stood there as we passed. I looked back quite frequently hoping it wasn't hungry. I was sure my imagination was playing games with me when Family Man asked if I heard that. "If you're talking about a lion roaring, the answer is no." There it was again. Somewhere out there a lion was making itself known, and we were not thrilled. When we came to our senses we concluded that the sound was coming from the valley close to civilization. Later we found out there is a wildlife sanctuary around that area. Reaching Soledad Canyon Road we walked 4/10 of a mile north to the KOA. It was late and no one was around, but we found a nice grassy area and set up our tents. We had hiked 70 miles in three days and were exhausted.

Chapter Twelve – Acton KOA to Bouquet Canyon Road

May 10th
Day 34 – 11.5 Miles
Total 455.5 Miles

What a great night's rest we had on the grass. We had to wait for the office to open at 9:00 a.m. to wash our clothes and pay our bill. Warm showers washed away the filth, and with clean clothes we felt renewed. They didn't have a restaurant at the KOA, but they did have ice cream and microwavable sandwiches along with all kinds of other food items we consumed. Jugs stayed at the KOA as well. The only difference is he got in four hours ahead of us. Leaving Acton for Aqua Dulce, we crossed through a nasty wooded area in the wash with lots of trash and bugs. As we crossed over the railroad we came to a monument marking where the blazing of the PCT was finally considered finished. Then it was time to climb, which we did for the next four miles. The weather was hot, and the terrain was desert. We did stop a couple of times for shade on the way up. Late afternoon we finally topped a ridge and viewed Interstate 14 below us. We have come to realize that just because you see something does not mean you are almost there. It was still about three trail miles before we descended below the highway into a concrete passageway over five hundred feet long.

At the far side of the tunnel we stopped for a break in the coolness of this underground breezeway. The Vazquez Rock Park was waiting for us on the other side along with the hot afternoon sun. Coming out of the tunnel there was some confusion on which direction to go. We started down one way until things just didn't feel right. Turning around we went back the other way, and sure enough just around the corner it became evident we were on the right path. We climbed a couple of miles out of the huge rock formations, which at times gave us much needed shade. Plant life is sparse in Vasquez Rocks, but they did have signs explaining what each plant was. We took special note of the one marked "Poison Oak." At the exit to the park we found a sign telling about all the movies and television shows filmed in this unique landscape. Leaving the park, the trail follows the road for a mile into the town of Aqua Dulce.

Walking two feet from pavement and the speeding cars was just about as scary as the roar of a lion in the wilderness. Passersby would honk their horns and cheer us on. We realized that we had become part of an elite group that the local population recognized. The 450 miles we had endured over the last five weeks had transformed us into official hiker trash. Stumbling into the Sweet Water Café we were greeted by a big sign welcoming the PCT hikers to Aqua Dulce.

We had been dreaming of good hot food for a couple of days, and the gourmet cheeseburgers took care of our hunger pains. To work out the dehydration of desert hiking we each consumed three quarts of ice cold root beer out of a mason jar. It was only about 4:30 when we finished eating. We were sitting there contemplating if we should continue on or go to the Saufley's place for the night. We had only put in just over 11 miles and it was still early. About the time we had decided to continue on, Jugs and Gavin came in with a couple from Washington (trail names Water Boy and Early Girl). They were helping the Saufleys. They offered us a ride down to Hiker Heaven, so we were officially sucked into the vortex. By the time they were ready to go, Moses and the Children of Israel arrived in town.

The Saufleys started Hiker Heaven in the mid 90's and have been a blessing to hikers for almost two decades now. From mid-April until the end of June they turn their garage into a mail room and their backyard into a resort. They welcome anyone with two or four legs and provide accommodations, showers, laundry, transportation hub, high-speed internet, telephones, and lots of information about the local area. They have found out over the years what a vortex this is for hikers and have limited stays to no more than two nights, with exceptions being made for injured hikers. There were ten hikers there the night we were. It was here we met Oakdale, whom we would run into a number of times between Agua Dulce and our final meeting place at the Canadian border. While we enjoyed spending the evening listening to others' trail experiences, we finally made our way to a large tent filled with cots. There we found rest, thanking God for sending trail angels like Jeff and Donna Saufley.

May 11th
Day 35 – 11.5 Miles
Total 467 Miles

It is so hard to leave a place of comfort; no matter if it's beside a bubbly stream or your own home. This backyard refuge in the desert was no exception. The roosters in the neighborhood have decided that four thirty is a good time to start the day, but I refused to get up until six. Water Boy was headed uptown at 7:00 a.m. and we did not want to miss the much appreciated ride. After a big breakfast of ham and eggs, biscuits and gravy at the Sweet Water Café we started the two mile walk up Aqua Dulce Canyon Road to the trail head on the north side of town. The hot sun reminded us of the reasons we should have started earlier or walked the night before. At the edge of town we found a stone wall under a shade tree across from a church. We sat down not even taking off our packs and drifted in and out of sleep. Then, what was starting to seem like an everyday occurrence, we started climbing. Just outside of town, as we climbed into the hills, we came across what looked like a large staging area for movie props. In the next three miles we climbed 2,300 feet with only a couple small dips. The trail was good though, and we only had to stop for extended rest a couple of times. At the ridge we found a nice grove of oak trees that gave us a grassy spot in the shade. Our resting spot in the grass gave us a view of the vortex of our recent past and a glimpse of the trail in our future. Rested up from the climb, we descended the three miles down to Bouquet Canyon road where Sharla was waiting to take us home for Mother's Day.

May 12th
Day 36 – 0 Miles
Total 467 Miles

What better way to spend Mother's Day than going to church? In the afternoon we watched the children so the moms could enjoy a day without the constant oversight of energetic youngsters. We spent the evening with the girls and preparing for the trail ahead.

Chapter Thirteen - Bouquet Canyon to Hiker Town

May 13th
Day 37 – 20 Miles
Total 487 Miles

As noon arrived on Monday the outside temperature read 93 degrees from inside the air conditioned car. We sat there in comfort looking up the hill we had to climb. After saying goodbye to Sharla we started the climb heading for the Oasis cache some 6.5 miles away. The trail treated us well; as it was gradual and clean. Arriving at the cache we found a dozen or so young hikers enjoying the shade and the coolers full of ice cold soda and beer. We sat for a while, sucking down three sodas. We headed west in hopes of meeting up with one of my old coworkers coming in from Francisquito Road. We never did see him and later found out he had turned around just a mile in front of us.

Around dinner time we arrived at Francisquito Canyon Road and hiked down to the ranger station to look for water. We found the place deserted and all the faucets shut off. Finally, we found some water in the water heater at the back of the station. A black widow quickly disappeared behind the tank while I filled our bottles. We kicked back under a picnic shelter, had some mashed potatoes, and took a little nap. Some of the young hikers arrived and hitched a ride down to Casa de Luna, a couple of miles south. The guys were the first to hitch a ride, and it took about a half hour before someone finally stopped. The girls showed up and asked about getting down to the trail angels. We told them how the boys did it, so they headed back out to the road to hitch a ride themselves. The first car that came along picked them up. What a demonstration of gender bias.

Trail angels Terry and Joe Anderson enjoy hosting hikers in a more party like atmosphere. We were told that some of the best taco salad on the PCT was being served at the "House of the Moon." While we would have loved to meet the Andersons, we pushed off the desire for taco salad and headed back to the trail. As we walked back up the road we met Grandpa coming off the trail. The sun was setting and the temperatures dropping. The cooler air allowed for an easier climb as we continued looking up the mountain at a trail that seemed so far away. Two miles into this section we were surprised when the trail topped a ridge, and instead of what we thought was going to be an additional climb up Grass Mountain, we found a fairly flat, clean trail around the north side. We were able to make good time, and I was happy to be following Family Man as he cleared the spider webs from the trail with his face. We figured that the spiders like to place webs across the trail after dark in hopes of catching insects for dinner. Crossing over Leona Divide Fire Road we started the descent down to Lake Hughes Road. Just before the road we found a water cache and a great spot to camp. It was 10:30 p.m. when we threw our packs on a picnic table and rolled our bags out on the grass.

May 14th
Day 38 – 24 Miles
Total 511 Miles

Sleeping close to a water source made a hot breakfast possible before starting out. As usual when we crossed a road we could expect a climb ahead. Early morning was a struggle, and Family Man seemed to have problems with a lack of energy. I don't know if it was from staying out too late or pain from his knee. A couple of times we stopped in cool grassy areas where he napped and I rested. It wasn't until we made it to the water tank at Ridgetop Junction that things seemed to pick up. As evening arrived we came across the 500 mile marker and stopped to celebrate the accomplishment. After thirty seconds of celebration we moved on. Stopping at 7:00 p.m. where the trail last crossed the dirt road, we ate a cold dinner and rested for another thirty minutes. Leaving the road, we headed into a wooded area with patches of grassy meadows. It was almost like an enchanted forest as the sun was setting. After dark we had a steep descent and eventually came across a burned out forest where downed trees littered the area. Part of the trail followed a jeep road that had been torn up pretty bad. Loose, ankle twisting rocks created a concern in the dark as we traversed the steep trail.

We had been in contact with another one of my old co-workers who had wanted to help out and was trying to meet up with us at Pine Canyon Road. We were running late, and I tried to make contact with him. I did see truck lights a mile to the east. Contact was never established, so we missed the cold sodas and water he was bringing for us. We descended via switchbacks to a small, unpaved parking lot where the folks from Hiker Town had placed a water cache. One of the hikers from Oasis Cache we had met yesterday, by the trail name Whitney Houston, was sleeping behind the cache but was a little incoherent. We rolled out our sleeping bags and again went to sleep under the stars.

May 15th
Day 39 – 7.5 Miles
Total 518.5 Miles

In the morning we were awakened by Whitney Houston packing up. We filtered a couple liters of water and headed for Hiker Town only 7.5 miles away. Our positive attitude, rooted in thinking that this was going to be an easy downhill walk, was crushed when we started climbing just past the paved road. Checking the GPS I saw we had over nine hundred feet to climb. The trail continued with its ups and downs, and seemed to go in and out around the hills for no apparent reason. It turns out one of the reasons for the extra miles was to allow the trail to circumvent a gun and hunting club. A mile from Hiker Town we came around a corner and spotted, like a mirage in the desert, the distant buildings below us to the north. By now Family Man was complaining about his shoes being too small, and his knee was hurting again. We decided to call on our trail angel to rescue us again and placed the call.

Hiker Town is a residential property where the owners are dedicated to supporting PCT hikers. They have set up a place to shower, wash clothes, relax, and sleep. We spent about an hour there drinking ice cold sodas and eating potato chips until Sharla arrived. By late afternoon we were home again in Wrightwood. Family Man went for shoes, and I rested. The next night we would tackle the long walk across the desert floor.

Chapter Fourteen – Hiker Town to Tehachapi

May 16th
Day 40 – 17.5 Miles
Total 536 Miles

      The day was spent preparing for an evening departure. By 4:00 p.m. we were loaded up and heading for Hiker Town. After stopping for some greasy food, we ended up at the trail head at 6:00 p.m. We said goodbye to Sharla and headed up the trail alongside the road. It was a hard goodbye as we knew it would be a week before we would see the girls again. As we left the car we were surprised by Moses and the Children of Israel just arriving at Hiker Town. After a couple of turns, we ended up on the aqua duct and shortly thereafter turned north onto the pipe that was our trail for over three miles. It was close to dark as the wind and clouds added to the chill in the air. We had expected a lot of heat going through the desert. It was quite a surprise when we had to wear coats. We came to Aqua Duct Road which follows the underground concrete waterway and turned northeast. Mile after mile we walked as the darkness deepened and the wind increased. Do you ever get tired? Does your mind go numb to the idea of even being in a remote place like this in the middle of the night? These are the thoughts that kept creeping into the doubtful part of my conscious as our steps took away the miles. Things just seem a little strange at night in the middle of the desert. It was eerie just seeing a truck driving down the gravel road. It brought our senses to full alert when a car came at us, speeding down the road along the aqua duct. We came upon a community of trailers in the middle of nowhere. The landscaping lights which spotted the surroundings created an eccentric atmosphere in the otherwise ghost town-like setting. We expected a dog to bark and a screen door to slam, but nothing. Rapidly we moved on.

Around 11:00 p.m. we left the concrete and headed down a parallel dirt road for another two hours. Finally, the lights and the sounds of windmills took away the doubt of ever reaching our goal. What goal could we possibly have out here in this waste land? That night, it happened to be the Cottonwood Creek Bridge where we heard there was a water cache. Arriving at 2:15 a.m. we found a flat sandy place to roll out our bags and soon fell asleep to the droning sound of large fan blades turning above us.

May 17th
Day 41 – 23 Miles
Total 559 Miles

We woke with great anticipation of a hot breakfast. Dave Schulist, the coworker we had missed a couple nights earlier, was bringing breakfast burritos from Palmdale and would be arriving around 7:00 a.m. Long Legs and his crew were at the water cache by the bridge which was now empty. The time for our burrito rendezvous kept getting pushed back due to GPS interface challenges and closed desert roads. Finally, at 9:30 Dave was able to find us, and we were soon sinking our teeth into much appreciated grub. The burritos, along with the soda we had previously missed out on, made for a great breakfast. Two of the hikers we had shuttled up to the trail in Wrightwood, Bristol Cone and Uber, came by and got some water. Once we had gone Dave found some other hikers coming up the trail and resupplied their water as well. He came out here to help us and ended up blessing a whole group of hikers. Our next stop was the Tyler Horse Canyon, which had a small but reliable stream. On the way up to Tyler Horse we were passed by a pair of cousins and the two British girls we had met at Oasis Cache.

We found the creek to be sufficient for our water resupply and after lunch started another climb higher into the mountains. The wind continued to strengthen the higher we climbed. Late in the day we entered a burn area and came across a water cache with a couple of plastic Adirondack chairs, thanks to Daniel and Larry, trail angels who are willing to haul all this water up here to the mountain. The wind continued to blow, intensifying after dark. We were pretty much exhausted by this time but decided to push on to Tehachapi Willow Springs Road eight miles away. At times the wind was so strong it would throw us off our feet and into the hillside. Many times I used my trekking poles to keep from being blown off the trail. We continued the struggle and were finally rewarded with a descent past more windmills coming alongside Oak Creek. We spotted numerous hikers camping in the trees along the creek. Crossing a rickety bridge, we found a camping spot. We cowboy camped again, putting our packs on a nearby picnic table. We had heard that a cooler was out by the road, so I walked on up the trail only to find it was empty. Even here at the lower altitude the wind continued to be strong as we fell asleep inside our cocoons.

May 18th
Day 42 – 8 Miles
Total 567 Miles

We woke up in the morning with hikers coming across the bridge. Family Man said he saw a raccoon run right by my head. I was still tucked away deep inside my sleeping bag and didn't see a thing. We were excited when we crossed the highway and started out across a pasture towards the distant hills. Our goal for the day was only eight miles and a meeting with another coworker who planned to pick us up at Highway 58. Family Man was not feeling too well, and I was hacking my lungs out from all the wind and dust we had encountered. By mid-morning we found a little protection from the wind behind a large bush. The challenge with doing this in a pasture is that the cows like the leeward side of bushes as well. So we settled in amongst the cow patties, and soon Family Man was asleep. I got a little nap, and we ended up spending an hour trying to get the energy necessary to continue on. Our little catnap was enough for us to push on through the pastures and over the hills to our pickup point at 1:00 pm.

Gary and Sally Schoelen were at the bridge when we crossed over Highway 58, and they took us into Tehachapi. After a big lunch at Primo Burger, they took us up to their home in Bear Valley Springs for the night. Sally washed our clothes while we showered. They fixed us a huge dinner of grilled steak, chicken and the fixings. Family Man slept all afternoon trying to get over whatever illness he was experiencing. My throat continued to get worse so Gary fixed me a hot toddy to ease the pain. It was getting so bad I had lost my voice. The Schoelen's are another example of God working through people to supply our needs.

Chapter Fifteen – Tehachapi to Walker Pass

May 19th
Day 43 – 23 Miles
Total 590 Miles

When you awake to the sound of an alarm and feel the comfort of a warm soft bed, momentary complacency is rapidly replaced by the cold reality of the day ahead. We left Gary and Sally's as the sun came up and were on the trail before 7:00 a.m. There was a massive amount of trash along Highway 58 and we're pretty sure PCT hikers were not the responsible party. I have it on my bucket list to stop and clean up the place on one of our trips over Tehachapi some time. After a little over a mile, we left the highway and started climbing into the hills. We climbed for the better part of the morning making pretty good time but still dealing with high winds. I was still coughing a lot and felt my lung capacity was reduced significantly. With altitude we traded sagebrush for wooded areas, and this helped reduce the wind. At our first water source we ran into a new hiker, for us anyhow. Bi-Polar is a 62 year old hiker from Wisconsin with a happy disposition. As we sat around the spring filling our bottles, Long Legs and his crew arrived. After a lunch of mashed potatoes we headed out. Within a mile we entered a burn area. Still dealing with wind farms, we seemed to be tortured with the ugly and the noisy for the afternoon. High on a ridge we acquired cell service and called the girls. Bi-Polar showed up and we let him use the phone to call his wife in Wisconsin. He had not been able to talk to her in over a week.

Early in the evening we became disgusted with some very nasty stuff on the trail and soon came upon the guilty party. Three cows stood there looking at us as if they owned the trail. We just kept going, and when we got close they turned around and ran up the trail to get away. All of a sudden they turned and crashed down through the brush in a pretty steep descent. By late evening, as the sun dropped below mountains, we were back in a burn area and kept hoping we would out walk both the windmills and the charred landscape. It did not happen, and as darkness set in we made camp at the top of an ash covered ridge with the "whooping" noise of turning props to sing us to sleep.

May 20th
Day 44 – 26 Miles
Total 616 Miles

We woke up to the blackness of soot all around us. It is always a discouragement to see what was once a beautiful forest turned into such desolate landscape. We walked about a quarter of a mile crossing another ridge to find the edge of the burn area and a nice place to camp.

The hot chocolate we'd had for breakfast temporarily helped the coughing, but it soon returned. By mid-morning we were passed by Bi-Polar and Long Legs with his crew. Ten miles into the day, we made it to the 600 mile marker during a strong steep climb on a section where the PCT co-existed with a four wheel drive road. Our water source for the day was Robin Bird Spring where we met a few other hikers and ate a late lunch. We passed through a valley and down along a stream bed, which had some stagnate pools of water and mosquitoes. By late evening, as the sun was setting we came out of another burn area. We had decided to stop around dark, but came across a sign showing the next water cache at Kelso Valley Road as only 4.6 miles away. This energized Family Man, and it was decided that we'd go for the water. It was all downhill, and fifteen minutes before midnight we were at the cache and into our bags, leaving the tents in our backpacks. It ended up being a record day of 26 miles. From the comfort of my sleeping bag I fixed a cup of hot chocolate to ease my sore throat.

May 21st
Day 45 – 21 Miles
Total 637 Miles

The sun appearing above the horizon jarred us from our dreams of soft beds, into the reality of lumpy sleeping pads. With fresh water at our disposal, we fixed a breakfast of mashed potatoes and hot chocolate. The late night translated into a late start, but by 9:00 a.m. we crossed the road and started climbing into the hills. The climbs for the day were moderate and we made good time. We met a big black bull standing regally amongst the Joshua trees, not more than a hundred feet off the trail. He kind of stared us down as we passed. In the middle of the afternoon we passed an old, abandoned mine with rusty vehicles and concrete foundations before descending down to Frog Creek Road then up another ridge. A couple hours later we started a descent to Bird Spring Pass. Crossing the side of the mountain under Wyleys Knob we spotted a hiker out ahead. This was our first sighting of Keymaster since the Baden-Powell spur. We passed him as he sat by the trail eating a snack less than a half mile before the water cache.

We sat under the afternoon shade of a Joshua tree eating what we could and drinking what we needed. The fifty or so gallons of water was literally an oasis in the desert. With this road crossing we would be climbing out of the arid mountains and into the more wooded area, leaving the desert behind us for good. The hill ahead looked scary as the wind was again starting to blow, and the climb up Skinner Peak was going to be around 1,700 feet. By 6:00 p.m. we were on our way, and within 600 vertical feet we hit the switch backs and turned back into extremely strong wind. Each turn back to the west was a grueling task. Not only did the wind get stronger with altitude, but the temperature also dropped. Family Man was well ahead as he likes to power up the hills, whereas Stagecoach's ponderous climb is nothing to brag about. As I turned back to the east on the last switchback, I spotted Family Man sitting high on a rock formation on the ridge.

We crossed just under Skinner Peak as the sun was setting and started our descent to a lower altitude. Once we had entered a wooded area the wind died down significantly. As darkness fell we started looking for a place to sleep. It took a while, but we finally found a somewhat flat and yet breezy place. We had to move a lot of dead branches out of the way and spent another night cowboy camping. It was another long day with many miles behind us. We became pretty sure we'd make it to Walker Pass on time the following day.

May 22nd
Day 46 – 15 Miles
Total 652 Miles

We were up early, anxious to make it to Walker Pass. With the motivation of a night with our girlfriends and a warm bed we made good time. I tried hard to keep up with Family Man, but he was on a mission and moving fast. By 11:00 a.m. we had the highway in sight and descended into the valley to arrive at the campground shortly after noon. As we waited at the campground for Sharla, we met a new hiker from Canada who was waiting for her hiking partner to arrive the next day. Sharla arrived at around 3:00 p.m., and we headed home for four days. This time off was a mandatory reprieve from the trail so we could be at our daughter Aurora's graduation.

Chapter Sixteen – Walker Pass to Kennedy Meadows

May 23rd-26th
Days 47-50 – 0 Miles
Total 652 Miles

Spending four zero days in civilization was not our idea of enjoyment. However, we did appreciate the time with our family and friends back in Wrightwood. This down time was also an opportunity to readjust our food supply. Our preconceived ideas of the perfect trail food had evolved with our experience. With our metabolism out of control we found a need for a more protein and calories. Family Man being the Chef, and having the ability to consume a vast amount of food, made the shopping list, and we headed for Winco. This trip was to serve a dual purpose. The first and obvious was to fill a shopping cart with instant mashed potatoes, beef jerky, tuna, spam, multiple bags of candy, food bars, drink mixes, and other edible items. It also tested our patience in dealing with humanity. We had come from an environment where conversations with a stranger were meaningful. Like, "Where's the next water source?" and "Are there any good places to camp?" In Winco all we found were strangers looking intent on finding Twinkies, hotdogs, and previously frozen salmon. There was not a smile or a nod or even an excuse me. We were blessed by an elderly lady willing to crop dust us in the cereal aisle. It wasn't pretty, and Family Man tried to blame Stagecoach.

May 27th
Day 51 – 14.45 Miles
Total 666.45 Miles

Leaving Wrightwood on this Monday morning was one of the hardest things we had ever done. We would not be returning until we had completed the trail. What made it even harder was the apprehension of the section ahead. Over the next 290 miles we would encounter the highest passes and experience a very remote and rugged trail. Trepidation may have been the cause of our anxiety, but the anticipation of taking on the heart of the PCT was really an exciting time.

Aurora joined her mother in chauffeuring us back to the trail. We dropped off our high country resupply box at Kennedy Meadows Store. This necessary side trip added a couple hours to our day but greatly reduced the weight we would have to carry out of Walker Pass. It was afternoon before we started the climb up around the barren mountain. Above the highway we watched as the car disappeared around the bend. We were committed to the trail ahead. An hour later we had conquered the handful of switchbacks and were on the ridge where the climb became more tolerable. We transitioned a burnt area before crossing a saddle just south of Owens Peak. As we descended to a small stream the clouds began to thicken. With the unlikely chance of rain, we welcomed the shady protection from the boiling sun. The trail was designed to cross as many water sources as possible, and that was certainly the case here. Once we crossed the trickling stream we climbed back up on a ridge, reaching the top as darkness fell.

May 28th

Day 52 – 22.78 Miles
Total 689.23 Miles

I woke up just as the day became aware of our existence. Nature called, but I was quick at returning to the warmth of my sleeping bag. Finally, an hour later, I packed and woke up Family Man. We descended to our first water source at Spanish Needle Creek. We had moved out of the shrubby brush covered landscape into groves of scrub oak trees. After getting water we again climbed to a ridge overlooking Ridgecrest. From here we were able to contact the girls and update them on our progress. We had a gradual descent moving in and out along the ridge. Just south of Sawtooth Peak, we did a switchback before coming to an overlook which opened up into the Inyokern Valley for the final time. Heading west, we descended to Chimney Rock Creek. As we closed in on the creek we caught up with Turtle Back. He was struggling, as most of us seemed to be doing. At the creek we found evidence that a trail angel had been there over Memorial Day weekend. A cooler full of empty soda cans disclosed what we had missed.

Fox Mill Spring was our next stop on the PCT. A quarter inch stream was flowing from a three quarter inch galvanized pipe coming out of the ground. Dumping into a trough, the water was clean and cold. It just took a long time to refill our hydro packs. After cooking up a dinner of mashed potatoes we climbed to a plateau and watched the sun set before hiking into the night. We set up our tents in an old burn area on the ridge, only eleven miles from Kennedy Meadows.

May 29th
Day 53 – 18.27 Miles
Total 707.5 Miles

The sun did its job and woke us up at 6:15. We had a cup of coffee and a food bar. The first five miles were gradual downhill. Family Man set the pace, making good time. The thoughts of a cheeseburger were on our minds as we raced towards Kennedy Meadows. From the hillside above Manter Creek we could see the ribbon of green to the northwest. The desert landscape east of the river offered no help from the blazing sun as the trail refused to go straight to the river. Instead, it stayed to the east and climbed over another hill. Eventually we entered a forest of scrub oak, which gave us some much needed shade. We didn't stay long as food and cold soda were on our minds. A mile beyond the wooded area we came to the North Fork of the Kern River and followed it upstream. It was along this river that I was introduced to rattlesnakes. Family Man was in the lead when all of a sudden he stopped and put his hand up. Pointing with his trekking pole, he showed me a four foot rattler lying in the grass next to the trail. He antagonized it enough that it headed for the protection of a boulder on the other side of the trail. The trail took us over a couple of hills and back down to the river before we arrived at the pavement.

There we were, just a mile from the Kennedy Meadows Store alongside Sherman Pass Road, and we still didn't want to walk all the way up to the store. So we decided we were going to hitch a ride. We had no idea how that hitching stuff worked, but we thought we'd put our thumbs out and the next passerby would pick us up. About five minutes later a truck came by, and we used this new found form of saying we wanted a ride. I guess the driver didn't understand our sign language and drove right by. We were devastated by the rejection and started making our way up the road. Walking up the road we met a hiker by the name of Whistler from Utah. You'd never guess how he got his trail name.

It's not easy walking on pavement after miles on the dirt, dust, and rocks. Arriving at this extremely remote store, we had the feeling of walking into a base camp for an expedition. A dozen or so hikers sat around tables on the covered deck. All were in various stages of going through their resupply boxes and their backpacks. Most were consuming food and beer as they shared stories of their trail experiences. Everyone had various levels of anxiety about the mountains in front of them. We found a table off to the side where we dropped our backpacks and headed into the store for our resupply box and a cold drink. The first root beer went down smooth and the second even smoother. After ordering cheeseburgers we unpacked our box on the table. Everything from ice axes to balsamic vinegar covered the table. It didn't take long before we realized that the weight and volume of our supplies was just a little overwhelming.

Chapter Seventeen – Kennedy Meadows to Forester Pass

The showers at Kennedy Meadows consisted of a couple of open air stalls located on the hill behind the store. For a few bucks we got hot water and a towel. The shower felt so good, washing the last three days of trail dirt from our tired bodies. Eventually we felt obligated to shut the water off. It was then that the chilly breeze blew up through the open bottom. This ice cold wind assisted in the drying process. Clean at last, we donned our rain gear and got in line to wash our clothes in the single washer. The clothes dryer consisted of three ropes stretched between poles. The lines were literally covered with hikers' semi-dry clothing. We had plans of an early afternoon departure, which was delayed by two hours while we waited on the clothes to dry.

As the restaurant was getting ready to close in preparation for the evening meal, we ordered an Italian sausage sandwich for our final high fat food for the next fourteen days. Delaware Dave, Robocop, Ice Axe (previously Just Lora), and Hikes A Lot were amongst those hanging out at the store. We met a couple of girls named Midnight Chocolate and Cowgirl whom we would see off and on during the High Sierra crossing. A few others arrived shortly before we left.

The recommended Kennedy Meadows departure date is the middle of June, but at 5:20 p.m. on May 29th we said goodbye to what civilization was there and with extremely heavy backpacks headed back to the trail. Our decision to leave ahead of the recommended date was due to the low snow pack on the higher passes. Our plans that day were to make it just up the trail to Kennedy Meadows campground. At the campground we discovered they wanted to charge us seventeen bucks for a flat place to set up our tent. With millions of other places to set up a tent for free, we axed the idea of a campground night. The last outhouse in almost two hundred miles had a door that wanted to swing open, causing a minor challenge which was cured by a big rock.

While we were filling up our water before leaving the campground, Cowgirl and Midnight Chocolate passed us. A mile later we passed them while they were setting up camp along the river. We hiked a few more miles, crossing a bridge where there were some campers with a big campfire. Campfires concern us, so we left the mosquito infested riverbank and climbed into the dark. About a mile up the hill, we stopped for the night excited that we had escaped the vortex of Kennedy Meadows and were on our way to the high country.

May 30th
Day 54 – 19.5 Miles
Total 727 Miles

As morning arrived, I lay there talking myself into getting out of the bag. After fixing a cup of coffee and eating a food bar we headed north. The first part of the day took us on up another 1,000 feet through 3 miles of burnt forest. Crossing a ridge we dropped into a valley where we walked through a meadow for about 2 ½ miles. The sky was clear and sun hot, but the occasional pine tree gave us shade. The trail took us around

Deer Mountain climbing for about 500 feet on the north side. Topping the ridge, we looked out across the valley where we could see the dark green splotches of the North Fork of the Kern River.

At the bridge we found Cowgirl, Midnight Chocolate, Brook, Deer Hunter, Iron Man, Stegosaurus and Shined Bright. The water was tantalizing as it was the first river of significance since we had left Deep Creek in southern California. The bridge across the river was guarded by a vortex troll and we were sucked in by the shade. We sat in the grass and ate potatoes and noodles, drank two liters of water, resupplied our hydro packs, and washed our feet and legs. What really lived under the bridge was a huge flock of birds. Considering what birds drop, we went upstream of the bridge to get our water. Not that it was any cleaner; it just made us feel better.

We finally paid the vortex troll with two hours of our time and were allowed to cross the bridge. The 2,700 foot climb up to over 9,000 feet started out okay, but the heavy packs and steep trail soon took their toll. We pushed on with frequent breaks and made it to the top after experiencing five sunsets. We would see the sun set behind a hill, and as we continued up around the mountain the sun would come back up. We rested at the top of the climb, just on the southwest slope of Olancha Peak, reflecting on the day's events before heading down another hill where a stream awaited us. Our goal of 20 miles for the day took us into the dark before we stopped, exhausted and ready for a good night's sleep.

May 31st
Day 55 – 23 Miles
Total 750 Miles

Waking up early, we got out of the sack before six. After a cup of hot chocolate, we put in four miles over mild terrain before arriving at Death Canyon Creek at 9:00 a.m. We took a short rest then climbed up to a ridge at 10,700 feet overlooking Owens Valley. From on the ridge we were able to make contact with our support team for an update. The mountains were getting bigger, making the views more spectacular. From time to time we could see a snow covered mountain to the north. For the most part we were in groves of pine trees, giving us plenty of shade. Leaving the ridge we descended to Diaz Creek which ended up being dry as a bone. It did not concern us much as we had plenty of water to make it to the next source. Climbing up the hill past Dutch Meadows, we arrived at a ridge that leads down into Horseshoe Meadows. Somewhere down there was a campground and a road. It wasn't for us though, and we kept going, arriving at Poison Meadow Spring which had some really good running water. Now, with a name like Poison Meadow Spring, it was a little disconcerting as to the quality of the water. We looked around and didn't see any skeletons or dead animals, so we happily filtered a couple liters of water each. Tanking up with the plans of dry camping that night we hiked on for another two hours arriving at Cottonwood Pass. The wind was blowing hard on the west side of the pass where we found an acceptable camping spot in a patch of gravel with a slight slope. After dropping his pack, Family Man walked over the pass to try to find a flat spot out of the wind. What he found on the other side was covered with snow. We set up camp in the wind and were in our bags as it got dark.

June 1ˢᵗ
Day 56 – 20.5 Miles
Total 770.5 Miles

It was the first of June, and we were heading deeper into the interior. While eating our breakfast of food bars and hot chocolate, Deer Hunter came by and told us the legendary Billy Goat was not too far behind. We had just hoisted our packs onto our backs when we saw a couple of hikers coming over the hill heading in our direction. Thinking they would catch up with us we headed on down the trail. They never did catch us, and we assumed they exited down to Horseshoe Meadows. A mile into the day we came to our first lake. Chicken Spring Lake, even as low as it was, brought with it a new attitude. From here to Hat Creek Rim we could expect plenty of water, which reduced the amount we needed to carry. Not only the quantity, but the quality of the water was changing as well. Leaving the lake we climbed over a small ridge and followed along the tree line on the west slope of Cirque Peak. Around 9:00 a.m. we crossed another ridge and entered the Sequoia National Park where a sign said we were at 11,320 feet above sea level. From there it was a gradual descent to Rock Creek.

Arriving at Rock Creek just after noon, we decided this would be a good place to wash our clothes. We spread our packs out on a grassy area next to the water, sharing the shady spot with a number of ants and other critters. Washing dirty clothes, and our grungy selves, with ice cold water was not idealistic. For the next two hours we rested and ate our lunch, allowing time for the sun to dry our clothes. Leaving the creek we started a substantial climb out of a canyon. We crossed a spine on the eastern base of Mount Guyot and down through the Guyot Flats. There in the open space of the flats we called the girls on the satellite phone. It was always good to hear their voices. Just the knowledge that everything was okay in the outside world dispelled the imaginary things that went through our heads in this remote environment.

We reached the trail heading up to Mount Whitney around 5:00 p.m. and ran across Keymaster. We crossed over the river on stepping stones and took off our packs for a break. While we were resting, Brook arrived. She was taking a side trip up to Whitney and headed east along Crabtree Meadow to join the John Muir Trail. Leaving the stream, we climbed about 1,000 feet to where the trail came down from Mount Whitney. The next hundred miles from this point would be familiar trail for Stagecoach from the previous year's adventure.

As the sun was setting, we made it to Wallace Creek amongst swarming mosquitoes. We quickly set up our tents while chatting with a hiker we named Just For Men due to his extremely dark red hair. He had hiked in from the west on the High Sierra Trail and was on his way up to Yosemite. He told us we would not be able to keep our mileage up now that we were in the high country. Comments like that to hikers who have 770 miles under their ever shrinking belts, normally turns them off just a little bit. While I have no desire to denigrate a fellow hiker, my attitude about what was possible was on a different plateau than Just for Men's. Not wanting to attract bears, we decided against fixing any dinner tonight, and the mosquitoes kept us in our tents. We did have a food bar to drive away the constant hunger pains.

June 2nd
Day 57 – 15.63 Miles
Total 786.13 Miles

We had been looking forward to this day ever since we first spotted the snow capped mountains. Our first and highest pass was less than ten miles away. We woke up early and quickly packed the bag before the mosquitoes could figure out we were available to supply them with blood. There wasn't a cloud in the sky as we climbed 1,000 feet to Bighorn Plateau. The plateau is above the tree line which gives you a great view of the surrounding mountains including Mount Whitney. A small shallow lake on the plateau looked more like a home for frogs than a water resupply for hikers. On the way down to Tyndall Creek we crossed a small stream where we fixed potatoes and stretched out on our pads for a rest. Crossing over Tyndall Creek, we started the five mile climb up to Forester Pass. Climbing the slope to Diamond Mesa, the trail took us across our first snow pack in the High Sierras. The snow melts at different rates leaving small hills and valleys in the snow called sun cups. It was only a hundred yards across, but it was just a brief taste of things to come. At 12,400 feet above sea level we were definitely feeling the altitude. Resting at the base of the pass we resupplied our water and teased the marmots that were looking for free handouts and contemplated how they would taste in a Jetboil.

As we sat there looking around at the massive granite walls that surrounded us, we were filled with awe. The mountains stood well over a thousand feet above our already high altitude. It brought so much peace to sit there watching the multiple streams which flowed out of the snow packs forming a bigger stream before plummeting down the valley. Looking up at the notch that dropped down about 300 feet from the ridge on each side, we were reminded of the over 700 feet we still needed to climb to the pass. This last 700 feet consisted of switchbacks moving up the right side of the chute. Unlike the previous year when Sharla and I had made our way over this pass, the weather was great and visibility was unlimited. Just fifty feet or so under the pass we crossed the chute covered with snow. The chute is on a 60 degree slope and harbors snow late into the summer. Fortunately, we were not the first ones across this snow pack. We made it to the top at 1:45 p.m. and were rewarded with a spectacular view of the other side and its many snow fields. The sense of accomplishment we felt sitting there on the highest point of the trail was overwhelming. Being emotionally overwhelmed had become a more frequent occurrence with each day that passed. For the next three quarters of an hour we rested, taking in the awesome view and talking to the girls.

Chapter Eighteen – Forester Pass to Mather Pass

Looking out across the snow fields to the north, we stepped off the pass and headed for lower altitude. On the first snow pack we tried to cross we sank up to our waists. If it wasn't for our oversized backpacks we may have gone deeper. So there we were, in the middle of a snow pack above 13,000 feet up to our waists in snow. Now what? We struggled up out of the snow only to sink again. It took a while, but we finally made it to some bare rocks where we rested. We decided to leave the trail which was mostly covered with snow and follow the bare stones down to a lake. It looked like the safest path to take.

The slope was steep and rocks unstable. You would step on a two foot diameter rock and it would give way and start sliding down the mountain. We slowly, step by step, made our way to the lake. As we approached the lake with soaking wet feet, we made the choice to go around the right side. The left side had snow fields and a 45 degree slope into the lake. That ended up being a poor decision. It took two hours to get around the lake as the rocks we had seen from up on the mountain ended up being the size of dump trucks. We ended up doing a lot of boulder hopping, some of which was quite dangerous. We would have to jump a four foot chasm, some 20 feet deep. This may not sound too bad, but add high altitude and a thirty-five pound pack and it gets intense. At one point a large rock rolled onto my foot, and I froze. A twisted ankle at this altitude could be disastrous. I hollered at Family Man to stop, and we evaluated the situation. Fortunately, the rock was balanced enough I was able to roll it back releasing my foot without any damage. It did make me think about being more careful.

We were tired and soaked when we found the trail on the north side of the lake. Once we were clear of the snow we stopped at a stream flowing across the trail and reflected on our accomplishments of the afternoon. As we waited for our shoes to dry, Family Man fixed spaghetti and meatballs in an attempt to reenergize our aching muscles. I'm sure you're thinking we didn't have it too bad eating entrées like that, but let me clear up any misconceptions of our culinary indulgences. These spaghetti and meatballs were small freeze dried meals. When rehydrated with boiling water they make enough to maybe satisfy a three year old, if he gets a cookie for dessert. We topped off our dinner with a hot cup of coffee.

After about a half hour at the creek we spotted a couple of hikers coming down from the pass. Evening was coming, and cold wind off the snow made it necessary to move on. Putting on our semi-damp shoes, we continued the descent to warmer temperatures. The trail improved and so did our speed. The many waterfalls along the headwaters of Bubbs Creek were mesmerizing, and we tried to slow down enough to enjoy them. Jeff, one of the two hikers caught up with us, said they had pretty much followed the trail out onto the ridge. Obviously that had been the right direction to go, regardless of the snow packs. He was planning on exiting Kearsage Pass and hurried on. We made it into the valley and followed Bubbs Creek to Vidette Meadows where we camped along the river. There a long way from civilization, deep in the wilderness, we felt God's presence and thanked Him for a successful day and protection.

June 3rd
Day 58 – 13.87 Miles
Total 800 Miles

In the morning we again witnessed God's beauty, His grace, His strength and His blessings. We awoke at the usual time but did not leave in a hurry. We had a 10:00 a.m. rendezvous point only 2 ½ miles away. Family Man's friend, Brett, was coming across Kearsage Pass with some much desired supplies. After following Bubbs Creek for a mile, we parted ways with the now raging river and made a right turn heading up the mountain. Switchbacks made for a rapid climb as the mosquitoes chased us up the mountain. A thousand feet higher we arrived at our previously arranged meeting spot at 8:30. We were not used to taking a mandatory hour and a half break and really didn't know what to do with ourselves. We found a great place to spread out our pads and relax away from the stream and clear of mosquitoes.

Brett and his friend Scott showed up at 10:00 am with the package from the girls. Banana bread, Mountain Dew, and oranges along with Nutella for Family Man were in the bag. We wasted no time consuming the oranges, Brittany's homemade banana bread, and the carbonated beverage.

Considering what we experienced on Forester Pass, we decided we did not need our ice axes. The guys were willing to pack out the axes along with our trash. At 12:30 we said our goodbyes and headed on up the mountain. Stopping at a shelf, we were overtaken by Iron Man who took a break and chatted with us for a few minutes. It was time to attack Glen Pass. The previous year, Sharla and I had struggled on this pass and it was still fresh in my mind.

Even with numerous snow packs on the climb up the eastern slope of the pass, it did not seem as dreadful as the last year's ascent. It may have been the eight hundred miles of training leading up to the pass that eased the pain of such a climb. The icy blue lakes which contrasted with the snow covered mountains were spellbinding. Where the snow had melted, the blooming flowers created an unbelievable palette of colors. We stopped a number of times to enjoy the view, which allowed us to again fill our starving lungs with oxygen.

A few hundred feet below the pass we heard Iron Man holler. As his bellowing echoed off the mountain walls, we pretty much figured it out that he had reached the top. The climb through the snow fields was not a challenge, but topping the pass we could see the trail down was full of snow. Having learned our lesson from Forester Pass, we decided to stick as close to the trail as possible. As we started down we could see Iron Man below us. He hollered up for us to enjoy the post holing. For the next half mile we plowed through the snow, constantly sinking in up to our knees. Again our feet and pants were soaking wet. An hour later we made it to the first shelf and out of the majority of the snowfields. Where the snow had melted, spring was revealed in the green grass and flowers. Streams of cold, clear water came together to create tumbling waterfalls making their way down to Rae Lakes. Before reaching the lake, the trail crossed the primary tributary. Family Man found this a good spot to wash his hair by sticking his head under the waterfall. I'm pretty sure the recently melted snow cooled him down a bit.

It was late afternoon when we reached Rae Lakes and started the long walk along the string of lakes. These are the lakes that make up the headwaters of the South Fork of Woods Creek. I really wonder why they call it a creek. This was a raging flow of water some twenty feet wide or so, with waterfalls that sounded like thunder. Is that not a river? After all, we found mere trickles of water in southern California which were called rivers.

We thought about stopping, but with so much daylight left we headed on towards the bridge six miles away. We picked some wild green onions at the closed Ranger station and considered eating dinner on the front porch. The mosquitoes were so bad we packed up and moved on. Storm clouds had followed us over Glen Pass and were now making noises consistent with a thunderstorm. God had protected us coming off the pass, and now He was giving us shade. We waded across a couple of streams, getting my almost dry shoes wet again. We entered mosquito infested land and made it to the suspension bridge by early evening. After washing up in the river, we wasted no time getting into our tents away from the blood sucking insects.

June 4th
Day 59 – 16 Miles
Total 816 Miles

The sun streaming through the trees transitioned us from a fitful sleep to the buzz of mosquitoes outside our tents. As we sulked over our breakfast of noodles and a cup of instant coffee, we found out Iron Man was running low on food. Sure, it was his fault for not carrying enough, but out there in the wilderness hind sight did nothing for a person. We went over our food supply and were able to give him some noodles and food bars. Family Man shared with him about the green onions. Iron Man was kind enough to take a couple of pictures for us as we crossed the suspension bridge.

We headed upstream along the North Fork of Woods Creek on a 3,300 foot climb to Pinchot Pass. Little over a mile up the trail White Fork Creek came tumbling out of the mountains. Though it was twenty feet wide, it wasn't all that deep, but boy was it cold. I crossed at the trail with the water up to my knees. Family Man came across on a row of stones, still about a foot deep. We were sitting there putting our shoes back on when Iron Man came through with his sandals and walked right through. He stopped and thanked us again for the green onion tip and the food.

It was another awesome day of spectacular landscape as God's creation revealed itself in the mountains around us. We rested briefly at a spot where Sharla and I had camped the previous year under the shadows of Crater Mountain. The deer, while keeping their distance, didn't seem overly concerned about our presence. You can never say a 3,300 foot climb is easy, but the one up Pinchot Pass was one of the more gentle ones we experienced. We reached the pass soon after noon and were rewarded with another spectacular view, not only out ahead but also from where we had come. The chain of icy blue lakes dwarfed by the snow covered mountains strung into the valley which was dotted with pine trees amongst the rocks.

Starting down the north side of Pinchot Pass, we were surprised to find it fairly clear of snow. At the bottom of the 2,000 foot, 4 mile descent we crossed numerous strong flowing streams. One of the streams lacked stepping stones or any form of downed trees and required us to remove our shoes and wade across. The cold water felt good on a hot day, but the mosquitoes gave us motivation to get our shoes on and head up the valley towards Mather Pass. Walking along the west side of the South Fork of Kings River, we crossed numerous streams flowing from the side of the mountain. One of the streams was only about ten feet across but was running fairly deep. Family Man found a place he could jump across, but there was no way I was going to try it with my short legs. I ended up hiking uphill about 300 yards before finding a spot to cross without getting wet. The rest of the four mile climb to the base of Mather Pass was mild.

We arrived at the basin below the pass at 6:00 pm and decided not to tackle the pass this late in the day for fear of getting caught on top. A cold northeast wind had started to blow, and dark clouds were rolling across the mountains from that direction. The threatening storm intensity gave us enough concern that I covered my tent with a light weight tarp and we fortified our tents with rocks to hold them in place. Thirty minutes later it started hailing and dropped precipitation on us for about twenty minutes. Family Man fixed up a Jetboil full of rice and we drank hot apple cider as the hail bounced off our tents. It is amazing how secure you can feel inside a warm sleeping bag in a tent. As the sun set, the storms moved on and the sky began to clear.

Chapter Nineteen – Mather Pass to Silver Pass

June 5th
Day 60 – 19.05 Miles
Total 835.05 Miles

The sound of a hiker's footsteps woke us up. At 11,500 feet, this would be the highest altitude we would camp, and it was downright cold. I had no intentions of getting out of my bag. It wasn't until the sun came over the mountains and warmed things up that we crawled out. By 7:30 a.m. we had the camp cleaned up and started up Mather Pass. Snow packs covered portions of the trail, but overall the 500 foot climb was not too difficult to navigate. During our climb on the switchbacks a young, lightweight hiker passed us. He had started twenty days behind us. In some ways it made us feel slow, yet we knew our limitations would not be able to handle that kind of speed. When we arrived at the top our new acquaintance was sitting on a rock smoking some weed. Maybe that's the way to pick up the pace.

The north side of the pass was still in the shade and half covered with snow most of the way down to Palisade Lakes. We were no more than twenty yards down the trail when we hit our first snow pack. Testing the snow, Family Man found it covered with ice from the rain the night before. We discussed the dangers of a direct descend over boulders, and from our experience on Forester Pass we were adamant about staying close to the trail. Small footprints broke up the otherwise smooth surface across this forty five degree slope. We questioned our previous decision to get rid of the ice axes.

Standing there testing the grip of our shoes on the ice, I made a decision that could have cost us our lives. I told Family Man to make sure he anchored his trekking poles with each step, and we would be okay. Three steps onto the ice we had a coming to God moment, knowing this was a bad choice. There was no way of turning around safely. Digging our poles into the ice, we would place our feet just above the pole to keep it from sliding. Doing this slowly, one step at a time, we inched our way forward. Only about a fourth of the way across I stopped with my left foot resting on a trekking pole stuck two inches into the icy snow. Fear was very real as I watched Family Man twenty feet ahead working his way along the small indentations. *What was I going to tell Brittany when her husband crashed into the rocks 200 feet below? Would I be able to tell his little boys what grandpa talked their dad into? Would his mother ever forgive me?* It was here on the side of this mountain that I experienced something I have never felt before and find really hard to describe. It was a strong presence that seemed to methodically move our feet and hands, not haphazardly but with confidence and control. On the other side we were both shaken from the danger we had just experienced.

As we continued north over the next three months we felt God's presence many times, but the presence we felt during this 150 foot patch of icy snow was by far the greatest. It strengthened our faith in God, and we learned we could trust Him to protect us even in our stupidity. Looking back up the mountain we vowed we would not make this mistake again. We discussed the influence I had on Family Man, being his dad, and how it was necessary for him to speak up when something I wanted to do was dangerous. Close to the bottom, where the snow pack leveled out to a more manageable slope, Family Man wanted to slide down to the bottom. It looked safe enough, so using his trekking poles for brakes he gave it a try. I laughed my tail off as he went bumping down the hill, bouncing off each little hump in the snow. He broke one of his trekking poles and hurt his bum. I told him I would come down the old fashion way, one step at a time.

Once out of the snow we stopped at the first stream for our morning break. Brook, Cowgirl, and Midnight Chocolate came by while we were eating breakfast and drinking our coffee. Cowgirl and Midnight Chocolate had had the same challenge we had on the ice, but Brook used mirospikes, making it considerably safer. As for the pot smoker, he came straight down the mountain, bouncing from boulder to boulder and staying clear of the snow.

The trail stayed some fifty feet above Upper Palisade Lake, giving us a great view of the snow packs that led down to the edge of the crystal clear water. Adding to this landscape were small fluffy white clouds in a rich blue sky, and I was enticed to bask in the sunshine like a lizard on warm rock. As I drifted into a state of complacency, Family Man again reminded me that the trail is not going to walk itself, and we moved on. By the time we got to Lower Palisade Lake, Family Man had left me far behind. The trail had descended to just a few feet above the water. Walking along the lake I was staring deep into the water, thinking about how inviting it looked, when I tripped on a flat stone sticking up about three inches. My trekking poles slipped on the stone, and I tumbled rolling down hill, stopping just short of the water. Other than a bruised knee, and my pride, I was unhurt. I had to laugh as I struggled back up on my feet and hobbled on down the trail. You should pay attention to where you're going, or you will go to where you pay attention.

Below the Palisade Lakes, we descended the Golden Staircase. The steep switchbacks take you alongside the ever growing river which plummets over multiple falls down a narrow gorge into the Palisade Valley. Just before I entered the tree line at 9,100 feet I found Family Man stretched out on a huge boulder sleeping. A lot of tempting ideas came to mind, but I resisted and woke him up. We continued the descent to 8,000 feet where the Palisades Creek flows into the Middle Fork of the Kings River. Before the rivers merged we went through a mile or so of old burn area. Some of the trees had already fallen and others looked close to doing the same.

The mosquitoes were thick at the Middle Fork Trail Junction, so we wasted no time in starting our climb upstream toward Muir Pass. This three plus miles up through Grouse Meadows and along the river to Bishop Pass Trail Junction was an emotional time for me. It was here that Sharla and I had decided to leave the John Muir Trail the previous year. I knew that once we passed the trail junction, the scenery would all be new. By 5:00 p.m. we crossed the Dusy Creek Bridge and the trail up to Bishop Pass.

The next two miles took us through another meadow before starting a moderate climb. We climbed Barrier Rock, where the trail has been chiseled into the side of the granite alongside a 70 foot waterfall. The waterfalls coming down from Muir Pass were spectacular as the mountains dumped their melting snow into the valley. The climb intensified as the trail got steeper. It was not quite dark yet when we stopped for the night on a shelf under the shadow of a 13,300 foot mountain named the Black Giant. We were getting pretty high, and it looked as if we were getting close to the snow packs. Brook and a couple of other hikers were camping on the shelf as well. We hiked over 19 miles that day, climbed over Mather, and descended to 8,000 feet before climbing back up to 10,500 feet, and I was tired. It was an emotional strain to look at the mountains ahead, but looking back at how far we had come made it all seem possible.

June 6th
Day 61 – 20.45 Miles
Total 855.5 Miles

Waking with the sunshine, we were on the trail just after 7:00 a.m. Three and a half miles and 1,600 feet to climb to Muir Pass didn't sound too bad. It became bad however when we hit snow around 1,100 feet below the pass and spent the next three hours climbing through snow fields. The pure streams coming out from underneath the snow packs and the ice floating on the pristine lakes reminded us of our high altitude. Cowgirl and Midnight Chocolate passed us at Helen Lake as we were entering a continuous snowfield. From there to the top we tried to follow the trail, but for the most part we climbed straight up the mountain, making stair steps in the snow. Adrenaline kicked in a couple hundred feet from the top as the Muir Hut came into view framed by the crisp, blue cloudless sky. The stone hut with its conical roof was built in 1930 by the Sierra Club as a shelter for hikers.

Cowgirl took our picture before heading north to catch up with Midnight Chocolate. A hiker named Juice arrived and hung out for just a few minutes before he moved on. We celebrated reaching the last of the 12K passes by calling the girls and eating Jelly Bellies. It didn't take long in the wilderness for candy to become a premium commodity. It was time to say goodbye to the pass and head down the other side.

For the next two miles we post holed through snow fields as we made our way past Lake Dermand. At the half melted Wanda Lake we stopped for a few minutes to enjoy the awesomeness of God's creation. The snow capped mountains and the few scattered clouds in the deep blue sky reflected off the water with amazing clarity. We crossed a couple of streams from the run off of Wanda Lake and followed the west slope of the valley on a fairly consistent descent around Sapphire Lake to Evolution Lake. We crossed back over the stream, which was now 120 feet wide, on a path of stones. If you were really good, you could keep your feet dry. Considering our feet were still wet from post holing in the snow, it didn't really matter. We joined Juice, Cowgirl, Midnight Chocolate, and Brook all sitting on a big boulder just past the stream overlooking the lake. We didn't hang around long as we had a goal to complete 20 miles. Things were going slowly, and it looked like it would be a long night to make this goal.

After making our way around Evolution Lake we descended a number of switchbacks into the valley along a rolling stream which turned into Evolution Creek. We had heard rumors that the spot we were to forge the river was dangerous. A section hiker we met said he was taking the alternate route through the meadow, and crossing upstream where it was wider and shallower than the forge. We talked about what we would do if the water was too deep or running too strongly to safely cross. We decided we would just make that decision when we got there. We had really stopped worrying about anything that was more than ten feet up the trail. A couple of south bounders gave us good information on the passes ahead and what we could expect at the river. Walking along the meadow we spotted a few deer grazing, but they paid us little attention.

Eventually we arrived at the forge, which was 80 feet wide and about 30 inches deep. We took off our shoes, socks and pants, putting them all securely in our backpacks and started across. Family Man being the tallest went first so I could see how wet I was really going to get. The water was extremely cold. I don't know how long it took for it to get here from the ice and snow, but it did not bother to warm up on the way down. After the crossing we walked through a small burn area and descended a couple switchbacks to the South Fork of the San Joaquin River. We had heard the thundering sound of water coming down the valley and were quite happy to see a footbridge spanning the river. It was a very scenic hike as we followed the river downstream three miles to our campsite. We felt relieved that the highest passes were behind us. It was the end to another God blessed day.

June 7th
Day 62– 23.2 Miles
Total 878.7 Miles

Like a broken record, I awoke soon after 5:00 a.m. and lacked any interest for getting out of my bag. It was warmer at this lower altitude, but the motivation was not there. Finally harsh reality won over comfort, and I started the long process of getting dressed and waking up Family Man. The mosquitoes were not too bad that morning when I exited my tent. We had another 500 feet to descend to the Muir Ranch Trail before starting the 3,300 foot climb over Seldon Pass. As with all climbs, it was tough but we made it up the switchbacks to a couple of meadows by 11:00 a.m. Again we were witnesses to God's creation as waterfalls cascaded from the side of the mountain. As noon approached we passed between the Sallie Keyes Lakes and around the east side of Heart Lake. There was not a lot of snow on the way up to Seldon Pass, but at 10,910 feet the pass itself was solid snow. The north side of the pass down to Marie Lake was spotted with snow packs, but it was crusted enough we were able to stay on top keeping our feet dry. Stopping at one of the snow packs, I made myself a snow cone, using Crystal Light for flavoring. It was my treat for having to traverse the frozen patches. Family Man was a little concerned about my habit of eating what could be contaminated snow, but they were always a treat for a dry mouth. Leaving Marie Lake we descended to Bear Creek following it for about 5 miles as the pleasing sound of the babbling stream turned into the roar of a rushing river.

Again we were misled, having heard the upcoming forge was dangerous. When we crossed the river, it wasn't bad at all. It was just another sans pants crossing. The biggest problem was the mosquitoes. They were vicious and hungry for blood. We forged two more rivers before climbing a thousand foot ridge which led steeply down to the Vermillion Valley Resort trail. All the hikers talked about going over to the resort for a couple of zero days. We had been out of civilization for nine days and we were craving a cheeseburger. The VVR vortex would take at least 24 hours. We checked our food supply, and even though our fuel was running low, we had plenty of calories for the 29 mile hike over Silver Pass and down to Reds Meadow.

We knew we may end up eating dry noodles, but we made the decision to push on the following morning. We found a great spot close to the bridge over Mono Creek to camp for the night and for feeding mosquitoes.

June 8th
Day 63– 22.3 Miles
Total 901 Miles

At 5:15 my inborn clock woke me up, and I decided not to ignore it this morning. Family Man wanted to get a big day in. I started packing and eventually woke him up. We were on the trail crossing the bridge at 6:15. Silver Pass was the pass of the day, and we had to climb 3,000 feet to reach the top. It was a multiple shelf climb which gave us several false assumptions that we were almost there. Experiencing too many of these optical miscues leads to depression. It was 10:30 a.m. when we finally made it to the pass which was clear of snow. Family Man whipped up some potatoes which we shared with the mosquitoes that had followed us up the mountain. Why they feel comfortable at 11,000 feet is beyond me. We were beginning to despise these little critters. Why did God create them anyhow?

Chapter Twenty – Silver Pass to Tuolumne Meadows

Leaving the pass we descended 1,700 feet through a few snow fields and into a deep valley. A short time after noon we crossed the Fish Creek Bridge where the water came cascading down the canyon. After a quick switchback we followed the creek up to Tully Hole, which ended up being just a big valley in a horseshoe shape. From there we climbed another 800 feet of switchbacks before passing by the uphill side of Virginia Lake and over a hill to Purple Lake. It wasn't purple that day, but maybe it was at one time. Leaving Purple Lake we climbed gradually along the contour of the mountain. In the late afternoon, as we made it to the highest point for the day, a few sprinkles started falling from a really small cloud. I told Family Man that it was heaven crying tears of joy that we had made it to the top. We had already climbed 5,700 feet and the day wasn't over. The trail descended a couple hundred feet to the Duck Lake outlet. Crossing a log, we started back up a hundred feet returning to the contour of the mountain.

All the hikers we met that day were south bounders. They told us the café at Reds Meadow served breakfast, which really cheered us up. Our bodies had been deprived of fatty, cooked foods for so long that it was constantly on our mind. Almost every conversation centered on a greasy highly caloric entrée. Passing the 900 mile marker, we hiked a gradual descent into a valley bringing us to the end of our day. We had just enough gas to cook noodles and hot chocolate for dinner.

June 9th
Day 64– 5.7 Miles
Total 906.7 Miles

There is nothing like the promise of bacon to get a hiker going in the morning. We were out of our tents and on the trail at 5:00 a.m. The day started with a mile of gradual climbing before descending the 4.5 miles into Reds Meadow. We made our way through a vast amount of blown down trees from the wind storm that had happened a couple years ago. Winds at 120 mph with gusts calculated at over 180 mph had blown in from the north and lasted over three hours. Literally tens of thousands of trees toppled like matchsticks across the mountains. Walking through the worst affected area was like going through a war zone. Huge trees lay in all directions across each other. Trail crews have done a great job cleaning up the trail. For the final mile we walked through a twenty year old burn area. Decomposing burnt tree trunks still spot the landscape where new growth is slow in coming.

Reds Meadow Resort consists of campgrounds, store, lodge, and most importantly a café. We walked into the resort at 7:30 a.m. and found the first sit down toilet in 205 miles. With hot water at our disposal, we spent ten minutes trying to wash ten days of crud off of our faces and hands before heading into the café. We were sure we heard angels singing "Hallelujah" when we walked through the door and saw the tables with their sunflower tablecloths and padded chairs. It is surprising how much we had begun to miss the simple things. A hiker friendly waitress and the smell of bacon coming from the kitchen added to our already euphoric emotions. The bacon and eggs were really good, and we dug into the home fries. Multiple glasses of milk and cups of fresh coffee were a hit. We devoured everything with a passion. After breakfast it was on to the showers and laundry room. Family Man's clothes were so filthy the dirt clogged up the washer. After fishing out his clothes, all that was left was a washer full of muddy water.

We spent the day in the store sitting on an overstuffed couch reserved for hikers. The free WIFI allowed us to update our Facebook pages and check our email. We cannot say enough about the hospitality of the resort. We showed our appreciation by continually purchasing chips, ice cream, soda and candy all morning. The waitress in the café promised us a ride to Mammoth once she got off work at one. Since we had to wait anyhow, we returned to the café for lunch.

Sitting around the store we met a lot of hikers, most of them either weekend or section hikers. One PCT hiker named Lefty came into camp, pointed at Family Man, and said, "I know you." He had found Family Man's driver's license lying on the trail. Family Man was not even aware that he had dropped it. Lefty was in a hurry, and after using my phone to call his dad, he quickly got what he needed and left. We heard from another hiker that Lefty, being true to his name, had taken off on his female hiking companion at VVR. Not sure how true that is, but it makes a good story. Iron Man and Jefe came into the resort before we left. Neither of them wanted to go into town. The waitress finally came through, and we made it down to the Motel 6 in Mammoth where she dropped us off around 4:45 p.m. We were thrilled to be kicking back in a soft bed. For dinner we walked across the street to John's Pizza Works for pizza and hot wings and drank way too much root beer.

June 10th
Day 65– 0 Miles
Total 906.7 Miles

After breakfast at the Breakfast Club we spent the day running around Mammoth hunting for smaller pants. We were not able to find any pants, but we did get our food resupply and some snacks. While at the 99 Cent Store we asked the clerk if she knew of anyone who could give us a ride back up to Reds

Meadow. She ended up arranging for her son to take us the next morning. We ran into Brook (now known as Peanut Butter Platypus) and the Canadian couple. They were hanging around outside the hotel getting ready to go across the street for pizza. We had our minds set on Mexican food and headed uptown for dinner. Our eyes were definitely bigger than our stomachs as we ordered, and we ended up leaving half of our food on the plate. At the grocery store we met more hiker trash. Mule, Snorts, and Story Teller were all part of the NOBO SOBO group we had seen on Facebook. They like to hitch north to a point on the trail and hike south one section at a time. On the trolley back to the motel a bunch of unruly preteens and teenagers were making a lot of noise. When some of them got off, I applauded. Shortly thereafter the driver kicked the rest off the bus. We had lost any tolerance for too much civilization. Back at the motel we packed our bags for an early departure and spent the rest of the evening resting.

June 11th
Day 66– 19.5 Miles
Total 926.2 Miles

We were up early and ready for our ride over the ridge to Reds Meadow. Logan, our chauffeur, showed up right on time and was a real gentleman. The Canadian couple rode with us back to the resort where we had breakfast at the café before returning to the wild. We met an elderly hiker named Lucky and his brother who was supporting him on the trail. Soon after returning to the trail we crossed the Middle Fork of the San Joaquin River and the Devils Post Pile. We met up with Lucky and hiked together for a while, but we let him move out ahead after a couple of hours. Our inclination was to hike alone.

Continuing the climb along the river, we eventually left the valley and climbed through Agnew Meadows and up about a dozen switchbacks below the San Joaquin Ridge. Stopping in the shade beside a stream I decided to get water as it was just below a spring and looked really clean and cool. Straddling the stream

I filled up my bottle. When I turned around my foot slipped, and I sat right down in the water. It was quite humorous except for the wet bottom and one soaked shoe. Fortunately, Family Man had stopped at an earlier stream and was not there to witness the good old butt soaking.

Climbing over Agnew Pass, we arrived at Thousand Island Lake late in the afternoon. We found a place overlooking the lake to stop and rest. Family Man had been looking forward to seeing this lake and had talked about swimming out to one of the islands. After 923 miles of backpacking and walking through streams of freezing water, he changed his mind. So we just sat there and enjoyed the view. Leaving the lake, we climbed over Island Pass and started down into a valley as a cold wind started to blow. We crossed a log over some really cool waterfalls and started the climb to Donahue Pass. Not wanting to get too high on the pass we stopped early for the night.

June 12th
Day 67– 16.3 Miles
Total 942.5 Miles

Back on the trail at 6:00 a.m. we climbed another 1,300 feet to Donahue Pass arriving at 8:45 a.m. The top was half covered with sun cupped snow, and we were treated to a great view up Lyell Canyon. I was able to make contact with Sharla, arranging our pickup for later in the day. Making our way down into the valley, on a trail consisting of rock steps, we crossed the watershed off the east side of Mount Lyell making up the headwaters of the Lyell Fork of the Tuolumne River. We forged many streams from the waterfalls cascading down the mountains. The mosquito infested meadows helped us keep up the pace for the ten miles down the valley along the now gently flowing river. The closer we got to Highway 120, the more day hikers we met. We were anxious to get to the highway, making it difficult to spend much time sharing with them our adventure. Our thoughts were on the near future, knowing that we would be back in the RV with our wives and the boys by dinnertime.

Arriving at the highway at 3:00 p.m. we hiked down to the store for something to eat. We met Spitfire, Dora the Explorer, Operator, and several other hikers. While we were there, Lucky and the Canadian couple arrived. It did not take long before we headed back to the parking lot where Sharla was to pick us up. It was just too noisy at the store and we were not thrilled with that much activity. Walking back to the parking lot, we reflected on the last seventeen days and looked forward to a couple of days off the trail with the girls. As we lay back on our pads in the shade of a pine tree we watched people come and go.

At around 5:30 p.m. we saw Sharla drive by. We picked up our stuff and headed out to the road. After finding out from the hikers at the store where we may be, she finally found us. The drive back to the RV at Mono Lake Campground was scary as the car seemed to be going way too fast. We had been on the trail long enough that anything over 2.8 mph seemed dangerous. It felt so good to get back to the RV where we were able to take a hot shower and put on clean clothes.

June 13th-14th
Days 68-69– 0 Miles
Total 942.5 Miles

The next two days were spent resting and reuniting with our support team. On the first day Family Man took his family over the mountains to Yosemite. He and Brittany had looked forward to showing off the boys to their old friends. Sharla and I hung out at the RV Park babysitting the dogs. We did make it up to the BBQ joint in town for some good hot food. On the second day we packed up the RV and headed up to Bridgeport. Sharla had had problems with the RV periodically kicking out of gear on the way up and wanted me to figure it out. Naturally it did not act up at all on the 28 mile trip. We used the rest of the day to organize our packs for the 76 mile section up to Sonora Pass and to play with the boys.

Chapter Twenty One – Tuolumne Meadows to Sonora Pass

June 15th
Day 70– 19.5 Miles
Total 962 Miles

Another long drive brought us back to the tourist infected mountains. Arriving at the Tuolumne Meadows store and café at 9:00 a.m. we were greeted by a long line. It took a half hour to get an expensive breakfast of dry tasteless biscuit, a little piece of bacon, and an egg. Sharla dropped us off at the trailhead at 9:38 a.m. It was the middle of June on a Saturday morning, and we did not have the trail to ourselves. Scores of clean pretend hikers, with high brand hiking clothes, obviously wanted to take a slow casual walk in the mountains. It was like traffic leaving a major metropolitan area. The farther we walked, the less perfume laced pedestrians we encountered. By the time we arrived at Glen Aulin the tourists had all but disappeared.

Other than our encounter with the slow hikers, it was a high speed, two hour hike to the high country camp. I do recommend this day hike for anyone who would enjoy a stroll along the Tuolumne River. The last two miles descend 500 feet along the cascading river to the camp. We sat on a bench watching the water roar over the 50 foot White Cascade falls and ate lunch. One of the cooks at the camp had been Family Man and Brittany's coworker in Yosemite Valley a few years before. In the early afternoon we left the camp, and any form of civilization, and hiked up a valley crossing a ridge into Virginia Canyon finding water again at McCabe and Return Creeks.

By the time we arrived at the creeks my stomach was churning like a washing machine trying to get the dirt out of Family Man's favorite hiking shirt. I was pretty sure by the regurgitating taste, that it was the peanut butter and honey I had eaten for lunch. By the time we started the descent down to the Matterhorn River I was downright sick. I was still convinced it was food poisoning and mumbled about never eating peanut butter again.

Arriving at the Matterhorn River we found a river some 48 feet wide and only about a foot deep. Starting as a trickle out of the snow packs some six miles east on Matterhorn Peak, it snaked its way 3,700 feet down the canyon with little opportunity to warm up before reaching the PCT trail crossing. The rocks were slippery and the water was freezing cold as we bare footed it across and found a nice place to camp in the grass. It was not yet dark when I crawled into my sleeping bag allowing it to push back the chill of the night. When Family Man inquired about my desires for dinner he got a negative response; I was well on my way to sleep.

The awareness of something drastically wrong brought me out of my fitful sleep. I was definitely sick. What was going on in my stomach was similar to what was going on in the bowels of Mount St. Helen in the spring of 1980. I crawled out of my tent to take care of business. The frost covered grass was painful to my bare feet as I got as far away as I could before the eruption occurred. Feeling better after spraying peanut butter all over the green frozen night, I returned to the comfort of my sleeping bag.

June 16th
Day 71– 12 Miles
Total 974 Miles

The normal morning time departure was delayed as Family Man was patient with a very weak Stagecoach. Ice was all over our tents and it was still cold when we crawled out at 8:00 a.m. Slowly we got our stuff together and moved along the river for a mile before turning up the valley towards Benson Pass. The lack of ability to keep any nutrition down reduced my strength to that of a wet noodle. A hundred feet below the pass I was surprised by my stomach's decision to again dispel its contents. The problem with this surprise was that I forgot to remove my mosquito net. Needless to say I had to clean a mosquito net, and Family Man got a good laugh.

By the end of the day I was feeling a lot better, and I'm sure it was God's healing from all the prayers going out. It was starting to get dark as we made it to the Benson Lake trail and considered the 3/10 mile down to the lake where there was a sandy beach which would be a great place to camp. We looked at the 1,500 foot climb ahead and decided to get as far up it as we could. A mile and 500 feet up the mountain we found a flat place to make camp. Family Man fixed soup and hot apple cider to ease the hunger pains that now had my attention. It was definitely the longest 12 miles on the trail for ol' Stagecoach. Happy Father's Day!

June 17th
Day 72– 26.25 Miles
Total 1000.25 Miles

Waking up at 5:15 and feeling a whole lot better we put off getting started until 6:30. We had a goal to make it half way to Sonora Pass and needed a good day if that was going to happen. The first two miles was a climb up a thousand feet to Seavey Pass where we found Flipper (later to become Mr. Clean). He was trying to dry his socks over a campfire. We spent a little time warming by his fire before descending into Kerrick Canyon. We followed the Kerrick Creek down the canyon four miles before starting another climb over a couple of ridges. While eating our mashed potatoes at lunch time I suddenly remembered this was a very important day. I wished Family Man a happy birthday, and he responded with a pouty, "I wondered if you would ever remember."

The gradual climb in the Jack Main Canyon along Falls Creek was filled with mosquitoes. They liked to hang out on our nets and buzz around our ears causing us to go insane. For eight miles we moved from one marshy area to another. It wasn't until we passed Dorothy Lake and up onto the pass that the blood suckers abandoned their quest and flew back to the marsh. We made it to the thousand mile marker just before 8:00 p.m. when the mosquitoes returned. A quarter mile later, with twenty-six miles in the bag, we stopped for the night just before the Cascade Creek crossing.

June 18th
Day 73– 18.25 Miles
Total 1018.5 Miles

We started the day at 6:20 a.m., following the contour lines for the first five miles and crossing over Walker River on a footbridge before starting a long climb up Kennedy Canyon. Once we left the tree line at 9,500 feet, the wind took over for the mosquitoes. Climbing the long switchback to Leavitt Ridge, we encountered large melting snow packs. An acceptable short cut trail was passed up due to its steep climb. On top of the 10,600 foot ridge we took a break as the 50 to 60 mph winds worked at drying our wet shoes. Fighting the strong winds, we worked our way north looking forward to crossing over to the east side of the ridge and hoping it would provide some protection. Two and a half miles later we did go over the top only to find a basin filled with snow.

Hiking across the sun cupped snow took time as we tried to step on the ridges. A periodic slip sent us into the cups which were normally only about a foot deep. The constant attention to the glaring snow started affecting my eyes. Sure, I had sun glasses, but they were buried in my pack. After a couple of crossings, black spots started appearing in my eyes. This caused me enough concern to pull off my pack. The sunglasses did help with the glare, but they did nothing for the wet feet the melting snow created. With two miles to go, we left the ridge for a thousand foot descent to Sonora Pass. The descent around the basin and down through the valley was about fifty percent snow again, soaking our feet. The shoes we wore were fast drying, but the wool socks were more like a sponge. To their credit, they did keep our feet warm, even when wet. We arrived at Highway 108 just before 5:00 p.m. and were standing at the road when Sharla arrived a couple minutes later. Within an hour we were at the RV enjoying a shower and looking forward to a good night's sleep.

June 19th
Day 74– 0 Miles
Total 1018.5 Miles

The plans were to move to the RV park at Truckee on Interstate 80. The girls decided they would rather stay at our son Ben's home in Fernley, Nevada, so we packed up the RV and headed north. Fernley had a Walmart giving us a place to replenish our consumables. Stepping on a scale, I found I had lost 47 pounds in the last 1018 miles. Sharla was concerned about this massive weight lost and encouraged additional calorie intake. Family Man had lost 30 pounds. We would just have to do more to tank up while in town as we could only carry so many calories.

Chapter Twenty Two – Sonora Pass to Donner Pass

June 20th
Day 75– 15.9 Miles
Total 1034.4 Miles

Our grandsons, Lucas and Wally, joined us for the 3 hour, 128 mile car ride back to Sonora Pass. As with all the other trips back to the trail, multiple calories were required. To fulfill this requirement we found the Hamdog Café in Minden, Nevada. Tucked back in a strip mall, this eating establishment treated us right and spoiled the boys. We did see our first bear that day. The only problem was it was lying along the highway after being hit by a truck. As we turned onto Highway 108 at Sonora Junction, none other than Slim was standing beside the road. Poor guy, there he stood all alone with a cardboard PCT sign begging for a ride. As much as the guy irritates ol' Stagecoach, I know I would have picked him up if the car wasn't already full.

Arriving back at the trail we were greeted by Jefe who was also being dropped off. Lucas joined us for the quarter mile hike up to the Sonora Pass parking lot. He thought it was so cool to use our trekking poles as he walked alongside some real hiker trash. We were going through our pre-departure check list when an SUV showed up and Slim jumped out. His hitch up the mountain was a corporate pilot and avid hiker who could not pass up a hitchhiking backpacker. He was heading south to do a section of the PCT and had a lot of questions about the trail.

It was shortly after noon when we said goodbye to Sharla and the boys and climbed the thousand feet up the slopes of Sonora Peak. After a couple of short-lived interactions with Slim, he disappeared. Four miles into the day we crossed over a pass marked by a sign stating it was the divide between the Walker River and Carson River watershed. The trail then descended into the valley along the East Fork of Carson River. Trying to get some miles in to make up for our late start, we took minimal breaks. Tributary streams provided plenty of water and raised our morale. The gradual descent into the valley led to a 700 foot climb over a ridge. On top of the ridge we called the girls on our satellite phone. Knowing that Sharla and the boys made it home safely eased our worries.

The funny story of the day came at my expense while crossing over a downed tree. On top of the three foot high fallen pine tree, I saw a branch about a foot off the ground to use as a step. It acted more like a mouse trap as the unattached branch flipped, throwing me face first to the ground. It scared Family Man, because from where he was watching it looked like a stick had come up and hit me in the face. Once he realized that I was okay, he couldn't stop laughing. For some reason after that fall, Family Man always had the camera handy when I crossed precarious logs or rivers.

The evening was spent hiking the contour line towards the top of the mountains with an occasional descent into small valleys. Stopping at a nice grassy area while it was still light, we set up camp. Watching the moon come up over Stanislaus Peak, we ate our bedtime snack. Family Man had brought along some Snicker bites all in a Ziploc bag. They had melted together during the day giving him a Snicker blob when they cooled down. It didn't stop him from chewing into it like a popcorn ball.

June 21st
Day 76– 23.6 Miles
Total 1058 Miles

The sun woke us up when it pushed its way through the leaves warming our tents. Considering how late we got up, we decided to eat breakfast before starting out. We did not like late start times, as our morale would go down when we only had ten miles in at noon. It was a quiet day, and the landscape was gentle and rolling. With almost every descent a stream would cross our path giving us plenty of water. After lunch, as we passed Asa Lake, Family Man spotted a bald eagle flying overhead. We met a couple of southbound section hikers and then were surprised to run into Super Dave, a trail legend and the owner of Mount Laguna Sports. Marie passed us a couple of times trying to catch up with Jefe. We had no idea if he was in front or behind us.

Crossing over Highway 4 late in the afternoon, we stopped for a break. While sitting there enjoying the rest, a pickup truck pulled into the drive. Our hopes of a cheeseburger from a trail angel were dashed when it became apparent they were just turning around. As daylight faded on the longest day of the year we found ourselves on the east slope of Raymond Peak looking for a flat place to camp. We ended up finding a spot about a hundred yards below the trail and put up our tents in near darkness. In the hiker community it is common knowledge that summer solstice is hike naked day. We did not conform to this ancient tradition, and thankfully neither did any other hikers we met.

June 22nd
Day 77– 26.3 Miles
Total 1084.3 Miles

Up at 5:15, we ate a breakfast of oatmeal and climbed the steep hill to the trail. We had gone no more than a couple hundred yards when we heard someone holler. "Is that hiker trash I smell?" Standing in the middle of the trail in his down jacket and thermal underwear was trail angel Papa Joe from Casa Luna. He had come up north to do some section hiking after the herd had come through southern California. The rolling hills gave way to mosquitoes as we leap frogged with George, a gentleman from Houston. We crossed Blue Lakes Road around noon before starting a climb up along the west slopes of a dry and barren mountain range. High on the ridge, above any form of water, we had to ration our dwindling supply. There were numerous snow packs below us that we could have descended to, but we felt the situation was not that critical.

In the valley we could see Upper Blue Lake filled with weekend boaters, and four wheel drive vehicles were kicking up dust as they traversed the fire roads around the lake. We walked along the ridge a thousand feet above it all thinking about how much we would love an ice cold soda. We met three elderly day hikers who were interested in our journey and rewarded us with three big homemade oatmeal raisin cookies. We sat down in a rare grassy area on the ridge and enjoyed the cookies. Just finishing up the first two homemade morsels we were about to split the third one when we spotted George making his way up the trail. We had one of those selfish thoughts of not wanting to share, but our conscience got the best of us. George enjoyed his soft chewy cookie as well.

Descending into a saddle, we crossed the dirt road that led down to Lost Lakes. I stayed with the packs in the shade while Family Man ran down to the lake for water. By the lake he found a pickup with a camp set up, but no one was around. He said the coolers sitting around the camp were tempting, but being the God fearing Christian man he is, he left them alone. Back on the ridge, we came to a snow pack, and I just had to fix a snow cone. As I dumped the liquid drink mix in my cup it spilled all over my hands and pants leaving some awful red stains, but I thought, *Oh well, maybe the appearance of blood splattered hands and pants will add to the fear civilians have of hiker trash.* Again we could tell we were getting close to civilization as the trail got wider and more populated. In the late afternoon we left the ridge and descended into Carson Pass.

The ranger station at Carson Pass was staffed by volunteers who gave us Snicker Doodle cookies and an orange. They made us weigh in and sign the logbook. I had lost about 50 pounds and Family Man had lost 30. As we were getting ready to take off, Marie arrived. A mile up the trail we stopped at a stream for dinner. Marie came by and stopped for a chat while Family Man fixed mashed potatoes and gravy. She could not get over the idea of fixing gravy in the wilderness. Marie told us her story, but for the sake of her privacy we will not share that here. Let's just say we started calling her Attorney.

We made another five miles up the mountain to Shower Lake where we found Attorney and a couple of other hikers setting up in a mosquito infested clearing. Continuing around the lake we met other campers and more mosquitoes. On the northeast corner of the lake, the water spills over the side and down a ravine. We lost the trail and thought it went over the outlet. A few dead end trails led to pulling out the GPS which showed we had to go down the ravine a bit and back up the other side. Yet another mystery when it comes to trail design. Once we made it back up to the lake we decided we had had enough. We set the tents up in a clearing while swarms of mosquitoes welcomed us to a night of buzzing.

June 23rd
Day 78– 26.6 Miles
Total 1110.9 Miles

With ten miles left to Echo Lake, we woke up early and got on the trail by 5:30. The mosquitoes had maintained their presence overnight and drove us down the trail. An hour into the day we caught our first glance of Lake Tahoe. As we descended to Highway 50 we met Tracker trying to clean up a bit so he could hitch a ride down to South Lake Tahoe. The word was the buffet was worth the trip. We were pretty sure we could get our food fix at the lake, bypassing the trip to town.

We crossed the highway and climbed a 400 feet ridge, arriving at the Echo Lake store just before 10:00 a.m.

It was Sunday morning and the place was buzzing with weekenders. Family Man finally met Maverick and Lodgepole, the other father and son team. They were ready to head out when we arrived. The store, while more than happy to take our money, was unfriendly to hiker trash. We badly needed to charge our phone, and even though I offered to pay for the service, they would not even consider it. Fortunately, a couple of southbound hikers let me use their solar panel for about twenty minutes to get some charge. We consumed a great turkey sandwich, ice cream, milk, and cookies. Each of us drank a whole quart of milk, which was probably not very smart. The remaining 4 cans of root beer were packed away for somewhere in the wilderness. George and Attorney arrived at the lake about an hour behind us.

The clouds were getting darker and white caps were whipping up on the lake as we strapped on our backpacks just before noon. Some weekenders we had talked to told us the storm of the decade was coming down on us over the next two days. George and Attorney were considering waiting out the storm in South Lake Tahoe. We talked it over, and while we could get the girls to come and get us, we decided we needed to move on to make a hard deadline of Sierra City by June 29th. Following the east side of the lake below Echo Peak we met a lot of weekend hikers coming off the trail. They too had heard the forecast and questioned our mental state as we pushed up into the mountains.

Three miles out of Echo Lake we were hit with the first rain shower which only lasted about a half hour. The clouds continued to boil over Ralston Peak to the west, getting darker with each hour. In the late afternoon we arrived at Aloha Lake. It would be a great place to camp in nice weather, and if you're a section hiker. We noticed a family with two young children at the lake. All we could think about was the six miles to Echo Lake and would they get there before dark or before the storm hit. After passing a couple of more lakes we started the long hard climb up to Dick's Pass at 9,400 feet, and Family Man moved out ahead.

Arriving at the pass, I found it covered with snow and no sign of the trail. Scouting around I found Family Man's footprints and for about a mile followed them across the snow. I figured that if he was on the wrong trail at least we would be there together. Once we got to lower altitude bits of the trail showed up between the snow drifts. After making our way across the Fontanillis Lake outlet, we climbed a small hill and set up camp just as it was getting dark.

June 24 *th*
Day 79– 27.1 Miles
Total 1138 Miles

After another restless night we woke up to rain falling on a not so waterproof tent. We quickly packed our stuff before it got too wet and started out. To reduce weight, we had left our oversized ponchos that covered our backpacks at the RV and brought lightweight trash bags. That worked pretty well until the wind started blowing. I could not keep the bag down around the pack. Family Man mentioned that what I needed was a bungee cord and no more than 200 yards down the trail a yellow and black bungee cord was lying in the middle of the trail. Again we were amazed at God's provision, even though I'm sure somebody was wondering what happened to their bungee cord. Rounding Phipps Peak we descended briefly before climbing along a ridge. The rain was coming down sideways now as the wind had picked up to a gusty 60 to 70 mph. Hiking along and just below the ridge we were constantly in the clouds, diminishing our view of Desolation Wilderness to the west and Lake Tahoe only five miles to the east.

The rain and wind became miserable and we became exhausted, but every time we stopped we got cold. Before lunchtime we passed Richardson Lake. We found out later that a shelter is located on the northeast side of the lake. It was probably a good thing that we didn't know at the time, as it would have become a vortex difficult to leave. The sound of revving engines caught our ears and excitement built as we approached a dirt road. Trudging along the muddy trail with soaking wet feet, I imagined the possibilities of some kind of comfort food. Maybe a breakfast burrito provided by a back country cowboy driving a Jeep. The sound of the double clutching vehicles got louder as we arrived at the road, so we waited. Three mud covered vehicles came to a stop when the lead driver noticed hiker trash standing beside the road looking like soaked rats. We shared our story to their amazement, and they apologized for not having any hot breakfast burritos. The beers they offered were not at all what we were looking for. After agreeing we were all crazy, we thanked the backwoods campers and moved on.

A hundred yards ahead, Family Man turned around and hollered for me to hurry. Not that I could hear through the howling wind, but I could see the excitement in his face. Topping the hill I spotted the source of this excitement. We had arrived at Barker Pass where the trailhead housed a pit toilet. The six foot square block building with a toilet in the corner and a door for privacy is a fairly common establishment at campgrounds and trailheads. This one was clean with little odor, and we dropped our packs thinking about how awesome it was to be out of the rain. I sat down on the seat with a sigh as we contemplated fixing some mashed potatoes and hot chocolate. We were finally out of the storm and felt that just maybe we could survive.

The sound of voices broke our silent pleasure of the new found shelter. We muttered some "Oh no's" and opened the door to meet an elderly southbound couple out hiking for a couple of days. The guy had kidney problems and needed to empty his external pouch. Fifteen minutes later he exited the previously odor free building. The noxious odor that now permeated from the block building caused us to hoist our water soaked bags and head down the trail. The restroom vortex had lost its draw, and we moved off into the storm.

Family Man had the maps protected from the rain, and I had the phone with its GPS in the water tight box so we had no idea where we were. Our southbound restroom friends had told us about the ridge we were about to climb and advised against getting caught on top. We talked it over and decided it was necessary to make it to the valley beyond the first ridge. We made it up the switchbacks to the ridge at 5:30 p.m., and fighting the 80 mph winds and cold rain we progressed along the rim topping out just below Ward Peak. A lot of things were hidden from our view as we hiked blind inside the clouds which continued rolling over the ridge and dropping into an unseen valley to the east. One of the things hidden was the building which housed the top wheel of the ski lift. It was probably for the best as it would have only lured us into a temporary shelter where we could whimper about the miseries that dampened our souls.

A mile north of Ward Peak, to our pleasure, we started down some switchbacks. Due to Family Man diligently studying the maps and his great memory, we knew we were getting close to a camping spot. The dark clouds deepened as we descended into the valley and the wind subsided. We crossed the creek and found six tents scattered throughout a clearing.

Only one of the hikers was outside, the rest all hollered greetings. Long Legs, Autobahn, Sasquatch, and the Canadian couple, were among those we recognized. We had decided, that due to my tent's inability to shed water, we would both sleep in Family Man's tent. The plan was to erect my tent for temporary protection and to store my backpack. Family Man would get his up and dried off inside as much as possible before I moved in.

It seemed like forever as I huddled there in soaking wet clothes while water dripped from the ceiling of the compact tent. Shivering, I knew it had to be down close to 45 degrees. At least we were out of the wind. Finally, Family Man was ready and I handed him my sleeping pad and bag before moving into a drier shelter. We ate hot mashed potatoes from the warmth of our cocoons and went to sleep.

June 25th
Day 80– 17.5 Miles
Total 1155.5 Miles

Waking in the morning after a fitful night of sleep, I could feel the moisture saturating the fabric of my sleeping bag. It had rained all night and was still raining. The motivation for getting out of our wet sleeping bags was hampered by the fears of the day that lie ahead. We ate some oatmeal, in an attempt to get some warmth and calories, before pulling on our wet pants and socks. Shivering, we crawled out of the tent and into the cold rain, shoving our feet into our soaking wet shoes. Even though the shoes were wet, it didn't take long before our body heat created a little warmth. A couple of other hikers were packing up as well. A number of others were going to wait out the storm in their tents. We quickly packed our tents, hoisted our now waterlogged backpacks, and moved out onto the muddy trail.

We still had seventeen miles to Donner Pass, and we knew it was critical to find shelter before the day's end. We descended briefly along the west base of Squaw Peak before turning north and climbing over a ridge which lay between Granite Chief and the Squaw Peak Ski Resort. Periodically, the clouds lightened up to reveal a little sunshine which gave us false hope of better weather. As quickly as it came, the sun disappeared again behind the menacing clouds. The rain continued without letting up as we struggled along not knowing how many miles we had come or how far we had to go. The climbs were only made worse by the despair of our environment. When we thought the worst was over, we started a climb up to the exposed ridge at Tinker Knob.

It was only 11:00 a.m. when we found ourselves on the 8,700 foot ridge where the wind was blowing between 70 to 80 mph with the rain going sideways. Our rain gear no longer protected us from the rain. I could feel the moisture permeating my rain coat and soaking the last line of defense, my down jacket. The wind was so strong we could not keep our hoods from blowing off. My fingers were so numb from the cold that I could not even tie the hood strings. All I could do was pull them tighter, but even that only worked for a short time. I did have gloves but, like my shoes, they were soaking wet. However they did hold my body heat in giving my hands some warmth. Family Man's fingerless gloves offered little protection, so he pulled his sleeves down over his hands. This method worked but reduced the grip on his trekking poles.

Up and down the saw tooth ridge we progressed like a never ending story. With only about a hundred yards of visibility, we were caught in a condition of physical and emotional anguish. The trail was made of decomposed lava rock which had turned to a mushy substance that caked onto our shoes. To walk parallel to the trail was even worse as you would sink in a couple of inches and destroy the fragile mountain plant life. Desperation was setting in as we battled with desolation and fleeting thoughts of defeat flashed through our semiconscious minds. Hypothermia started setting in as our core body temperature started to drop. As tired as we were, we needed to keep moving. Periodically Family Man would hide behind a rock to find some protection from the wind. The previously two pound tent now increased to six pounds with water weight and swung on my back like a pendulum. This irritation caused irrational thoughts of throwing it over the ridge into a godforsaken crevice. Dehydration started to take its toll on us as well. We had been walking in the rain all day with water running off our faces and had little desire to drink the water our bodies really needed.

In my semi delusional state I seriously considered pushing the search and rescue button on the SPOT. "What would that accomplish?" I muttered to myself. No helicopter was going to come out in this storm, and to put others at risk to save two seasoned hikers from their struggles was not an option, so we walked on. A real strong gust of wind hit us at the most inopportune time, and I watched Family Man almost blown off the cliff on the right before he dug in and jumped left. After that he walked a little more on the left side of the trail. As my feet got heavier from the accumulation of mud and the depletion of much needed nutrients, I talked to God. Oh boy, did I talk to God. I gave Him an ear full, if there is such a thing. After I exhausted my vocabulary explaining my disdain for our current situation, a small voice filled an empty mind. "I'm only watering my trees. What are you doing?"

As we progressed towards Donner Pass, time seemed no longer to be relevant. The experience of walking eleven hundred miles kept riveting in my mind calculations of time and distance. *You have the answer, and it is the next step. Just keep putting the next foot forward. On and on we go nothing seems to change. What does hypothermia feel like? Will I know when my body is ready to shut down? Or do you just fall asleep?* Thoughts like these raced through my mind.

I thought of our geographical significance. In the spring of 1846, a wagon train headed west from Missouri. Due to a number of unfortunate circumstances, they found themselves arriving at the base of the mountain range late in the season. They had started up towards the pass when a big snow storm brought their progress to a halt. A large number of the party perished over the winter and a few even turned to cannibalism of the dead. Now the pass has become a tribute to the group of emigrants who suffered so much agony and loss over a hundred and fifty years ago.

Tree Boo flew by, bringing my mind to an alert and present time. I knew my feet were moving, but climbing the hill in the slippery mud was like tires spinning. In his shorts and thin plastic poncho, Tree Boo must have been freezing. I caught up with him and Family Man in a small grove of trees where they were getting a little relief from the howling wind. He told us we only had one more hill to climb, which gave us some slightly misinformed hope. It ended up being two hills. The second hill, which would normally not have been a factor, became quite treacherous. On the climb we crossed a large snow pack. On the far side we found a twenty-five foot shear drop off where the trail appeared out from underneath the snow. We ended up having to work our way three hundred feet up the mountain over the snow to where we could get back on muddy soil again. After sliding back down the muddy mountain, we started a slow descent.

Crossing around the east side of Mount Lincoln, we entered a wooded area and came to a sign that said we only had 2½ miles to Donner Pass. Relief set in as we knew everything would be all right. The rain was still pouring down and the wind was still whipping through the trees, but our spirits were high. The rest of the way down the mountain we were in and out of the trees which gave us relief from the wind. As we passed by the top of a ski lift, a pickup truck was sitting there. We considered asking the maintenance worker if we could get in and warm up, but the thought of food and dry clothes moved us onward. For the final half mile, the trail consisted of well maintained stone steps. The torrential rain had turned these steps into hundreds of waterfalls as four inches of water joined us in the descent. I tried to walk along the edge for a while stepping from stone to stone trying to keep my already wet feet out of the water. Looking ahead at Family Man, I noticed he was walking right down the middle of the trail. Maybe it was the lack of oxygen, or dehydration, or just plain not thinking. Whatever is to blame, it made perfect sense. For the rest of the descent I, too, walked down the middle of the trail.

When we arrived at the Old Donner Summit Road we found a dumpster, and the first thing I did was toss that disgusting water soaked tent hanging off my back. Arriving up at Highway 40, we found a maintenance building with an overhang. We had just dropped our backpacks to get the phone out when an SUV pulled up. The driver inquired about the trail conditions and then told us his son had come off a side trail with hypothermia. He just wondered if it was as bad as his son had said. I don't know if it was our answers or the wet rat look, but he was satisfied with our response and offered to take us down to Soda Springs. He dropped us off at the grocery store and while Family Man went inside, I called Sharla. We were trying to figure out what would warm us up when our ride from the trail came back. He had stopped at the restaurant down the road and shared with them our situation.

It was three in the afternoon as we dropped our wet backpacks in the entryway of the Summit Restaurant and Bar. We pulled our tired, storm battered, trail worn bodies up on the barstools and ordered two hot chocolates. They had offered us a table but the cloth covered chairs did not deserve the abuse we would have given them. They let us plug in our phone to charge and I was able to call Sharla again for an update on our pickup. While we waited we ate cheeseburgers and Buffalo wings and drank a number of hot chocolates. The bartender almost cut Family Man off when he spilled a cup of hot chocolate all over the bar. Sharla arrived ninety minutes later and we put on dry clothes and returned to Ben's house. Those will be two days we will long remember. The physical toll that it took was just starting to reveal itself.

It would be awesome if I could write this book in fairytale fashion and leave this part out. This dream of the ideal was overridden by those who witnessed the pain experienced. Having spent two days drinking very little water and a body fat level well below normal created an extreme intestinal challenge better known as constipation. Great! Now you know that sometimes long distance hikers have trouble doing what needs to be done. The pain was so severe the night we came off of Tahoe Rim that I was unable to sleep. The pain lasted for about a week. It would have been nice to curl up in a corner for this time, but we still had a deadline. So we found some medication and an extra roll of TP just in case and moved on, or at least attempted to move on.

June 26th
Day 81– 0 Miles
Total 1155.5 Miles

After just one night at Ben's place, we moved the RV up to Sierra City where we had reservations at the Sierra Skies RV Park. On the way we stopped by a sports store where I picked up a smaller backpack. The 85 liter that I had been using was just too big for my now 167 pounds. It would be strange strapping on this smaller pack after all the miles of carrying the big green monster that I had come to hate. The campground set us up in a nice spot, and we spent the rest of the day relaxing. Late in the day we put together a two day supply in preparation for the 42 mile section up from Donner Pass. With a store across the street, and the trail just a mile east of town, it was a perfect place for the girls to call home for the next week.

Chapter Twenty Three –Donner Pass to Sierra City

June 27th
Day 82– 20 Miles
Total 1175.5 Miles

My pain subsided somewhat, and I was able to get a half decent night's sleep before Sharla drove us back down to Donner Pass. Arriving at the pass at 10:30 a.m., we found sunshine and mild temperatures. The last couple of days on the trail were still fresh in our minds as we looked back across the highway at the maintenance shed. We were still amazed at how God had sent a trail angel to rescue us. We left the highway and hiked over to the rest area on Interstate 80. We met a lot of elderly hikers who were part of a seniors hiking group on this four mile section. One of the ladies gave us some fresh fruit after we shared stories of our journey. We stopped by the rest area for a short time to eat a snack and fill up with water. We were sorely disappointed at how filthy the restrooms were and that the state of California had shut off the drinking fountains to preserve water. We ate our snack at a dirty picnic table as we mumbled about the trash lying around. The humans who came rushing in and out of the rest area caused us to question if humanity could even survive.

133

Back on the trail, we were in high spirits over the sunshine and the solitude of the trail. The grades were gradual and the tread was well kept. Later, as we tried to fix dinner, we discovered our new butane gas container would not fit our Jetboil. Thankfully this was only a two day stint. As we were sitting there tinkering with the stove, a young man from Ireland named Hooligan stopped and chatted for a while. We continued to climb after a cold dinner, arriving at the top of a ridge as darkness fell. We set up our tents, and because the stars were shining we did not even put on the rain flies. This was my first night in the new bigger two man tent, and it was great to be able to bring everything inside the tent for the night.

June 28th
Day 83– 22 Miles
Total 1197.5 Miles

With 22 miles left to Sierra City, we wanted an early start. I set the alarm for 4:30 a.m., but preempted the sleep depriver by waking up ten minutes early and shutting it off. I brought Family Man out of dreamland by playing "I Would Walk 500 Miles." We were on the trail at 5:35 a.m. and completed 10 miles by 10:00 a.m. We were taking a break at the Henness Pass Road when along came the English girls. We had been hoping a passing camper heading down to the Jackson Meadow Reservoir would find pity on the hiker trash and drop off a couple of sodas. We had also somehow overlooked our TP supply and were running low. We laughed about how funny it would be to wave down a passerby and beg for this necessity. After further review, we decided we could always use our hankies if it came down to it. That would be a suicide mission for the hanky, but it would die doing a noble deed.

The afternoon went well with minimal altitude changes. It warmed up considerably in the afternoon to the point that Family Man came close to a heat stroke while climbing an exposed hill. His inability to sweat was a hindrance in these situations. We were only a couple of miles from the highway but stopped to allow him to cool down. As we sat there enjoying the shade, the English girls came by again. The trail started down, crossing a foot bridge over the Yuba River before paralleling the highway for a half mile to the trail head. While we were sitting at the trailhead with the English girls waiting for our ride, Long Legs and another couple arrived. I talked their driver into giving the girls a ride into town, and a short time later Sharla arrived.

We had hiked 831 miles since we had set the goal to make it to Sierra City by the end of June. To meet this date we had put ourselves through some moderately tough situations. Now it was time to relax and celebrate God's grace and protection. Ben and his family arrived to help us celebrate Sharla and Sawyer's birthdays.

Chapter Twenty Four –Sierra City to Old Station

June 29th
Day 84– 9.5 Miles
Total 1207 Miles

On Saturday morning Ben and his oldest son, Lucas, joined us for a 9.5 mile, 3,300 foot climb up the mountain to Packer Lake Saddle. It was already heating up when we arrived at the trail head at 10:30 a.m. It was not going to be an easy day, especially for the two new members of our hiking team. The first half mile took us slightly up hill to the east side of a slope before switchbacks started the grueling climb. About 1.5 miles in Lucas realized the camera had fallen out of his pocket. Family Man headed back down the trail and returned thirty minutes later with the camera. He would have caught up with us sooner, but he noticed a spring off the trail and picked up a liter of water. We reached the 1,200 mile marker at noon and celebrated this milestone by eating lunch.

The hot day was responsible for increased water consumption, and by the time we left the shade of the pine trees, it became a serious factor. We had taken what we thought was plenty of water for the day. Now with only a third of the way completed over half the water had been consumed. Trading shaded switchbacks for moderated exposed grade only increased the need for water. Five and a half miles and 2,100 feet into the climb we came across a small dripping spring. While the water was cool, the sun was baking off the granite walls, turning the mountain into an oversized pizza oven. Ben and Lucas found a shade tree a couple hundred yards up the trail where they could cool down during the twenty minutes it took to coax two liters of water from the side of the mountain. Attorney, Tree Boo and Hooligan (in his kilt) stopped by bringing us up to date on all the trail gossip.

The heat was starting to get to Lucas, so I told him to go fast in the sun and slow down in the shade. He got the "slow down in the shade" thing down so well that it didn't even look like he was moving. We added two and two together and figured out we were not going to get to the saddle before dark. Family Man handed me his backpack and gave Lucas a piggy back ride for a couple of miles up to the crest of the mountain. Reaching the top of the mountain, Family Man and I took off leaving Ben and Lucas to finish the downhill trail on their own. Two miles later we found Sharla waiting at the parking lot. We dropped off our packs and continued the mile on to Packer Saddle Road. Ten minutes later, as we approached our pickup point, Sharla drove up with the boys.

June 30th
Day 85– 0 Miles
Total 1207 Miles

Today we celebrated Sharla's birthday at the RV park with all the grandchildren.

July 1st
Day 86– 0 Miles
Total 1207 Miles

On Monday morning Sharla and I took off on a road trip. On Tuesday she would be picking us up on a logging road in the middle of nowhere. If the pickup wasn't going to be possible, we would need to carry full packs and two extra day's food. We figured the only way to know was to drive the 150 miles around the mountains, and hunt down the trail crossing. While a three hour drive may seem a little overboard, it also gave us time alone. We had no problem finding the trail, and the stage was set for a thirty mile day. We spent the evening celebrating our youngest grandson Sawyer's first birthday.

July 2nd
Day 87– 30.5 Miles
Total 1237.5 Miles

We woke up with the alarm. After two full days of rest we were anxious to get moving. Sharla dropped us off at Packer Lake Saddle just as it was getting light. With a pickup scheduled at day's end, we only carried our daypacks, which contained water, minimal food, and a medical emergency kit. It's what we call slack packing. The purist backpackers consider this is a form of backpacking infidelity. We were not hiking the trail for these berry eating, poison oak wiping, and "I carry the world on my back" individuals. So we walked on.

Following the ridge with little altitude change, we put in six miles in the first two hours. When we stopped for a break at the top of a small hill we had cell service and were able to update my parents on our position. Family Man wasn't thrilled with the 45 minute break, but he understood. We had given them a large map of the PCT and with each update they were able to follow our progress north. Sometimes they said it looked like we didn't make it very far.

Thirteen miles into the day, it was approaching noon when we arrived at the A-Tree Springs where we found an angle iron upside down making a trough. It was stuck back into the bank, and fresh water poured out at about a gallon a minute. The rest of the day was just as fast, moving up and down small ridges all afternoon. At 6:00 p.m. we arrived at the first road where we found Sharla waiting so patiently. We had only 28 miles in, so we headed on down the trail in a gradual descent another 2.5 miles to where we were picked up at another logging road crossing. She had brought a bag of oranges which we hung on a PCT sign. It was a long ride back to the RV at Sierra City, but we were happy. We had busted through the 30 mile physical and mental block. It changed our outlook on what was possible.

July 3rd
Day 88– 13.1 Miles
Total 1250.6 Miles

It was moving day for the RV. We left Sierra City at 10:30 a.m. and drove up to Caribou Crossing RV Park a mile east of Belden, California. Tucked back into the shade in the 100 degree temperature we were quite satisfied with sitting in the air conditioned RV. Finally at 2:15 p.m. we said goodbye to Brittany and the boys and left the comfortable vortex for the trail. We arrived back at the trail at 3:30 and headed out for the 51 mile section to Belden. The trail was a gentle downhill to start the afternoon. Eventually, we did have to climb a small ridge where we met Chameleon and Tree Shadow taking a break. Chameleon picked up his trail name because of his ability to imitate any accent. Continuing the gradual descent down the spine of a ridge for eight miles, we came to a deep valley where the Middle Fork of the Feather River ran. An eight hundred foot steep switchback descent took us down to a foot bridge crossing the fast running river. Crossing the 185 foot bridge we noticed hikers down by the river on the far side getting water. We made our way down a side trail to the water where we found over a half dozen tents and found our own secluded place to camp.

July 4th
Day 89– 29.4 Miles
Total 1280 Miles

In the real world it was Independence Day. On the trail, we took an early morning holiday and slept in a little later. It was a hot night down at 3,000 feet, but it did cool down by morning. There were somewhere between 8 to 10 hikers in the area, and we could hear them one by one packing up. We only knew Brownie, whom we had met at Oasis Cache. We were on the trail at 7:00 a.m. with a climb out of the deep valley to start the day. By the time we had reached the top of the ridge, some eleven miles later, we had climbed 4,600 feet. We leap frogged with Double It and Gumby for awhile and ran into a south bound hiker at the Buck Lake Road trail head. When we saw John Deere at the parking lot our hopes spiked as we hoped he was a trail angel with root beer. When we introduced ourselves he laughed about the root beer. Sharla had given him a ride up at Caribou Crossing and had told him about Stagecoach and Family Man, so he had been looking for us. Leaving the road, we climbed 1,500 feet to the ridge between Spanish Peak and Mount Pleasant. On the ridge we picked up cell service and called the girls to arrange a 9:00 a.m. pickup time in Belden. By the time we stopped for the night we had climbed over 7,700 feet in 29.4 miles. We are definitely pushing ourselves to the limit trying to increase our average miles. The only fireworks we experienced that evening were our legs burning from too much exertion.

July 5th
Day 90– 26 Miles
Total 1306 Miles

We were up at the break of dawn and skipped breakfast in our hurry to make it down to Belden. It was a long slope down the mountain to the small river town. Family Man was getting antsy, so we agreed to meet in town, and he quickly left me in the dust. Four miles out we started the 3000 foot descent down the switchbacks to the river. After going through a mile of overgrown trail, things cleared out and we were able to pick up speed. When we reached the railroad tracks all signs of the trail disappeared. The GPS confirmed my suspicions that the trail followed the paved road into town. Walking the third mile into Belden at 8:45 a.m. was like walking into some spaced out hippie commune. Little did we know our schedule coincided with the "Priceless 2013 Campout," which appeared to be a very free spirited event and a weird display of humanity. We arrived just as some of the zombies were awakening from their post party stupor. A few individuals were communing with the spirits in a large dome tent filled with pillows. I had thought maybe they would think we were the strange ones. The weirder things became, the more I pictured what Sodom and Gomorrah really looked like.

Family Man was sitting outside the store eating chips that Postholer had given him. We had not thought about needing money and had left our billfolds in the RV. We sat on the bench outside the store for as long as we could handle the bizarre gathering of humanity. With fifteen minutes before our pickup time we walked across the bridge and headed east. We had only gone about fifty yards when a pickup truck with a large slide in camper pulled up and asked if we needed a ride. Maureen, the awesome wife of Chief, had seen hiker trash and knew she just had to offer us a ride. Chief was somewhere behind us and she was just waiting on him. Sharla pulled up behind her, so we thanked Maureen but happily threw our packs in the back of our car.

The first thing we did was eat a big, high calorie breakfast at the café followed by a long, hot shower. If I remember right, the sign on the showers said there was a five minute limit. We figured that counted each day the RV was parked at the campground and added them up. The air conditioner in the RV fought off the 100 degree temperatures outside and caused the vortex to start spinning. Complacency set in and as we ate some ice cream, we made the decision to leave again at 1:00 p.m. that afternoon.

Brittany bought us cheeseburgers for lunch. We said goodbye at the appointed time and headed for the trail. There is a bridge without a sidewalk on Highway 70 where the PCT crosses. We decided that due to the amount of traffic, we would have Sharla drop us off on the west side of the bridge.

The temperature read 101 degrees when we got out of the car at 1:30 p.m. As we climbed away from the town, we could see the muddy river filled with clothing optional partiers. We were so glad to get away from this environment, even as we headed up into the burned out mountains. The burnt trees and dry grass made the three digit temperatures feel even worse. We longed for shade. Finally, two miles in, we found a single tree to give us a little reprieve from the heat. Family Man needed it badly as he had unintentionally left his hat in the car. We consumed a liter of water by the time we arrived at our first water source, three miles from the highway. It was right in the middle of the burn area, and we were surprised to see the volume of clean water flowing in this seasonal stream. There wasn't any shade by the stream, but we stayed long enough to tank up (drink as much water as possible), and fill our bottles. We continued up the valley, and by 13 miles in we had climbed 5,800 feet. We topped out as the sun sank below the horizon and continued walking in the dark for three more miles.

July 6th
Day 91– 30 Miles
Total 1336 Miles

We woke up early in an attempt to get to Highway 36, which was thirty miles away, before the end of the day. A couple of miles up the trail we came to Cold Springs. Clean, cold water was coming out of a pipe into a horse tank. Someone had constructed a bench next to the tank and we sat there enjoying breakfast when a truck pulled up out on the gravel road. Two gentlemen on their way to their favorite fishing hole stopped to pick up some drinking water. They said it was the best tasting water around, and they had always made it a habit to stop by here when out fishing. They were chatty fellows, so we spent 45 minutes listening to their stories. Mid-morning, while Family

Man was busy in the woods, a group of three cowboys came a riding up. I was hoping he was far enough off the trail not to get too embarrassed. They were in the process of riding the PCT one section at a time and were finishing up California. At Little Cub Spring I told Family Man it was my turn to get the water which ended up being a third of a mile down a side trail. I use the word down, because that's exactly what it was. The climb back up to the trail gave me plenty of opportunity to grumble about the fresh, clean water with which we had been blessed.

As with every trail, there has to be a halfway point. At 4:00 p.m. we reached that point on the Pacific Crest Trail. The concrete post stood beside the trail and shouted out our achievement, while also quietly reminding us of what lay ahead. How can a person deal with three months of intense physical trauma without it affecting their mental state? What we had just gone through is what still lay ahead. Fortunately, we were able to look beyond the miles still to come, to the here and now with anticipation of a soft, warm bed that night.

We stopped only long enough to take pictures and read the register. Family Man again left me in the dust with the plan of meeting at the highway nine miles ahead. At Soldier Creek I found him getting water and chatting with Postholer, Maverick, and Lodgepole. I took the water Family Man had already filtered and moved on, knowing he would catch me soon enough. Thirty minutes later, while crossing a logging area where the trail had been messed up by the heavy equipment, he did catch up. We hiked together for the last mile, making it to Highway 36 at 7:30 p.m. Sharla was waiting for us at the trailhead, and we headed into Chester for a pizza before returning to the RV at Caribou Crossroads RV Park.

July 7th
Day 92– 0 Miles
Total 1336 Miles

We were in no hurry to get out of Caribou Crossroads and even enjoyed breakfast at the café. Our plans for the day only involved repositioning the RV up to Hat Creek Rim RV Park in Old Station, CA. We were not real thrilled with the dust at the Hat Creek RV Park. It would be a dirty mess for the boys and the dogs. The rest of the day was spent packing up the backpacks for an early morning departure.

July 8th
Day 93– 25 Miles
Total 1361 Miles

We left the campground at 6:00 a.m. for the hour and a half drive back down to the trailhead at Highway 36. We stopped at the grocery store in Chester in search of deli sandwiches and Gatorade. We found Whistler whom we had met down at Kennedy Meadows. Stopping by a café for a breakfast burrito we ran into Brownie. We offered him a ride, but he still had things to do in town. At the trailhead, we were unloading our packs when Cowgirl and Midnight Chocolate crossed the road.

The trail was gentle with minimal altitude change for the first ten miles. With one stop at Stover Springs for water, we made it to the North Fork of the Feather River by 1:00 p.m. We found shade under the bridge where we kicked back on the rocks and ate our deli sandwiches from the market. We watched as a couple of riders tried to get their horses to drink from the river. The horses were more interested in the fresh grass.

Approaching Boiling Springs Lake, we came across a section where the trail crews had cut in a new trail. I have no idea why they moved the trail, but no one advised the GPS and it kept telling me we were in the wrong place. The smell of sulfur was getting stronger, giving me confidence we were approaching the sulfur filled lake. I caught up with Family Man as he read a sign which said it was unlawful to go beyond this point. I don't know if he was considering ignoring the sign, but the boiling water and the previously acquired knowledge of unsure terrain helped convince him otherwise.

We again knew we were getting close to some sort of civilization as we started running into day hikers. A mile later, we found ourselves on a boardwalk making our way into the Drakesbad Resort. According to the Drakesbad Resort website, Edward Drake settled this valley in the late nineteenth century by acquiring 400 acres. He opened up the land for campers seeking the hot water from the springs. Alexander Sifford, a frequent visitor to the valley, purchased the resort in 1900. In 1958 the resort was sold to the U.S. Government for inclusion into the adjoining Lassen Volcanic National Park.

As we made our way into the resort, Family Man was stopped by a young family who had a lot of questions. I continued on to the restaurant in hopes of scoring some root beer. The staff was preparing for dinner but was kind enough to get us a couple cans of the special brew. We had considered joining the resort guests for dinner, but the twenty-five dollar price tag discouraged the white table cloth experience. I found a rock to sit on and waited for Family Man who was still giving his new found friends a hiking seminar. He got paid with a can of Sprite and a bottle of water. We headed down the gravel road returning to the trail. At the trailhead we found a pit toilet, trashcan, and a water fountain. It was a great place to eat our $1.29 tuna and fix up a bottle of Gatorade. We ate our dinner while a vacationing family warned us about a bear they had encountered. Naturally the bear ran, because it had just had an encounter with humans.

We tanked up with water and were about to leave when Midnight Chocolate and Cowgirl arrived. At the campground, not even a mile down the trail, we came across Maureen and finally met her husband, Chief. They had set up their camper not more than 10 feet from the trail. Maureen had her back to us and we had not met Chief, so I jokingly asked if we were too late for dinner. Maureen turned around and hollered, "Stagecoach! Family Man!" They invited us to join them for some bread and fruit along with, as always, a soda. Getting to know them was great, but we needed to move on. We were just trying to spin out of this vortex when Midnight Chocolate and

Cowgirl rolled into the campground. We said goodbye and headed up the mountain for a 1,500 foot climb. It was getting dark as we crossed the ridge. We sat down for a break and watched the shallow valley darken. We pushed on late into the night to reach our goal, and as my headlamp started screaming for new batteries we found a great camping spot. We had a goal, and we were able to reach it.

July 9th
Day 94– 23.5 Miles
Total 1384.5 Miles

The late night hiking rewarded us with an amazing view as we crawled out of our tents. Lower Twin Lake was smooth as glass and mirrored the trees to perfection. With very little climbing and 2,200 feet of descent, we expected the 17 miles to the Hat Creek RV Park to be a breeze. We wanted to move quickly as it looked like water was limited. Crossing north of Mount Lassen, we encountered miles of old burned out forest which was coming alive with new growth. The young pine trees, some ten feet tall, gave hope of a thriving forest to come. We made our way around Badger Mountain and started a two mile hike across a terraced landscape which had obviously been excavated by some logging company in the past.

Family Man was somewhere out ahead when I made it to Hat Creek at half past noon. It was refreshing to see a nice cool river flowing along the trail. Heading downstream, I hadn't walked more than a mile when I came across a sign that read "Hiker Fool Hangout." I don't know if it was exhaustion or because I was brain dead, but it never registered that I should go down and check it out. I was climbing the hill on the east side of the campground when someone woke me out of my stupor by hollering, "Stagecoach, come on down!" That's when I saw Family Man and a couple of others sitting around a fire pit in lawn chairs. Family Man was busy sucking on a soda and eating fresh fruit.

Legasorus and Pocahontas, a couple of hikers turned trail angels, had set up camp and were doing some trail magic. Even though we were only 3.5 miles from the campground and the girls, we enjoyed the hospitality with the angels before making our way to Old Station. Legasorus was trying to see how brain dead I was by guessing what kind of soda I liked. Even in my bewildered state I knew Family Man must have revealed my addiction to root beer, which our host finally produced.

We walked into the RV Park at 2:30, staying only for about a half hour. We wanted to make it up to the parking lot on Hat Creek Rim before dark. Family Man decided to take Whiskey with us for the seven mile climb. As we left we met Chief, Cowgirl, and Midnight Chocolate on their way into the campground. Whiskey overheated a mile later and started upchucking all over the trail. We made a phone call, and Sharla picked the lazy dog up at the highway. Whiskey wasn't the only one to have an emergency on this section. It must have been all the ice cream he had eaten at the RV that caused Family Man's sudden departure from the trail. He caught up with me a little farther down the trail with a quarter of his shirt missing. Upon further explanation, I found out that he had forgotten to put TP in his day pack and ripped off a piece of his shirt for the occasion. By 6:30 we had climbed the 600 feet to the parking lot on the rim where Sharla picked us up a few minutes later.

Burney Falls

Chapter Twenty Five – Old Station to Mount Shasta

July 10th
Day 95– 31.2 Miles
Total 1415.7 Miles

We arrived back up at the rim at 5:40 a.m. for an early start. We were only carrying day packs for the 31 mile hike along the extremely arid rim. We carried a couple extra gallon jugs of water a quarter mile down the trail for Chief, Midnight Chocolate, and Cowgirl who were coming up later that morning. We were cautiously optimistic that we would find water at Cache 22, thirteen miles down the trail. Cattle occupied the first few miles of the day giving us the blessed opportunity to skip over cow dung on the trail. We caught up with Mr. Clean at the communications tower and found him again at the cache. Cache 22, a three sided shelter built of sticks and brush, is located just off the trail within a hundred yards of a dirt road. When we arrived it was stocked with a few lawn chairs and 25 gallons of water. We did inventory on our H2O and after calculating our time/water situation decided I had enough and Family Man needed a liter. Water is heavy, and to carry more than necessary is just an added burden.

The sound of vehicles in the wilderness always gets the attention of hikers and that day was no exception. We could hear it coming for a couple of minutes before it popped over the rim and came to a stop where the trail crossed over the fire road. A dog was the first to arrive at the cache before it took off back down the trail towards its obvious master. A short time later, a lady arrived asking if we would be interested in some trail magic. Of course we answered in the affirmative and made our way down to where the truck was backed in under a shade tree. Backpackers Lee and LeAnn Clark had come down from Washington to do some trail magic, and we were their meeting with destiny. We sat there in folding lawn chairs enjoying soda and sharing stories with Lee while LeAnn fixed us an awesome taco salad. We were making our way through some chocolate cake when a British fellow arrived. The hour and a half break at this remote taco stand was unplanned yet much appreciated. With cell service unavailable, I sent out a SPOT message pushing our pickup time back to 8:00 p.m.

According to the National Geographic Society, the name Hat Creek came from a surveyor who lost his expensive hat in the swift waters. His partners, finding much humor in his loss, named the stream accordingly. Hat Creek Rim formed from a fissure being forced up from the valley floor some 900 feet and paralleling the stream. It might have been the afternoon sun, or the energy required to escape the taco vortex, but water consumption increased as we continued along the rim. Family Man was somewhere out ahead when I realized my water was not going to last to where the next water source was advertised. Each time I took a sip from my bottle I looked at the little that remained. The inner grumbling about my lack of planning at the water cache led to the realization that my faith was wavering. Now, in reality, a person could go three days without water, but not while hiking thirty miles a day. I turned my thoughts away from my imagined emergency to all the times God had provided for our needs. This change in attitude released the weight of exhaustion from my tormented mind as I crossed a ridge and could see the waters of Baum Lake in the valley to the north. Just the sight of this water was an emotional relief.

A quarter mile after I decided to let God provide, I came across a 24 inch pipe. I had no idea where it was coming from or where it was going, but the eight foot geyser coming from a small hole on top was God's answer to my prayer. At first I was concerned about not having the filter, but I decided if God answered my prayers the water would be safe to drink. Was it the physical exhaustion of 27 miles in 12 hours or the heat? Either way, my mental capacity obviously was out of kilter. I turned my bottle upside down over the geyser and stood there watching the water enter the bottle only to succumb to gravity. The thought of God saying, "So you want me to change the law of gravity for your thirst?" made me chuckle. Cupping my hand, I was able to divert the water spout into the bottle.

Less than a quarter mile later, at the bottom of the hill, I came to a power plant and crossed a foot bridge. I was finally able to find Family Man lying in the shade beside the road. He filled up his bottle from a hose at the fish hatchery, and we headed for our pickup point four miles away. Hiking alongside the water, we were attacked by swarms of mosquitoes, which destroyed the ambiance of the lake. Once we had climbed 300 feet over a hill we had a gradual descent to Highway 299.

In preparing for our pickup, I had loaded primary and secondary pickup points into the GPS. I even named them accordingly. Cell service was scratchy so I sent a text message for Sharla to meet us at the primary pickup point. She misunderstood the message and thought we were at the closest pickup point. Eventually, through scratchy messages and an occasional text, it all got sorted out. Ten minutes later, as she approached, Family Man talked me into throwing down my hat and stomping on it in a sign of disgust. This dispelled any grumpiness from the 31 mile day, and we were happy to be in the comfort of an air conditioned car.

Our plans had been to continue on to Interstate 5, which was 91 miles away. At that time we would return to Hat Creek to pick up the RV. With the girls not at all thrilled with the dust at the campground, we gave them the option for plan B, which would be for us to pack up the girls in the morning and they would drive themselves over to the KOA at Mount Shasta. After much debate, they decided on plan C. The nonexistent plan C had to be developed, so over a half gallon of ice cream and a two liter bottle of root beer we figured it out.

July 11th
Day 96– 9.3 Miles
Total 1425 Miles

We got up early, packed up the RV, and headed up to Burney Falls State Park. Parking the RV in the day use parking lot, Sharla ran us back to Highway 299 for the eight mile hike up to the park. A half mile in we came to where a family had set up a table with some nice patio chairs and coolers full of soda, beer and candy bars. There was a cooler with a digital camera with a note for the hikers to document their visit with a selfie. With the girls waiting at the park, we didn't waste any time and moved on. We arrived at the falls at 1:15 and spent a few minutes relaxing before moving the RV over to Mt Shasta KOA. The afternoon was spent setting up the RV and swimming with my girlfriend and grandsons. Evening time found us in the car on the way back to Burney Falls with anticipation of the next section to Interstate 5.

As darkness was setting in, we said goodbye to Sharla and headed out onto the trail. It just seemed strange to be leaving civilization and heading out onto the trail at that time of day. It was dark by the time we crossed over the dam which held back the waters of Lake Britton. Climbing a half mile up the hill from the dam, we found a flat spot to set up the tents. We had hiked less than ten miles but felt like we had a big day.

July 12th
Day 97– 32.5 Miles
Total 1457.5 Miles

We were on the trail at 6:15 a.m., climbing over a hill and following the ridge above Pit River. Reaching Rock Creek, we crossed over a footbridge where the water cascaded down the valley. The ups and downs of the day were minimal with no big mountains to climb or valleys to descend into yet, over the thirty-two and a half miles, we still climbed over five thousand feet. For most of the day Family Man was somewhere out ahead. I would say it was kind of lonely, but loneliness didn't seem to bother me anymore. Over the miles of solitude I had developed a process of training my mind to create projects. I would start with an idea for a building, and then step-by-step I would build that building. Another time passing exercise was to think up ideas for a novel and work through the plot. On days when depression was trying to get the best of me, I would work on lyrics for songs about my demise on the PCT.

Walking through an old burn area, I came face to face with a hiker who was carrying a contraption on her back that looked like she was trying to contact aliens. Tina Lippke, trail name Seminole, was hiking with a Trimble GPS Survey system to map the trail. The data gathered during her hike through this part of the country resulted in tracking at sub-miter accuracy.

Lon Cooper's maps are the standard bearer when it comes to navigating the PCT. The name of the maps, and Cooper's trail name, comes from the half mile waypoints on the map. In 2012, while Tina was hiking the PCT, her husband David Lippke, a retired AOL senior vice president, was paralleling Tina on his bike. His frustration about the lack of quality mapping led him to join up with Mr. Cooper and an app was born. A year later, we found the advantages this app brought to navigation indispensable. Our gratitude goes out to these three and all the others that worked on this project.

About an hour later, I crossed the Summit Lake Road and found Family Man sound asleep on a log. The fiber energy bars were doing their thing and the temptation was too much. He woke up with a start as I "crop dusted" the airspace about six inches from his nose. For the next ten miles we made our way along a ridge in a big sweeping half circle around the headwaters of Kosk Creek. The Kosk gathers its water from all the other tributaries and moves south down to Big Bend where it dumps into the Pit River. Late in the day, we paralleled the summit road which looked pretty rugged. We planned on stopping for the night when we found a flat spot on the ridge. Coming out of the trees and onto the crown we found the only flat spot occupied by our friend Mr. Clean. We could have squeezed in, but out of respect we moved on down the trail. After all, it wasn't dark yet. The trail followed the ridge, descending slightly for the next mile and a half until we came to a big flat gravel parking area by the dirt road. We found out that dirt roads with quarter sized stones do not make for good sleeping.

July 13th
Day 98– 33 Miles
Total 1490.5 Miles

Waking up at the first hint of light, we were rewarded with a great view of Mount Shasta's snow covered peak. The fourteen thousand foot volcanic peak stood out in an otherwise six to seven thousand foot terrain. For the first seven miles we followed the contour lines with minimal climb. As we started our descent along the steep slopes of Grizzly Peak we came across three trail workers. They told us they were part of a larger team with a camp a couple more miles down the trail. They encouraged us to stop by the camp for fresh fruit. With this mouthwatering vision clouding an otherwise beautiful day, we picked up our speed. We met more trail workers, spending time with each one and thanking them for the volunteer work they were doing. They loved hearing our stories as many had spent time hiking the trail, either in sections or a thru hike in some previous year. Many were retired, including a volunteer who was working close to the camp. He was eighty years old.

He had had heart surgery a couple of years before, and the others made sure he didn't overdo it. At the camp we met John, the team cook and bottle washer. He invited us to sit down and relax. He brought us each a Ziploc bag full of fresh cut fruit and a can of root beer.

John spent forty-five minutes chatting with us before we excused ourselves and moved on down the trail. Leaving the camp, we came across a number of additional trail workers. We made it a point to spend time thanking each of them. We continued a descent to McCloud River where we found vehicles at the Ash Campground. A concrete footbridge crosses the McCloud River a mile south of the dam that holds back Lake McCloud. We followed along the river for three miles before it turned southwest and headed back up over a mountain. Fifteen hundred feet later we made it back to the top, and for the next ten miles did the up and down thing. We ran into a section hiker named Lance-a-Lot, a trail name derived from the way he handled his numerous blisters. He liked to hike fast, then stop and read his book for awhile. We leaped frogged with him a better part of the afternoon.

Family Man and Lance-a-Lot were hiking together when they were suddenly startled by a rattlesnake making noises beside the trail. Lance-a-Lot had just been telling Family Man about his multiple encounters with the slithery serpents. Family Man had the honors of dispatching the snake down the mountain and they moved on.

Crossing over the Squaw Creek Bridge at 9:30, we were unable find a flat enough spot to camp. Lance-a-Lot headed down a side trail looking for a camping spot. That went against our grain, so we headed on up the mountain knowing that somewhere out there in the night was our spot. Climbing 400 feet over that last half mile just about finished us. We had beaten our previous record with 33 miles and had climbed 9,300 feet. A small clearing in a wooded area next to a fire road looked ideal. That is, until I kicked a rock out of the way and found it had been covering something special. It was fairly fresh and smelled worse than Family Man after a week on the trail.

He could not stop laughing as we both relocated to a different campsite.

July 14th
Day 99– 17.5 Miles
Total 1508 Miles

We woke up later than normal the next morning as the previous big day took its toll. The only thing that motivated us to get on down the trail was the knowledge that it was a resupply day. Interstate 5 was only sixteen miles away. We continued our climb by a handful of switchbacks to the ridge. The continual climb was interrupted only with periodic dips into small ravines. We passed around the north side of Girard Ridge for some unknown reason, other than for a couple of water sources. The GPS said we had 3,900 feet of descent and 1,500 feet of climbing to get to the interstate. This is where we started using the term "dissipating climb." Sometimes the program would register a hill that we did not actually go over, so as we passed by this hill, the altitude it showed we had to climb would just go away. There were times it would do the same thing while we were climbing, giving us "dissipating descent." This was more depressing than the dissipating climb. However the trail conditions were excellent, and we made really good time.

Family Man was somewhere out ahead when I had a rattlesnake encounter. We had descended below 2,500 feet ASL, and I was walking through a grove of oak trees. In my peripheral vision, I saw what looked like a rock sliding down on the leaves beside me. As I took another step, I wondered what would cause a rock to slide down the mountain. Turning around, I saw about a 30" snake coiled up on the trail. Using my trekking pole, I convinced it to continue its journey.

I crossed over the Sacramento River via the Soda Creek Road bridge around 1:00 p.m. and found Family Man resting underneath the overpass. We waited there in the shade for about twenty minutes as thousands of vehicles roared overhead.

Finally, we spotted Sharla walking down the road from the exit ramp. She had been in the parking lot hidden from our view.

Mount Shasta from the west

Chapter Twenty Six – Mount Shasta to Seiad Valley

We spent the afternoon resting at the campground, playing with the boys, taking showers, and packing up for the next section up to Seiad Valley. It was decided that Sharla would take us back to the trail before dark. As a sendoff, Brittany made us an awesome steak dinner. At 8:00 p.m., with full stomachs and backpacks, we headed back to the trail. It was getting dark when we said goodbye and started the climb away from the freeway. We only climbed for about a mile and a half before coming to a clearing where power lines crossed the trail. There we set up camp. We had only put in a little over seventeen miles but the time with the family was worth it.

July 15th
Day 100 – 29.5 Miles
Total 1537.5 Miles

In the civilized world it was Monday morning. On the PCT, the day of the week had long before lost all significance. We started this morning like all the others. At 6:15 we were walking down the trail. We found our first water source six miles into the day on the west side of the crags. Burstares Creek was shallow yet flowing, surrounded by umbrella plants. A half mile up the trail, at Disappearing Creek, we met a hiker carrying a folded lawn chair. Camp Chair, his obvious trail name, is Operator's uncle. He had come out to meet up with his nephew for a few days of backpacking. As we pushed our way up the now exposed hot mountain, we met Wendy hiking southbound. She gave us excellent water source details. First hand water reports less than a day old can usually be depended upon.

We had only put in eleven miles by noon but had climbed over four thousand feet. We made it to the crest by late afternoon, and enjoying the cooler altitude, we were able to pick up our speed. It was early evening when we came across White Ridge Spring coming out just below the trail. The trail workers had been kind enough to wedge a copper half pipe in the rocks, giving us a nice flowing stream of clean, cold water. The plans of a thirty mile day were cut short by a half mile when we came upon Mr. Clean set up on a null. As we stood there looking out ahead at the darkening trail cutting across the steep ridge, we decided to stop as well. We were tired and didn't want to spend half the night looking for another suitable camping spot.

July 16th
Day 101 – 34.75 Miles
Total 1572.25 Miles

At 4:30 a.m. we woke up to the sound of raindrops hitting the mesh top of my tent. The challenge with this is that mesh doesn't deter rain. We had checked the ten day forecast before leaving Mount Shasta and it showed a zero percent chance of rain. This convinced us to leave our rain gear in the RV, including the rain flies that cover the tent. It was still pitch dark when I hollered at Family Man who was already stirring. By the time I got my sleeping bag in my back pack the rain stopped. We were awake now, so we decided to head out. Fifteen minutes later we were walking a hundred yards back to the trail, still in the dark.

Reaching what we thought was our trail, we made a right turn and started a descent. Why we didn't remember the ridge we had to cross is still a mystery. A half mile down the trail, things just seemed wrong. When we arrived at a lake we knew we were somewhere other than the PCT. An outhouse in bad need of repair sealed the deal. I dug my phone out of my backpack, and the GPS was kind enough to tell us we were at Toad Lake and a third of a mile off the trail. Six hundred yards doesn't sound like much, but when it's straight up the mountain it becomes a challenge. By now it was getting light and it was a drudging climb back up a mountain we were not suppose to have come down. Shortly after 6:00 a.m. we made it back to the trail and headed around the ridge. A short time later we stopped under a tree as another rain shower dampened our already cloudy enthusiasm.

The clouds moved away and the tread was good as we followed the contour. We arrived at Parks Creek Road where we found a parking lot with numerous vehicles. We sat under a shade tree waiting for some human to feel sorry for hiker trash and give us a root beer. After eating our snack and watching a few people come and go, we came to the conclusion that none of them were trail angels. We headed north with plans of getting water at Chilcoot Creek but found it undesirable. It was just past 6:00 p.m. when we crossed Highway 3 with 29 miles behind us, plus the two mile detour we took down by Toad Lake. We were getting tired as we climbed back up the thousand feet to the ridge. We came across a herd of cattle. One cow was given the responsibility of carrying a cow bell. The cows found it amusing to go running along the road just above the trail with the irritating bell clanging for the next two miles.

159

Late in the day when we were starting to look for a place to camp and water, we came across a stream coming out of a swamp. A dirty sock hung on a branch, but the smell we were experiencing was far worse than the smell of a dirty sock. Looking around, we spotted a dead cow in the swamp. It looked like it had died standing up and then just fell over on its side, stiff as a board. Getting water out of this stream suddenly became a bad idea. Three quarters of a mile later it was getting dark when we arrived at a nice, flowing stream coming across the trail. A hundred yards past the stream we found a nice spot to camp. The sky was full of stars as we went to sleep to the sound of the cattle in the distance making their obnoxious sounds while somewhere nearby the coyotes howled.

July 17th
Day 102 – 34.35 Miles
Total 1606.6 Miles

It's another day of hiking. Am I getting tired of hiking? That is kind of an understatement for the mental state of someone who has revolutionized his life after fifty years. It was like a never ending story as we set out on another day of endless climbing and descending. We were running low on food and made the decision to attempt to get a ride into the town of Etna at Sawyer Bar Road. That would make for another thirty plus mile day.

In order to cut down on our weight, we had not only left our rain gear behind, but also we had left our cook stove. We had talked through the weight to calorie issue, but we did not take into consideration the sugar content of our food selection. Once on the trail, we discovered almost everything we carried was high in sugar and low in protein. The challenge with this scenario is that sugar burns quickly, leaving you still feeling hungry. This caused a considerable increase in the amount of food we ate. What was intended to last five days was dwindling after three.

The trail continued southwest. By the time we had stopped the previous night, we had been heading southwest for over twenty miles. Anybody that knows anything about geography knows that Canada is not southwest of Northern California. Sometimes the trail gets to a person. We could get discouraged if we were looking for the shortest distance between Campo, California and Manning Park, BC. Yet, knowing it was 2669.5 miles, we only had to take that next step with the faith it would eventually get us there. Ten miles into the day we turned north and crossed Highway 93. Sometime around noon we ran into Backup. He got his trail name by carrying a backup for almost everything. He had two spoons, two headlamps, two water filters and numerous other spares. He hiked with us on and off for the rest of the day. There seemed to be a lot of climbing which led to a lot of descending as well. Just before we crossed over the ridge heading along the east slope above South Russian Creek, we ran into Forrest. Forrest was one of the hikers we had met in southern California when he was getting ready to return home for his brother's wedding. We spent some time catching up on his hike. He had come back on the trail at Crater Lake and was hiking south to Wrightwood.

Continuing north along the ridge we came to a long hard climb up an exposed granite mountain. I could see Family Man about a quarter mile out ahead enjoying a few minutes in the shade of a pine tree. He saw me coming and took off. This caused mumbling about lack of respect for old people. As I went around a corner I looked back and spotted Backup a quarter mile back climbing hard. It was a struggling hot climb as the afternoon sun baked the granite walls. I only stopped for half a minute at the shade tree before pushing on. I'm sure Backup mumbled as well. Finally, I hit the top and found Family Man sitting on a rock in the shade. I was so exhausted that I threw down my trekking poles and peeled off my backpack. With great exasperation I uttered a couple of unnecessary choice words that required an apology. My unexpected outburst brought laughter to Family Man. Ten minutes later Backup made it over the hill and joined us for a few more minutes of rest. He was

161

kind enough to share some steak jerky as he shared his struggle up the hill as well. He had seen ol' Stagecoach climbing and figured he could make it too.

Backup took off ahead of us, and we pushed on to Paynes Lake Creek four miles away. Family Man and Backup were already there when I arrived, and Family Man walked up a side trail 150 feet to Payne Lake while I filled my bottles. Backup and I left ahead of Family Man, and a short time later we spotted Family Man coming up the trail following three fast moving hikers. We stepped aside and let them pass. We found out it was Josh Garrett attempting to beat the trail speed record. He had two guys hiking with him trying to keep up. Stopping a short time later on a ridge with a great view of Smith Lake, I was able to get cell service. We called Hiker Hut at Etna and arranged a pickup for the next morning. The lady who took the message had to be a little confused when I told her it was for Family Man, Stagecoach, and Backup. I'm sure the relay went something like this, "Some family man called and wanted you to backup the stagecoach."

We still had three miles to the highway when it got dark. Backup desired to conserve batteries and walked ahead of me, using my beam to light his trail. The problem with this technique is it darkened the trail in his shadow. I started feeling sorry for him after he had kicked a handful of rocks. He didn't seem to care and hiked on.

We arrived at Sawyer Bar Road around 10:00 p.m. to find Josh and his entourage sitting on lawn chairs beside an SUV. We joined them as they were getting taken care of by Tish who was the one person support team for the record attempt. Josh was gracious in sharing his dream and story with us, and Tish was kind enough to give us a bag of BBQ chips and Gatorades. Josh ended up beating the supported record at 59 days 8 hours and 14 minutes. One day before Josh arrived at the northern terminus another hiker, Heather "Anish" Anderson, beat the unsupported record at 60 days 17 hours and 12 minutes. We did not have the privilege of meeting Anish. She past by us while we were at the RV in Mount Shasta.

The high speed hikers set up camp on top of the hill, while the rest of us camped down on the parking lot. Tish was headed to Etna for the night and had room to take one of us, but we had no desire to split up. Another 34 plus mile day and we were extremely tired, so the rocks under the sleeping pad didn't matter.

July 18th
Day 103 – 23.4 Miles
Total 1630 Miles

I was lying in my sleeping bag tossing back and forth just trying to figure out which hip hurt the least. My internal clock was telling me that daylight was getting close. The sound of a vehicle approaching removed any possibility of further slumber just before bright headlights flooded the area. We heard Tish apologize and back away. She had come back up to the trail to feed the guys breakfast. Awake now I told Family Man to pack up and I would try to talk her into giving us a ride into town. While the high speed hikers ate their breakfast and prepared for the day we ate watermelon Tish had given us. She had room for two of us, so Family Man and I were on our way to Etna two hours earlier than expected. We left Backup on the mountain to wait for the ride we had arranged earlier.

We were sitting on a bench outside the closed Wildwood Crossings on the corner of Main Street and Collier Way when a couple of ladies stopped by for a chat. They said that while the coffee shop and deli served good food, we were most likely looking for a café that served a big hearty breakfast. They gave us directions to Bob's Ranch House about six blocks down Collier Way. The ranch house was like most cafés bustling with morning activity, but the service was great. The waitress was understanding of the hiker trash fashion and served us up a big plate of bacon, eggs, hash browns, and pancakes. All during breakfast Family Man kept pointing out the lemon meringue pie in the display cabinet. Temptation overcame ol' Stagecoach, so for dessert, the mouthwatering pie made my morning. Finally a craving was satisfied. I was just finishing the pie when Backup arrived. He had caught a ride from a passerby. I called Hiker Hut with the update so they wouldn't make an unnecessary trip up the mountain and to arrange our return. We were walking out of the restaurant when Operator and his uncle, Camp Chair, arrived. They had made it to Hiker Hut where they borrowed bicycles. Family Man talked a lady into giving us a ride to the grocery store even though it was only five blocks away. I think it was more of a challenge than a necessity.

Tucked in behind the newspaper stands next to the grocery store we found an outlet and plugged in the phone and battery pack to recharge. For the next hour we sat there on the sidewalk like two bums eating ice cream and drinking root beer. We had already walked the aisles picking up about as much food as we could carry. With full stomachs and heavy backpacks, we set out for the Hiker Hut hostel and our ride to the mountain.

Hiker Hut is a cabin behind the Alderbrook Manor Bed and Breakfast owned and operated by Dave and Vicki Harrison. It is best suited for hunters, fishermen, bicycle groups, and the like. During hiker season it becomes a haven for those who hike 1600 miles to get there. The B&B is well maintained and is now on our bucket list as a place to visit. Dave was out of town on a vacation he received for his 70th birthday. While he was gone, volunteers had come in to help Vicki deal with the hikers. One of them took us to the trail head and gave us chocolate chip cookies, another example of the kindness we experienced on and around the trail. At 10:00 a.m., as the day started heating up, we found ourselves back on the trail. The sun continued to climb in the sky, and it got hotter. The food in our stomachs only weighed us down as we climbed the thousand feet back up to a ridge.

Our goal for the day was to get to the 1,630 mile marker. That would leave us thirty miles to Seiad Valley. At Seiad we would be taking a five day break. Family Man needed to live up to his trail name by taking his family up to Salem, Oregon for his boys' yearly doctor appointment. Earlier on the trail a thirty mile day would have made us cringe but not any longer. We had broken through that barrier. What used to be a dream was now the normal. Ten miles into the day, the runoff from Shelley Lake resupplied our water. Four miles later we crossed a ridge where we had a great view of a high altitude lake called Man Eaten Lake set in a basin. Pushing north along the ridge, we walked through fields of flowers leading to tougher climbs up additional ridges into the night. We still had four miles to go when it got dark, so we turned on the lights and kept walking. Family Man's shoes were getting thin, and I started kidding him about not having a sole. It was just before midnight when we crossed a small stream and found a ranger's cabin. It looked uninhabited so we found a spot in the grass to set up our tents. I returned to the stream and filtered water. We noticed tents uphill from us a hundred yards, and another hiker showed up and camped on the other side of the cabin. We had reached our goal, and it was time for a good night's sleep.

July 19th
Day 104 – 30 Miles
Total 1660 Miles

Where there's grass there is dew. You would think we would learn to set up our tents under trees. As we were packing up our stuff, the two hikers up the hill hollered a morning greeting. We were on the trail at 6:20 with a 2,500 foot climb ahead. Early on we met up with a hiker named Happy whose disposition had won him his trail name. Happy was on his second attempt at the PCT, the first ending with an ankle injury. This time he was hiking with some major sized hiking boots. He had found the added ankle support was worth the weight. Family Man quickly left us behind and it wasn't until three hours later that I caught up with him at Paradise Lake. He had located a great spring flowing into the lake and was busy eating whatever snacks he could find in his stuff sack.

Leaving Paradise Lake we ran into some southbound hikers, and as Family Man stopped to chat, I headed on to the top of the ridge. The bottoms of my shoes were getting thin and the trail was getting rockier. Every time I stepped on a rock I started feeling intense pain with my left big toe. It would not stop complaining, so I stopped to take a look and found it had pushed its way through the bottom of my shoe. There was nothing but a sock between my big toe and the trail, and the other big toe wasn't much better. I didn't have enough duct tape to tape up the shoe, so I taped up my toe instead. I was starting to understand what Family Man was going through. He had now lost most of his soles and was walking on paper thin rubber. Professional hikers would have known to check the soles while in civilization. The good news was that we had less than twenty-five miles to highway.

Family Man caught up on Buckhorn Ridge which we followed north, stopping at the Buckhorn Spring for water. The spring was in pretty bad shape, so we only got what we needed for the 5,000 foot descent to Grider Creek seven miles away. We did our calculations and sent off a SPOT message for a 6:00 p.m. pickup at Grider Creek Campground. I was somewhere out ahead of Family Man when I crossed the Cold Spring Creek. In my desire to keep my feet dry, I stepped across on the rocks. The dark green moss did not ring a bell until my treadless shoes no longer maintained any form of traction. In a split second I found myself sitting in eight inches of water. As quick as I went in I jumped up and pulled my phone out of my side pouch. Fortunately, I was not in the water long enough for the phone to get wet. All but my shoes were dry by the time Family Man came up behind me.

Arriving at the campground we found a nice RV without occupants. We made our way out to the parking lot and found a satellite dish in front of the outhouse. We didn't go inspect, but we figured it most likely was hooked up to the RV in the woods, not the pit toilet. We had just dropped our backpacks and sat down on a rock when Sharla showed up. With a lot of daylight left, we threw our bags in the back of the car and started the five mile road walk to the highway. It felt weird not having the weight of our backpacks on our shoulders. Imagine yourself all of a sudden thirty pounds lighter. Your arms and legs would flop around with little control. We sent Sharla off to the Seiad restaurant to buy us cheeseburgers and root beer as we battled the sensation of floating. Keeping us tethered to the earth were fresh sweet blackberries growing alongside the gravel road. Sharla found the restaurant closed, but not wanting to return empty handed, she bought us root beer and snacks at the store. We reached Highway 96 at 8:00 p.m. and headed for Mount Shasta and a warm shower. Another thirty mile day was in the books with only a thousand miles left to the Canadian border

July 20th – 24th
Day 105-109 –0 Miles
Total 1660 Miles

We woke to the sound of Sawyer ready for the day. That was okay as today was the beginning of a five day hiatus from the trail. We packed everything up and headed north. Sharla and I were in the RV with the two dogs and heading for the Holiday RV Park just south of Medford, Oregon. Family Man, Brittany, and the boys were in the car headed for a five day reprieve back home in Salem. These five days would also give us much needed rest and time to find new shoes.

After a couple of days of rest, we loaded the dogs into the RV so they would not cause a ruckus and headed out on foot to find the REI. We only had to walk a couple of blocks before catching a bus taking us north into town and close enough to the store that another block got us through the front door. They had my Morrell® Moab Ventilators in the right size. I tried to tell the employees mine should still be under warranty since they were less than three months old. They seemed skeptical as we put them side by side and the new shoes were a half inch higher. After all 1,294 miles on a pair of shoes through some rugged territory is impressive. With a short, emotional eulogy I dropped the old boys in the trash can and walked away feeling like a hiker with new shoes.

Family Man showed up on the afternoon of July 24th. The boys had checked out okay, they celebrated Brittany's birthday, went to church, and Family Man got some new shoes. We spent the evening catching up on things and laying out plans for the state of Oregon. We had been on the trail for a hundred days, and in thirty-eight miles we would cross over into Oregon. We were so looking forward to this milestone. We finished the evening packing up supplies for a 66 mile, three day section which would conclude at the Callahan's Lodge on Interstate 5, just north of the state line.

Chapter Twenty Seven –Seiad Valley to Ashland

July 25th
Day 110 – 10.33 Miles
Total 1670.33 Miles

It was 11:30 a.m. when Sharla dropped us off at Grider Road. The 80 mile trip down from Medford was uneventful, but the thermometer showed temperatures closing in on triple digits. While we walked the 1.4 miles of pavement to Seiad, Sharla waited at the café nursing a mouthwatering cheeseburger. We walked into the crowded restaurant for our greatly anticipated burgers shortly after noon. We found Maverick and Lodgepole hanging out at the campground next door. They were going to spend another night in the grass with a handful of other hikers with plans for an early start in the morning. They thought we were crazy climbing out of the valley in the afternoon's heat, and we probably were. It was like Belden all over again. At least this time Family Man had his hat.

It was difficult saying goodbye to Sharla. She was doing such a great job driving all over the west to get us on and off the trail. Many times, as we watched her drive away, we would ask

God to watch over her and Brittany as they continued to do the unimaginable.

Leaving the store, we hiked west on the highway with temperatures above a hundred bouncing off the pavement. Only a half mile down the road, under a big shade tree, we plopped down and questioned our motivation. Finally, after much soul searching, we struggled to our feet and made our way onto the trail another third of a mile down the road. As expected, immediately after leaving the highway, the PCT climbed like a homesick angel. Needless to say, we looked like turtles as we inched our way to higher altitude. Each step brought with it both emotional and physical torment. We stopped frequently to cool down and rest. The charred trees reminded us of the many miles of forest we had passed through in the previous three months. Two hours into the day we made it to Fern Springs where a one inch galvanized pipe dribbled water into a five foot by three foot concrete horse tank. The tank was full of water and laced with slimy green moss. We had gone less than two miles, yet we made the decision to take a two hour break. The sound of the water dripping into the tank added to the coolness of the shade. Taking off our new shoes to let our feet breathe, we wondered if we would ever find the motivation to keep going. All of a sudden Family Man stripped down and crawled into the horse tank, spilling water all over the side. He didn't spend much time in this mossy mountain spa as concerns grew about hikers that might be coming up the trail.

After more than two hours, we continued our climb back and forth up the mountain. We met a couple coming down the mountain who told us about Lookout Springs along the ridge. By 6:00 p.m. we made it to the ridge 3,000 feet above Seiad Valley. The temperatures were considerably lower when we arrived at the spring which was running, however slowly. By the time we tanked up it was dark and, with headlamps aglow, we headed on up the mountain. It was getting late and Family Man kept asking what time it was. He didn't care to hike late into the night as he tends to get grumpy when he's tired. So I would tell him it was almost 10:00, regardless of the actual time. He had proven his ability to maintain trail awareness with the snakes in southern California, and tonight wasn't any different. This time it was a scorpion making its way across the trail. The little black thing was just trying to get to the other side, but it did make me look around and under rocks before I sat down. We made it to the top around 10:30 p.m. where we found a flat ridge overlooking Seiad Valley 4,500 feet below. We were thrilled to have made it to the top in such adverse conditions. We took satisfaction in not having to face this hill in the morning.

July 26th
Day 111 – 34.12 Miles
Total 1704.45 Miles

It was a relaxing and surreal night as the 94% full moon lit up the inside of the uncovered tent. We woke up at 5:15 a.m. and had an awesome view down both directions from the ridge. The only sound coming from the neighbor's tent was that of a snoring, contented hiker. I cranked up the volume on my phone and played "I Would Walk 500 Miles." Playing a song in the morning accomplishes two things: first, it wakes up Family Man; and second, it gives him a song that keeps playing over and over in his head all day long.

We needed to go farther that day and set about doing just that. Already at altitude, and after a good night's rest, we made three miles in the first hour. Crossing under Red Butte, we started a thousand foot descent to Cook & Green Pass. Stagecoach was doing a high speed descent, but not fast enough for Family Man. He left me in the dust with plans to meet at a spring located near the pass. I arrived at the pass and had trouble locating the trail leading to the spring. Finally, I found it behind a tent next to an old dusty car.

The young couple occupying the tent said Family Man had come through a few minutes earlier in a hurry heading on down the trail. I was surprised he had not stopped for water as we were running low. The water looked clean so I went ahead and filled up my bottles unfiltered and went looking for Family

Man. I found him only a quarter mile down the trail wondering where the spring was. He had totally missed the side trail but now felt he had enough to make it to the next water source. We climbed 1,500 feet back up to the ridge, and by noon we had 13.5 miles behind us. We ate lunch under the peak of White Mountain. Hiking along at full speed I came across a hiker napping beside the trail. Double Zero was section hiking during his summer recess from teaching college in Japan.

Shark Bite and Faucet were at the Oregon state line when we arrived at 7:30 p.m. What a relief! After walking 1,698.93 miles and climbing 313,298 feet of mountains, we were finally out of California. We were so excited about getting out of the state which had caused us so much pain. We rested for a few minutes as Family Man signed the register and posed for a couple of pictures. The day was not over, so we continued to climb another 1,200 feet. We had crossed the ridge and were on a long gradual descent to Siskiyou Summit Road when we started hearing dogs barking. In the dusk we could see the dogs running out ahead around a couple of vehicles. Three guys were setting up camp for a trail marathon scheduled for the next day. They were interested in our journey and gave us cokes, food bars, and apples. We visited with them for a half hour before heading down the trail totally stoked. It was dark when we got to the spring which was one of the strongest running springs on the PCT. The water was shooting out of the two inch pipe like it was trying to put out a fire. Numerous other hikers were camping under the nearby trees, so we decided to tank up, fill up, and move on. With all the water we could handle and headlamps shining, we continued the gradual descent for another mile. Entering a group of trees, we found a spot to clear away the branches and set up for our first night in Oregon.

July 27th
Day 112 – 22.55 Miles
Total 1727 Miles

Before daylight could bring about another day, the moon found a gap between the leaves and shone directly into my eyes. It was after five, so I started getting around and woke Family Man up by throwing sticks at his tent on the other side of the trail. We had just started down the trail when the sun revealed itself from behind the hills. With a mild 23 mile day ahead of us, there were 2,800 feet to climb and 5,300 feet of descent. Soon after day break we started meeting trail runners competing in the race. The 14th annual Siskiyou Outback Trail Run was raising money for the Pacific Crest Trail Association and had over 500 runners participating. We were hiking in the opposite direction of the race and would step aside each time we heard someone coming.

Ten miles into the day, we heard a lot of cheering and the sound of someone blowing a horn. Arriving at an aid station we were greeted with the same fan fair as the runners. The volunteers treated us like heroes and invited us to enjoy all the good stuff they had spread out. We had a soda and some potato chips while sharing stories of the trail. On down the trail, the faster runners blew by us returning to the finish line. They told us to stop by the parking lot for more food and drinks. The temptation was thwarted by our desire to stay on the trail. We came across another cooler filled with soda a couple more miles down the trail. We were ecstatic with all the trail angel encounters, and the cold beverage sucked us into the shade of the oasis. Faucet and Shark Bite arrived just as we were getting ready to leave. Around noon we crossed the paved road that led up to Mount Ashland Ski Resort. While eating our lunch, Gumby and Double It came across the road and joined us. My left knee started hurting, and I blamed it on the side stepping all morning. Each step to a lower altitude was causing extreme pain. It didn't take long before we realized that I was experiencing what Family Man had in southern California.

The IT band runs from the hip to the ankle and is attached at the knee to help stabilize and move the joints. When the IT band gets inflamed from overuse and stops working properly it can cause severe pain, especially going downhill.

Because the symptoms are normally swelling and pain on the outside of the knee, most hikers think it is a knee injury. We were fortunate to have Gumby there to give us some medical advice and a couple of pain killers to mix with our Ibuprofen. One kills the pain while the other reduces the swelling. Is it a healthy thing to do? Probably not, but it did help.

A couple of miles and 700 feet of descent later we arrived at the Ashland Inn. The inn was closed, but the owners had left a faucet on for hikers to get water. We spent a half hour resting in hopes we could make it down this mountain. We thought about getting a ride from one of the many cars now coming off the mountain, but there was so much daylight left we wanted to get this done. Family Man, Gumby, and Double It volunteered to divide my pack between them. I thanked them for their desire to help, but knew that to shun my responsibility because of pain would be detrimental to completing the trail.

It was not good. At times I would back down the steeper slopes to reduce the pain. With three miles to go and 1,200 feet of downhill left, we took another break. I lay there whimpering about my lot in life, despondent about the pain I must endure. I don't know if Family Man felt sorry for me, or if he was tired of my whining, but he jumped up grabbed my backpack and headed down the trail. I yelled at him and took off after him the best I could. As bad as he wanted to help, I don't think he understood the emotional damage that could come from having someone else carry my load. Finally, a quarter mile down the trail he let me have it back, deciding I would make it one way or another. We progressed slowly but steadily, only stopping to read a big metal sign which told us this was the Siskiyou Mountain Wagon Road and that the last stagecoach had crossed in 1887. The humor from this now outdated sign, now that ol' Stagecoach had come down the trail, brought some relief from the pain.

We passed the cutoff trail to Callahan's Lodge and hiked the additional mile and a half up to the highway. The toughest part was the three quarter mile walk back down the paved highway to the lodge. Our plans had been to just have the girls drop off our resupply, and we would set up our tent in the back yard of the lodge with the other hikers. However, the package price for dinner, breakfast, take a shower and wash our clothes was more than we wanted to pay, so we called the girls with a backup plan to spend the night in the RV. They were already on the way and had to go back and drop off Brittany and the boys. Sharla showed up at 5:45 p.m. and drove us the twenty miles back to a night in the RV.

Chapter Twenty Eight – Ashland to Crater Lake

July 28th
Day 113 – 26.65 Miles
Total 1753.65 Miles

It was Sunday morning at the RV, and we slept in until 6:30. Taking our time, we spent an hour eating breakfast and drinking coffee. Back at the trailhead at 8:10 we climbed away from Interstate 5 for the last time. This highway was the subject of our conversation frequently when we grumbled about the mountains we had to climb. When one of us would make negative comments about having to climb over mountains instead of going around them, the other would say, "If you want easy, hike Interstate 5."

A couple miles up the trail, while we were taking our first break, Gnome God showed up. This was our first meeting. He was previously called Tick Tock due to his walking method. I don't know how his name got changed. It could be that, with facial hair, he resembled a gnome. He told us Gumby and Double It were at Callahan's and were concerned about Stagecoach. We had told them we had planned on spending the night there and when we didn't show up they were asking if anyone had seen us. We leap frogged with Gnome God the rest of the day, even having lunch with him at a water faucet in the middle of nowhere.

The day was filled with a lot of normal. It was just a two foot wide dry dusty path leading up and down the hills. Late in the afternoon we made it to the spillway for the Little Hyatt Reservoir. By now we were looking at information on the restaurant at Hyatt Lake Resort. Our desire for a cheeseburger was tempting us to walk three quarters of a mile off the trail. Fortunately, we did the math before going and realized they would be closed before we could get there. We met a group of brothers out for a day hike, and Family Man entertained them with stories of our hike for a while. We were running low on water when we made it to the road leading into Hyatt Lake. A hydrant beside the guard gate gave us clean easy water.

While we were filling up our water bottles a couple of section hikers, who obviously were not seasoned, showed up. They were just starting out to hike the whole state of Oregon. Family Man asked if they had started at the state line, which they had not. Maybe we were getting a condescending attitude from too many months on the trail. One of the differences between section hikers and thru hikers is in the length of the days. It was before 7:00 p.m. and they were stopping for the night where they could take a shower. We still had four more miles before we would call it a day.

Crossing a dirt road half way between Interstate 5 and Highway 140 we had reached our goal and started looking for that elusive campsite. Family Man found a nice spot under a tree where he could cowboy camp. I was not too keen on that idea and set up my tent. That was a wise move, for later we would find out he was sleeping in a patch of poison oak.

July 29th
Day 114 – 26.35 Miles
Total 1780 Miles

With the second half of the section to go, we started out at normal time with good trail. The terrain was fairly flat when it comes to PCT standards. The 26 mile day only had 3,500 feet of climb and almost the same in descent. My left knee started hurting from the very beginning of the day and worsened as we progressed. Even with the knee brace on, we still made pretty good time in the morning hours. Gumby and Double It did catch up with us and were happy to see we were still on the trail.

As always, Family Man was somewhere out ahead with plans to wait at Big Springs. When I got there and headed down the path to the spring, I couldn't see his tracks. I got my water unfiltered from the black plastic pipe and hurried on down the trail. Still I could not make out the print of his Cascades in the dust. There were plenty of shoe prints, just not his. I slowed to a normal pace as my doubts about the whereabouts of Family Man were sorted out. Fifteen minutes later I heard someone behind me, and sure enough it was Family Man running down the trail with a two liter Sawyer bag of water. He had stopped at an unmarked spring just before Big Springs thinking that it was the one where we were to meet. When I didn't show up he went back out to the trail and found my foot prints and the sign to the piped spring.

Following Family Man's footprints in the middle of the afternoon, I came to a note in the trail for Stagecoach to take the side trail off to the left. I guess he didn't want a repeat of the morning scenario. I found Family Man and a handful of other hikers at the Brown Mountain Shelter eating lunch. A hand pump provided fresh water from a well. After leaving the shelter, Family Man went on ahead to the road and I limped along. We had ten miles to go and it was not easy going anymore.

Brown Mountain, located just south of Highway 140, is the results of a shield volcano. Its exact age, while debatable, does not deter from the fact that a couple thousand years ago lava flowed down its sides. Arriving at the base, we started encountering these flows where the chunky lava had hardened in a way that no person should desire to cross. It was only the hard work of the trail crews who had blazed a trail across these moonscapes which made it passable. For a majority of the volcanic trail, volunteers had carried crushed stone and gravel into the lava flows, filling up the gaps between the chunks.

Circumventing the mountain on the western slope took us up and down, in and out of the ravines. I had to take frequent breaks to relieve the throbbing pain in my left knee. My right knee started acting up, so I moved the knee brace hoping it would help. Still a mile and a half out, I had to sit down and rest. The twenty minutes it took to let the swelling subside, was spent doing some real soul searching. Here we were once again dealing with the same issue we had fifty miles before. Was completing the trail even possible? The emotional price I was paying to deal with the pain was immense. Emotionally we were just about bankrupt. I had read enough about IT inflammation to know what I had to do, but I was unwilling to take the time off the trail to let it heal. Sitting there with tears swelling up inside, I did what I knew worked. I talked to God. Like so many other times on this trail, He answered, "Get up and walk." When I finally made it to the road at 6:00 p.m. Family Man was kicked back in the ditch under a shade tree. He had been there for an hour and a half. About twenty minutes later Sharla flew by hitting the brakes as she passed.

We were happy to find out that, during our two days on the trail, our friends had helped the girls move the RV to their ranch north of Medford. A hot shower, clean clothes, and elevated feet are unquestionably good things after such a painful day. *What about tomorrow? Let's rest tonight and worry about tomorrow, tomorrow.*

July 30th
Day 115 – 17 Miles
Total 1797 Miles

We woke up when we were tired of sleeping. Oh, the comforts of the RV. *Why do we do this to ourselves? Why do we go out there and walk the narrow strip of earth? Why do we leave our families for such an endeavor?* Laying there on the pillow top mattress I questioned a number of things, but that morning the real question was my ability to walk. There was a little stiffness in both knees, but the Ibuprofen 800 had done its job. The swelling had gone down. Soon I was chatting with Family Man about our intended departure time. The decision was made to rest throughout the morning with hopes of an early afternoon trailhead time. Our friend Rich was at work, but his wife Gail visited with us and spent time with the boys showing them how to milk a goat. Sawyer wasn't real thrilled unless he could eat it, but Hunter loved being with the farm animals.

Lunch time came too soon, and then we were on our way, arriving back at the trail at 1:45 p.m. Warner Springs Monty and a hiker we hadn't met named Number Two were hanging out at the trailhead. We hadn't seen Monty since April down in Warner Springs. Number Two, who got his trail name from a previous job of studying some sort of animal dung in a far off country, was northbound and we would leap frog with him throughout the evening. We climbed 1,300 feet around the north side of Mount McLoughlin before starting the normal up and down. We pushed hard to advance our mileage considering we had such a late start. As darkness closed around us we met our goal of seventeen miles and set up my tent.

Family Man wanted so badly to do forty miles. Yes that's right, a forty mile day. The next day was to be our first attempt at that goal. I know, you are asking: "Stagecoach, you were going to try to walk forty miles in one day when just the day before you were crying in pain with each step?" The answer for the naysayers was vitamin I. Yes sir, 800 milligrams of some of the best Ibuprofen on the market. Even while it was eating out the walls of my stomach, it was reducing the swelling up and down my legs allowing them to run like the wind, or at least walk like a tortoise. Anyhow with it being our first attempt, we decided if we stayed in one tent we would be more motivated for an early start. The mosquitoes started their attack runs as we set up so we wasted no time in getting inside the mesh. The alarm was set for 3:00 a.m.

With stars shining overhead and concerns about the next day fading from our consciousness, we slept. At 3:05 we were crawling out of our sleeping bags and packing up. It was the last day of July, and at 3:26 we were on the trail with lamps burning brightly. A half mile down the trail Family Man pointed into the brush where a tent stood. Quietly we passed by the sleeping hikers. By daylight we had 6 miles behind us and were going strong. Everything was going well with the knees not causing any problems. We laid out the forty mile plan to stop every five miles for a ten minute break. At lunch time we would rest for a full hour. While the total vertical for the day was a massive 6,000 feet up and 5,000 feet down, divide that by forty miles and we only had 150 feet up and 125 feet down each mile. We consider these numbers to be flat.

July 31th
Day 116 –40 Miles
Total 1837 Miles

At 6:45 a.m. the sun worked its way through the scattered clouds as it came up over the distant mountains. We stopped for just a brief moment to thank God for another beautiful day as we turned and headed down off a ridge to the west. Water was plentiful on the way down from the ridge, and we were moving fast. At noon we pulled out the GPS and found out we had already gone 22.5 miles. This was good, and we were well ahead of schedule. When things are going well is when people become complacent. We started doing the math and came to the conclusion that if we reached Highway 62 by 4:00 p.m., we would have time to run down to Mazama Village for a cheeseburger.

It was two minutes before four when we walked through the trailhead parking lot and onto the highway. We had 32.5 miles behind us and only 7.5 miles to go. The thoughts of cheeseburgers were melting our resolve and we headed down the road to the restaurant. "Let's hitch a ride," we said as we stuck out our thumbs. The first vehicle passing by was a tour bus and it didn't stop. So, like our other attempts at hitchhiking, we gave up and walked the mile of pavement.

Walking into any resort or restaurant as hiker trash, we looked a little out of place. That didn't seem to bother the hostess, and they were happy to seat us. Our side trip rewarded us with a mushroom Swiss cheeseburger and fries which we washed down with lots of root beer. It became embarrassing how many times I asked for a refill of this carbonated pleasure. Family Man felt inclined to top off his afternoon with a cup of fresh brewed coffee. During dinner we charged our phone from an outlet under the table. As we were leaving the restaurant Faucet and Shark Bite were arriving.

Over at the village store we found Chief, Gnome God, and Backup sitting around picnic tables. We found a place to finish charging the phone while we drank more root beer and ate ice cream. Chief invited us to his cabin where everyone was going to hang out for the evening. We would have loved the interaction with other thru hikers, but the 40 mile day called us back to the trail. We remembered we still had 7.5 miles, plus a mile of road, to go.

Reaching the trailhead at 6:00 p.m. we started the climb towards Crater Rim. The four mile, 1,000 foot climb up the side of the rim was torture. The vitamin I was wearing off and my IT band was not happy. Limping into the Crater Rim Resort at 8:00 p.m. we found a water fountain and filled up our bottles. The maps showed the next water source was 27.3 miles to the north. By the time we had finished filling our bottles the park was pretty much deserted. We moved into the restroom where we found hot water. A half hour sink bath cleaned up a couple of dirty hikers. As best we could, we cleaned up after ourselves, but I am sure the janitor noticed something different.

Leaving the visitors center just as the sun went down we followed the rim up and down the jagged mountain. By now my knees were going haywire. The pain was back with a vengeance, and two miles north of the visitor center the trail climbed a sharp hill only to drop off the other side in a steep uncontrolled descent. As we approached the road a ranger stopped and inquired about our camping plans. He didn't want us sleeping on the rim and gave us an alternative on the other side of the road. We thanked him and moved on. Family Man was concerned and asked if we were going to listen to the ranger. My response was, "No," to which he replied that he didn't think so. Our goal to get forty miles in was in jeopardy with only a half mile to go. We climbed over another hill as lightning flashed in the west. As the trail again descended back to the road the lightning was getting close.

With the two extra miles we had hiked on the side trip, we were well over the goal. So, to avoid teaching my son bad things by disobeying the law, we crossed the road and found a place to sleep. As I was putting on my rain fly it started sprinkling. Once we were inside the tent the rain started beating down. God sometimes sends people into our path to slow us down at the proper time, regardless of our rebellion. Pulling out my phone I checked the GPS, and it showed we had hit our goal of forty miles on the trail plus the two mile side trip. I heard Family Man mumble something about an early start to do a back to back forty. Tucked deep into my sleeping bag, I only chuckled in pain as my throbbing legs tried to cool down.

Chapter Twenty Nine – Crater Lake to Highway 20

August 1ˢᵗ
Day 117 –15 Miles
Total 1852 Miles

I woke up at 3:15 a.m. with the consideration of another forty mile day. Sticking my head outside the tent all I saw was billowing clouds blocking out the stars. The moon was desperately trying to reveal itself from behind the fast moving clouds. We were both awake at 5:00 a.m. and started our routine of trying to talk each other into getting started. The only thing that got started was the rain. So we went back to sleep. By 8:15 the rain had moved on, the sky had started to clear, and we were on the trail. Making our way around the west side of Watchman Peak the trail returned to the rim. We stopped for breakfast at the parking lot, making use of the restroom. We made our way around Hillman Peak and ended up at a lookout on the west side of Crater Lake. An RV sitting in the parking lot had the appearance of a trail angel. I guess our hiker trash mentality was getting the best of us. The people returning to the RV didn't invite us in for a hot cup of coffee so we moved on leaving the park behind us.

Heading towards Highway 138 twelve miles away, we found the trail littered with fallen trees. Every hundred yards, sometimes less, we found ourselves crawling over trees. About eight miles from the highway I started feeling a slight knee pain. I put on the knee brace and kept going. Family Man leaped over the trees like he was jumping hurdles in a race. Stagecoach crawled over like he was getting on a horse. Six miles from the road, I came to a screeching halt. The forward progress slowed from 2.5 to 1 mph. Climbing over the blown down trees was most likely the culprit in causing this sudden agony.

I knew at this point there was no way of making this a big day. Limping along at a blistering speed I heard the sound of footsteps rapidly approaching. Stepping aside I was greeted by a young lady named Siesta. She was going about three times my speed. Later B-Rad passed me up as well. I gave him a message for Family Man as he sped off down the trail. Struggling on, I realized that we needed to change plans.

Our plans were for Sharla pick us up at Shelter Cove up on Odell Lake, 60 miles past Highway 138. We would take the RV up to Family Man's hometown in Salem, Oregon. "That's the answer." I was always talking to myself on the trail. "We will get off the trail at Highway 138 and reposition the RV while my knees heal." SPOT messages are limited to 145 characters and it takes 20 minutes for the process to complete and another message can be sent. Hitting the send button I knew "Pick us up at Highway 138 ASAP" would cause some anxiety, but at least it would get wheels rolling.

Reaching the highway I found Family Man talking to Siesta and B-Rad. He was not happy that I had sent the message, but he understood. Fortunately by now I had cell service and got in touch with Sharla. We found out she had been out shopping with Gail and it would be at least ninety minutes before they could be there. We talked them into picking up ten gallons of water to add to the cache that was at the road. Soon Moses, Gnome God, and Operator made their way across the road followed shortly by Shark Bite and Faucet.

We lay there in the bed of pine needles sharing trail stories until Sharla and Gail arrived at 6:30 p.m.

August 2nd
Day 118 –0 Miles
Total 1852 Miles

The next morning we decided that I could rest my knees anywhere, and Brittany wanted to spend another day at the ranch. The boys were enjoying being around all the animals, and we were happy to spend time with our old friends. So, recharging our physical batteries was all that got accomplished that day.

August 3rd
Day 119 –0 Miles
Total 1852 Miles

On Saturday we packed up the RV for the trip north, but before we took off I just had to give Hunter a ride on Rich's John Deere tractor. He was about as excited as his grandpa, getting to ride on such a fine piece of machinery. Before the sun went down we had the RV parked along the street in front of Brittany's dad's home in Salem.

August 4th
Day 120 –1.75 Miles
Total 1853.75 Miles

It was a Sunday morning, August 4th, and we got to go to church. This was the first time I had been to church since May 27th. We were to come home from church and leave immediately for the trail. "Immediately" was soon replaced by "shortly," which turned into "sometime this afternoon." Just the thought of leaving the family brought on gloominess. This mentality only strengthened the vortex which held its grip on our progress.

It was 4:00 p.m. before we drove away from Salem for the 3 ½ hour trip back to the trail. The route we had to take to get back to Highway 138 took us over Willamette Pass on Highway 58. This route took us past Odell Lake and Shelter where we dropped off a resupply box. It was close to 8:00 p.m. when we got back to the trailhead. I don't know if it was the emotional stress of returning to the trail or the excitement of putting miles behind us, but Family Man started giving me trouble about a bottle of drink mix. He thought I should take it, and I didn't want it. After about three times of his harassment I picked the stuff up and threw it on the ground. He pulled my trekking poles out of the car and threw them on the ground. That started a hissy fit and before we finished all our stuff was everywhere. Sharla was walking her dog and returned to see our gear scattered all over the side of the road and we were laughing. She had no idea what to think.

I was overly concerned about Sharla's long drive back to Salem so late at night. We watched as she turned around and headed the 185 miles back to Salem. I do miss her when we're apart. We walked a couple miles up the trail before setting up our tent in the near darkness.

August 5th
Day 121 – 30.68 Miles
Total 1884.43 Miles

I crawled out of my sleeping bag at 5:15 a.m. and started packing up my tent. As I was strapping on my pack, Family Man woke up and said he would catch up somewhere down the trail. As I started in the predawn light I spotted a couple of hikers leaving their camp a couple hundred yards ahead. Within a couple of miles Family Man caught up, and six miles into the day we ran into Maverick and Lodgepole. Our other hiker encounters that day included a southbound thru hiker named Vogue and a couple of brothers named Purple Moon and Northern Wolf, both section hiking.

187

Early evening found us at the trail down to Six Horse Springs. We sat there debating our need for water. Nobody likes to go down off the trail for water and this side trail looked steep. We finally decided it was necessary and dropped our bags for the quarter mile, 250 foot descent to the spring. The number of mosquitoes we encountered increased the closer we got to the malaria infested watering hole. We had read on the map to bypass the first spring and go on down the mountain to find better water. That became obviously true when we came to the first pool of water that was heavily populated with flies and mosquitoes. The ground around the water looked like a watering hole in the Serengeti during migration season. Descending another hundred feet, we found a spring flowing out of the ground and over some logs. We had to wonder if it was fresh water or the runoff from a herd of wildebeest. With our bottles full of fresh, filtered water we headed back up the trail again, having to pass the hole filled with toxic waste. On the way up we met Maverick coming down to get water for himself and Lodgepole. They were stopping for the night. This ended up being our last meeting with these guys.

Picking up our packs, we headed north wishing to put a few more miles in before dark. The trail followed the contour lines for the next seven miles to Windigo Pass where we found a flat spot to set up camp. The final mile had been rough as the medication started wearing off, and the pain in my knees returned. We had cell service at the pass allowing us to make contact with the outside world.

August 6th
Day 122 – 27.57 Miles
Total 1912 Miles

I woke up early. It was 3:45 when I rolled out of the bag and started packing. Family Man woke up and followed suit. We wanted to make it to Shelter Cove twenty-seven miles away before the store closed. The first four miles of the day took us on a 1,400 foot climb up a ridge to the west base of Cowhorn

Mountain. Our first water source of the day was a small pond about half way up the ridge and down a short side trail. We were starting to miss the pristine streams created by the melting snow packs. On the north side of Cowhorn Mountain we sat down on the edge of the ridge where we had a spectacular view to the east watching the sun come up through the early morning haze. Crescent Lake appeared 2,500 feet below us in the valley. We had talked about taking the Oregon Skyline Trail down by the lake. It would have made it a lot easier to make it to the store in time. This alternate trail, hiked by a number of thru hikers resupplying at Shelter Cove, was 10.4 miles shorter and saved a thousand feet of climb. Other temptations to pull you off the PCT included the campgrounds at Crescent and Diamond View Lakes. The running water and working restrooms also had their appeal. Again we went back to our intentions of staying true to the PCT whenever possible.

Struggling to our feet and starting our 1,500 foot descent to Summit Lake, my knees told me they were unhappy with the short night's rest. At 8:45 we were standing on the south side of Summit Lake where the glassy water reflected Diamond Peak six miles away. The trail took us down to the shoreline, around the west side of the lake, to the Oregon Central Military Wagon Road. The road was built just after the civil war to transport military freight and troops. A large number of emigrants used this route to migrate into the Willamette Valley and along the Oregon coast.

By noon we had gone eighteen miles and were on the slopes of Diamond Peak. Finally, we were coming across streams flowing down from the snow packs up on the mountain. I was walking along, minding my own business, and enjoying the landscape enhanced by the snow packs hanging over the trail. All of a sudden there was a pop, and acute pain shot across my left knee. I stood there wincing in pain trying to figure out what caused this sudden degradation of ol' Stagecoach. I was sure the problem somehow came from the weakness caused by the continual use of inflamed IT bands. I finally forced myself into taking a step and was surprised my leg could handle the weight.

By now it was quite evident I would not make Shelter Cove in time to get our package. With nine miles to go, it was decided Family Man would make a run for it, and I would get there when I could. Each step caused the pain to shoot up my leg. If I swung my leg instead of picking it up, the steps were tolerable. Finally, I moved the knee brace to my left knee, and about a half mile later my right knee popped, doing the same as the left. About now I was again questioning the eight hundred miles left between us and the Canadian border. While I did not doubt a completion, I did wonder how long it would take.

With still eight miles to Shelter Cove and 2,000 feet to descend I sat down on a rock in the shade and spent twenty minutes, not begging, but just asking God for help. As I continued to sit there the pain was still present but apprehensions dissipated as peace drove out fear.

It wasn't until I was willing to get up and move down the trail before the pain subsided, and I was able to pick up speed. An hour into the descent I realized I could possibly make Shelter Cove before they closed. With four miles to go, I finally stopped for a short break where I sat on a log for three minutes before the vision of eating ice cream drove me on. I had made it to the road and was walking the mile down to the store, when a guy drove up in a golf cart and asked if I was Stagecoach. I assured him I was and he let me know that Family Man was looking for me. I am still puzzled why I didn't ask him for a ride back to the store. At 5:15, a full forty five minutes before closing time, I hobbled into the store and pulled an ice cream bar from the freezer.

Family Man had been there since 3:45 p.m. He did not have a watch, and without the knowledge of time, he had run practically all the way to make it before the store closed. He was still in pain as the push had caused a lot of damage to an already tired hiker. He had been eating pizza, and not knowing what time I may arrive, he had saved half for me. We spent the next four hours eating and going through our resupply box. When we packed the box back in Salem our stomachs must have outweighed our backpacks. There was no way we could carry everything we had packed. We took the choice stuff and put the rest in the hiker box. There were a number of other hikers hanging around the store and all were looking for places to plug in phones. The staff at the Shelter Cove Resort and Marina treated us well and their hospitality was greatly appreciated. We repaid their hospitality by buying all kinds of food and beverages.

Evening time was rapidly approaching when we headed through the campground back to the trail. We had been invited to stay at the campground with the others, but we had a strong desire to be back on the trail before morning. We did stop by the hiker trash campsite for about a half hour, listening to their stories and sharing some of our own. There were Moses, and the two we had called the Children of Israel (now known as The Hashbrowns), Gumby, Double It, Texas Grit, and a couple of section hikers. With full packs, we trudged a mile up the fire road to where Family Man had left the trail. I had hiked the additional half mile to the side trail that led down to the cove, now I was getting the opportunity to hike it again. We found a flat spot shortly after rejoining the trail and called it a day. Lying there, looking deep into space in my uncovered tent, I wondered what adventures the next day would bring.

August 7th
Day 123 – 20 Miles
Total 1932 Miles

Was I dreaming or did I hear thunder? The longer we were on the trail, the harder it became to define the difference between the dreams and reality. Sometimes I wondered if I was in a constant hypnopompic state. Another thunder boom completed the transition to extreme awareness. While my eyes were adjusting to the surroundings, the lightning flashed. I frantically searched around for my headlamp as I hollered for Family Man. I could see Family Man in his boxers running around his tent, duplicating my actions as we fastened the covers over our tents. Just in time we crawled back into the tents with minimal moisture on our backs.

For the next hour we were hit with a nasty thunderstorm as rain pounded the forest. It's easy to sleep when it's raining, provided you are warm and dry. So, as the lightning flashed and thunder rolled over our heads, we drifted back to sleep. We were up at 7:00 a.m. The storms had moved on, leaving dark rainless clouds hanging overhead. We found out later that a lightning strike had started a forest fire on the east side of the lake. We crossed Highway 58 at about 8:30 a.m., stopping behind the Highway Department building to eat a snack. It could have been breakfast, but it didn't matter anymore.

Breakfast, second breakfast, pre-lunch snack, lunch, second lunch, afternoon snack, pre-dinner snack, dinner, after dinner snack, night time snack: all of them came out of the same bag and did one thing, they gave us energy. We had been on the trail for four months and had given up on the ability to appreciate trail food for anything other than necessity. The only thing that broke this monotony was candy. Candy was the bright spot for our taste buds. While hard candy kept our throats moist, soft candies gave that instant sugar rush. Smarties were a favorite. I would open a package in my side pouch and pull them out three at a time. Just letting the sugar dissolve on my parched tongue brought this hiker to life.

Family Man's leg was giving him fits from the previous day's run, and though my legs had improved significantly, they were not 100%. After a gentle three mile climb, we came to Lower Rosary Lake. The camping site beside the lake was a great spot to relax and enjoy the view. We were only driven on when we noticed rain drops disrupting the smooth surface of the lake. Passing by Middle and Upper Rosary Lakes, we climbed onto a ridge where we followed the contour for a couple of miles. Before starting back down, we came to the Maiden Peak Shelter. Built by the Eugene Nordic Club, in partnership with the Willamette National Forest, as a shelter for cross country skiers, it took five years to complete. We found it to be clean and well kept. The octagon shaped cabin had one big, hand crafted door which was made to naturally swing shut. It was furnished with a big wood stove, a table made from two by sixes, benches along the walls which could double as beds, and a loft that could sleep a handful of people. Even though if it were hikers, I'm not sure the odor would be worth it. A solar panel powered a few dim fluorescent lights.

We spent 1 ½ hours at the shelter stretching out on the benches and eating lunch. We found a deck of cards and played a few rounds of poker, using candy as currency in our high stakes betting. Needless to say, distance was not an issue today, at least not in our minds. Finally, we spun out of the mini vortex at 1:30 p.m. with reduced expectations for the day. As we made our way through the heavily wooded forest, we were greeted with a lot of fresh horse poop. It stunk about as bad as anything I had smelled lately; even worse than Family Man after a week on the trail. It was really disgusting and frequent. A couple of miles from Lake Charlton we met two cowboys carrying stuff sacks and walking southbound in cowboy boots. They told us they had rode in last night, but during the night their horses had gotten loose and run away. They had been hunting for the horses all day, but they finally gave up and started the long walk to the truck. I felt sorry for the cowboys and concern for the horses, but I also found humor in the situation. For the next two miles, every pile of poop I stepped over I said, "Here's looking at you Mr. Horseless cowboy." Even though it was still daylight when we walked along the west shore of Lake Charlton, we decided to stop for the night. Both of us were still nursing sore legs from yesterday and decided twenty miles was enough. It did make us feel like failures, putting in such a short day. The camping spots along the lake were occupied, and even though there was room to set up our tents, we prefer seclusion. Finally, on the northwest side of the lake we found a spot right on a trail that could handle our tents. It was getting dark and threatening rain, so we called it good enough and hurried to get inside.

August 8th
Day 124 – 27 Miles
Total 1959 Miles

We were up at 5:00 and on the trail at 6:15. Right away we came to a gravel road where a camper was set up in a parking area. Our hopes were dashed when no one hollered for the hiker trash to stop by for bacon and eggs. This thought got our saliva running, and we started thinking about a cheeseburger at Elks Lake Resort. A number of the hikers had planned to take the mile plus side trip down to the lake, but it was not a scheduled stop for us. A mile and a half into the day, we hit the Charlton Butte Burn, and for the next three miles we walked through a wasteland. Seventeen years ago 10,400 acres had been toasted in an extremely hot fire. It has been slow at returning with minimal growth.

Back into the forest we encountered one lake after another with names like Taylor, Irish, Brahma, Desane, Porky, Horseshoe and many more. In between the lakes with names were a number of mosquito infested ponds. There were plenty of lakes, but streams were hard to come by. It's considerably more difficult to get water from a lake and stay dry in the process. We made 13.5 miles by noon and were feeling good about our progress. Late in the afternoon we met Gumby and Double It. We were in the process of falling for the temptation of a good meal. Calling the resort, we found out the restaurant closed in 1½ hours. Could we do 3.5 miles in that time? That's what stood between us and a cheeseburger. Despite bad knees and sore legs, the race was on. We were doing over three mph when we got hit with a heavy rain shower. It cooled us down, but the vision of French fried potatoes drove us through the downpour.

Soaking wet, we hit the trail leading down to the resort without slowing down. The rain had stopped, but it looked like more was on the way. We hurried down the mountain through more burnt out forest. This was the scar from a fire fifteen years before our arrival. It was sad descending through the devastated area. Small trees were doing their best to make a comeback and will someday put life back on the hillside above the resort. Crossing the road above the restaurant, we were not only racing the clock, but the dark cloud overhead was ready to cut loose. Dropping our packs on the porch, we made our way into a restaurant full of activity. The patrons gave us a "more hiker trash" look and went back to their eating. A hiker from the Class of 2012 was hanging out at the resort and offered to buy us a beer. We settled on a Mountain Dew and were led to a hiker table where we found Texas Grit, Backup, and a lady we had never met named Peter Pan. I ended up with a big hot turkey sandwich laced with bacon and a pile of fries to die for. The waitress kept the root beer coming long after the kitchen had shut down. After waiting out another rain shower, we made our way the three hundred yards back up the mountain to a campground. In the dusk we set up our tents for the night.

August 9th
Day 125 – 19.5 Miles
Total 1978.5 Miles

The overnight rain had dampened our spirits, so we took our time waking up. By 7:00 a.m. the idea of bacon and eggs won against getting on the trail early. The restaurant, for some unknown reason, didn't start serving breakfast until 9:00 a.m. But what is two hours anyhow? We could make it up by hiking later into the night. Backup and Peter Pan joined us for breakfast where we consumed a lot of fatty food and numerous cups of hot coffee. Before we left I bought a prepackaged lemon pie weighing in at 420 calories. Halfway up to our tents I opened the thing to find out it should have been bought by the PCT Class of 2010. It was more rubber than lemon. Too lazy to walk back down to the store, I threw it in the trash. We packed up our now dry tents, and at 11:00 a.m. we headed up the mountain to the trail.

Backup started out with us but soon fell behind. Leaving the burn area at the top, we took a break for lunch. We were

195

about to take off when Backup showed up, and a few minutes later Peter Pan arrived. We left Backup to entertain Peter Pan and took off. Two miles down the trail, we had four horses pull out in front of us. It looked like a couple of moms with their daughters. Family Man kicked it into gear and made just enough noise that they heard him and moved to the side. It still tickles him that he passed up horses. We stopped at Mirror Lake and were filling up with water as storm clouds started rolling in. The horses arrived before we finished, but we didn't mind sharing. It was a big lake.

Leaving the lake, we moved into the Wickiup Plains. For close to two miles we walked across the exposed flatland as the storm clouds made their presence known with lightning and thunder. We could see a couple of guys following back behind us. Family Man recognized one fellow from Israel with the trail name Hakuna Matata. As soon as we made it to the trees the rain started, and we did what any well trained person would do in a lightning storm. We got under a tree. The pine trees did pretty well at protecting us for awhile, but eventually the water started dripping down our necks. Lightning was striking the ridge across the valley, giving us quite a show.

Concern of lightning striking the tree we were under did cross our minds, but the knowledge that we were in God's hands somehow made us feel safe. Throughout the afternoon, a couple more thunderstorms did their best to keep us wet. With the ground sopping wet it was hard to find a place to sit down and rest our knees. They continued to get worse as the day progressed. As the sun was setting, we climbed up around Obsidian Falls and found some awesome spots to camp at the top. The only problem was the signs strongly discouraging this behavior. Not desiring to be fined by an overzealous ranger, we continued. A short hike later we found Sister Spring. The strong flowing spring, coming out of the base of a cliff, was clean and cold. With full water bottles, we only made it another five hundred yards before finding a suitable place to spend the night.

We woke up in the morning with about 30 miles to Highway 20. My knees were aching and I hadn't even gotten started. It was damp and cold, so we waited for the sun to come over the hill before crawling out of our bags. On the trail at 6:30, we moved nicely despite the sore knees. Two miles into the morning we hiked up the Collier Cone lava flow, giving us a good taste of walking on crushed lava rocks. Past Collier Cone we descended down to Minnie Scott Spring, where we again found fresh clean water. Moving on north, we came to the Yapoah Crater and followed along its west and north slopes before descending off the lava and into trees. It was about lunch time, and we had ten miles behind us, when Family Man let out a holler that could mean only one thing. The note on a cooler from a previous year's thru hiker welcomed us to enjoy the contents. It was still full of soda, beer, and blueberries. We were sitting in the grass eating our tuna and enjoying a cold soda when Boomer showed up. This guy was an instant hero in our book. He had hiked the quarter of a mile in from a campground carrying a cooler full of cold drinks and two hot pizzas. Boomer, who graduated with honors as part of the PCT Class of 2009, had recently moved to Bend, Oregon to be closer to the trail.

Before Boomer had arrived we were talking about how we had hit a mental brick wall. By the time we entered Oregon an emotional cloud had begun to build around us. It was something both of us were experiencing without explanation. We knew it wasn't the miles as we had averaged over twenty-one miles a day over the last two weeks, even with knee problems. Physically we were getting healthier every day. With less than seven hundred miles to go, the goal was becoming realistically achievable. So anything that could lift our spirits was always welcome.

It was as if God answered our prayers by sending Boomer. Boomer shared how during his hike he had experienced the same thing we were going through. He told us that calling family during this emotional challenge is the wrong thing to do. They don't understand what you are going through and will encourage you to get off the trail. "Nobody will blame you," they would say. "After all, you have hiked two thousand miles." He told us to keep pushing north, and the feelings would go away.

By now we were accustomed to meeting challenges as they appeared around the next bend or over the next hill. So far this day was no different. Little did we know what we were up against over the next eight hours. We left Boomer sitting at the trail waiting for more unsuspecting hikers and moved out across the rugged lava field. A half hour later we crossed Highway 242 as it started sprinkling. The sprinkling turned to rain as we walked into the trailhead parking lot. Again I saw the excitement in Family Man's face as he pulled a donut from a box beside a water cache. Some trail angel out there had just put the dessert on our spirit boost.

The intensity of the rain increased as we moved across the lava and continued up the mountain. I don't know how many years ago the volcano erupted and spewed molten lava creating the Belknap Crater, and I don't even know if this lava was from that crater. All I know is that climbing through this seemingly godforsaken landscape is extremely rugged. It was two miles of ankle twisting navigation as we climbed nine hundred feet through a thunderstorm. At the top we moved from lava rocks into burnt out forest. For the next five miles we made our way through this devastation as the sky continued to put on a show which left us soaking wet. Over a five hour period we were hammered by seven thunderstorms.

Family Man was somewhere out ahead when I made the decision. Soaking wet and tired of dealing with thunderstorms, I decided we would return to Salem to dry out. After all, the next day was Sunday and we could attend church before returning to the trail. A couple of times, when the rain lightened up I attempted to send out SPOT messages. Neither one was successful.

On the west side of Mount Washington, we finally left the burned out forest behind and entered the lush green forest. A couple miles later I was walking along, minding my business, when around the corner rode a southbound cowboy on a big healthy stallion. He met every stereotype imaginable when it comes to a cowboy on a horse in the wilderness on a rainy day. This guy would have made John Wayne proud. I stepped aside into the wet underbrush. I couldn't get any wetter. He stopped and addressed me, "Stagecoach?" I assured him that I was and asked about Family Man. "Family Man's doing fine. He's about a quarter mile out ahead." Cowboy continued, "I told Family Man to watch out for the cougars. I have shot six in this area." I let him know that was much appreciated and that I hoped he got the last one. He offered to let us spend the night in his horse trailer five miles out ahead. He said just to scrape the (insert colorful word in here) off to the side and set up our tents. In some circumstances that might have been a good thing but not that day. I thanked him, and with renewed hope I picked up my pace in hopes of finding Family Man before the cougars found either of us.

I ran into Family Man talking to a southbound hiker. I stopped only long enough to introduce myself and moved on. Family Man caught up shortly, and we laughed about the authenticity of the cowboy. He had asked Family Man if he was carrying a gun. That, combined with the cougar information, kind of put a little apprehension in Family Man.

Four miles from the highway it stopped raining and warmed up a bit. Those four miles seemed to take forever, and mosquitoes took over the job of administering misery. Crossing Highway 20 at 8:00 p.m. we climbed the hill to Santiam Trail where our two awesome trail angels walked us back to the car. It took a little talking to convince Family Man we needed to go to Salem. When we got back to the RV and I unpacked, I was glad we had made this stop. My sleeping bag was soaking wet.

Mount Hood

Chapter Thirty – Highway 20 to Timberline Lodge

August 11th
Day 127 –2.1 Miles
Total 2009.8 Miles

For the second Sunday in a row we were able to attend church, and just like the last Sunday, we kind of felt out of place. Our scrubby beards and long shaggy hair made us look more like hobos than upstanding citizens. Sometimes in life we get so caught up in our routine that we lose the true value of what we have. Growing up in a Christian home, going to church on Sunday was just part of my life. Although there have been times when it was not a priority, deep down the foundation had been laid. At times we went to church only because we had to or were expected to attend. Four months in the wilderness had concreted our faith in a God who is definitely not confined to a building. While we praised God everyday as we walked our narrow trail, we missed the experience of collective worship.

Standing there, singing songs of praise, we felt apprehensive about being surrounded by hundreds of civilized people in their khaki slacks and flowery dresses. We had become accustomed to ragged and trail stained convertible hiking pants and fast drying breathable shirts with a distinct sweat stain leading to eventual rot. We wondered if we would ever be able to transition back to this way of life.

We spent the rest of the day with our sleeping bags and tents spread out over the driveway drying in the sun. We took this time to rest and enjoy the family as we prepared for the next three weeks. Prior to this trip back to the RV, the plans had been for the girls to meet us at Mount Hood. With Mount Hood now only three days away, we decided to skip that one and go for Cascade Locks on the Columbia River. At 4:30 p.m. we took off for the Santiam trailhead, and after stopping at an A&W to fulfill our cravings for a chili dog and root beer, we arrived back at the trail at 7:00 p.m. On the trail at 7:30 we hiked for a couple of miles gaining altitude as we climbed towards Three Finger Jack, a group of peaks named for its distinctive shape. Finding a place amongst the fallen burnt out trees, we were in our tents before dark. We had been in the B&B Complex fire area ever since a mile south of Highway 20. New growth, still in its infancy, was pushing its way up through the skeletons of years gone by.

*August 12*th
Day 128 –31.7 Miles
Total 2041.5 Miles

When we woke up at 7:00 a.m. the dew was so thick that we didn't want to disturb it. So we waited for the sun to come up to dry the tents. It finally made its way over the hill, and we were able to pack things up and get on the trail. We did a lot of climbing and descending as we made our way around Three Finger Jack. The Ibuprofen 800 did the trick. I had minimal pain all day. Not so sure that medication was the healthy way to deal with the pain, but it was working. By 10:30

we were north of Three Finger Jack and looking at Mount Jefferson which stood tall at over ten thousand feet with a lot of snow. Then it was back into burnt out forest for the next five miles. It was after noon. I was getting hungry, and we needed water. Something about walking through toasted forest that does that. We did see a number of lakes down off the ridge. I had left Family Man back down the trail to take care of business. We agreed we would meet at Rockpile Lake for lunch and to fill up with water.

You never know who you're going to meet out in the wilderness, but let me introduce you to the ladies we called the Steel Magnolias. As I arrived at the south side of the lake, I spotted a group of four ladies in their late fifties to early sixties. They were on the north side of the lake about two hundred yards away. One of the ladies standing beside the water all of a sudden decided it was time to go skinny dipping. She pulled off her clothes and stepped down into the water. Still in and out of the trees, they could not see me yet, but I could hear her trying to talk the others into following her lead. About that time I exited the trees on the west side of the lake. I knew I had been spotted when the skinny dipper dropped to her neck in the water. I had to keep a straight face as I imagined how cold that water must be. I nodded at the other three and moved into a group of trees. Being the gentleman that I am, I turned my back to give the lady an opportunity to get out of the water and get dressed.

Family Man was a ways behind, which saved him from experiencing this awkward situation. By the time he appeared from behind the trees our swimmer was on the shore fully dressed and looking quite sheepish. I don't know if she thought this was a seldom traveled trail or what, but over the next half hour three southbound hikers arrived for water as well. Did we filter the water? You bet we did. We were still there when the Steel Magnolias headed north on the trail. Our skinny dipper was still wearing an "I've been caught" expression. I don't blame her for wanting to swim, but next time she may want to get a little farther away from a well traveled trail.

202

For the next five miles we followed the ridge toward Mount Jefferson. When the spine started climbing towards the 10,000 foot mountain, we turned west and did a lot of up and down to get onto the west slope. We traveled through some stands of huge trees, and late in the evening we crossed Milk Creek. This would not be the last Milk Creek we would cross as there is another up in Washington. The name comes from the milky water caused by erosion that slowly brings silt off the mountain. Once across we stopped to make dinner. Forty minutes later we were back on the trail making use of what sunlight we had left. Around 10:00 p.m. we came to a creek that was fairly deep and about ten to fifteen feet wide. Russell Creek is the accumulation of two large snow fields high on the northwest side of Mount Jefferson. All I know is we had to search around quite a while before we found a way to cross. Family Man did not seem to have a problem, but ol' Stagecoach, with his sawed off legs, kept looking at the water rushing down between the rocks and started freaking out. Finally, with a lot of encouragement, I took the leap and made it. Dry and happy, we continued on a couple more miles. At 11:00 p.m. exhausted and sore, we found a flat spot and rolled out our mats for a night of cowboy camping along a stream. By the looks of this well used campsite it was also frequented by wildlife. All night long I kept hearing things that made a deep sleep impossible.

August 13th
Day 129 – 36.5 Miles
Total 2078 Miles

It was August 13th and my mother's birthday. While I would normally give her a call, this year would be different. Looking at the maps, it was doubtful that we would pick up any cell service. Cowboy camping normally makes for an early start, and at 4:00 a.m. I was wide awake negotiating with Family Man about a departure time. He wanted to try another 40 mile day, so we crawled out of the bags and were on the trail at 4:30. Climbing a thousand feet over the next mile and a half, we arrived at a ridge where we entered the Mount Hood National Forest. We took a break on the ridge as the sun was coming up; we had a great view of Mount Hood 45 miles to the north. Coming down off the ridge, we crossed some smaller snow packs that were frozen and slick. This is where I found it was nice to use my backpack as a cushion when my feet flew out in front of me. Family Man turned around just in time to see me flat on my back.

The rocky trail slowed us down as we made our way down to Olallie Lake. It took over seven hours to do thirteen miles. The 40 mile day wasn't looking too good. When I arrived at the Olallie Lake store, Family Man was sitting on the porch overlooking the lake and drinking a Mountain Dew. He had already bought me one of these high caffeine drinks and a lemon pie. He knew the previous pie had done nothing to satisfy my craving. The folks at the store were generous and kind as they let us recharge our phone. While we waited, we drank more Mountain Dew and listened to a southbound "thru" hiker as he explained why he was becoming a "through" hiker. He was six hundred miles from the Canadian border, and he had had enough. He was quitting and going home. This was the first time we had experience with a hiker during a meltdown. It was an amazing thing as he tried to explain to us his failure. We felt as if our success was a spit in the eye to his inability to endure the struggles of the trail. He ranted and raved about how he didn't care what people thought. I am pretty sure he was more concerned than he wanted to admit. The only person he really had to convince was himself.

Around 12:30 p.m. we left the store and headed north. Family Man was somewhere out ahead when I checked my progress and found I was doing three miles per hour. The trail ran moderately flat over the next twenty miles with an average of 100 feet per mile climb and 150 feet per mile descent. The tread was in good shape, and my legs were feeling good. It looked like we could achieve our goal by 8:00 p.m. I picked the speed up to 3.4 mph to catch Family Man and soon found him sitting on the side of the trail in the power line clearing. He was waiting to use my phone and try to call Brittany. I quickly told him that if we could do 40 by 8:00 p.m. we could do 50 by midnight. The puzzled look on his face was priceless as I handed him the phone and took off down the trail at a high speed.

The plan was to stop every hour for a five minute break. Over the next three hours we put in ten miles. Family Man had caught up and was doing his best to stay there. At the end of those three hours Stagecoach, powered by Mountain Dew, ran out of fuel and came to a screeching halt. We sat there laughing about how caffeine can alter our thinking. There was no way we could do fifty miles when we had only thirteen in by noon. We still had hopes of forty, so we continued on at a modest 2.5 mph throughout the late afternoon arriving at the Warm Springs River about an hour before dark. Gumby and Double It were camped beside the footbridge. We sat down to get water and fix dinner. They offered to give us a couple of liters of water so we could keep going to make our goal. Considering that nobody likes to filter water, we thanked them and I filtered while Family Man fixed couscous.

Leaving the river, we started a gradual climb through the heavy forest as darkness closed in around us. We became accustomed to this particular kind of eeriness as we continued on in the semi-darkness without our headlamps. We tried to walk as long as we could into the night without the lights to conserve the batteries. Your eyes can do pretty well with adjusting to night vision, as long as no one turns on a light. Once a light is turned on your night vision fades rapidly. We knew it was time for the artificial light when we started kicking roots or rocks. The climb, while not steep, was constant, and with over thirty miles in sixteen hours I was getting tired. We kept our breaks short as Family Man continued to encourage me to push on. Finally, after four miles and eight hundred feet of climbing, we topped out on a knoll. By now we didn't care about forty miles, we both just wanted a flat spot to put up our tents. For a half mile we looked back and forth on both sides of the trail at the thick underbrush begging for a clearing. Finally, we had enough and made our own clearing. It was 10:00 p.m. and we had come up three and half miles short of our goal. Somehow we justified our failure by looking at what we had done, instead of what we had not done. To date it was our second highest day at 36.5 miles.

August 14th
Day 130 –29.5 Miles
Total 2107.5 Miles

Waking up at 6:00 a.m. seemed like oversleeping. We were on the trail at 7:00 a.m. on a gradual descent for quite a distance on the approach to Timothy Lake. I came across Family Man sitting in an old wooden row boat reading his maps. Clackamas Lake, a little water and a whole lot of marshland, was close by and probably the home of the deteriorated boat. We made it to Timothy Lake around 10:00 a.m. and walked along the eastern shore. A number of campers were enjoying their summer vacation camping along the lake. We talked to one lady who was cooking something that smelled real good. We tried to pan handle a couple sodas, but she either didn't have any or didn't want to share.

At the north end of the lake we crossed the inlet on a long wooden footbridge and shortly came to the Little Crater Lake trail. We considered the quarter mile side trip to the micro crater style lake, but we were in the zone. It was a zone that had Canada written all over it. Considering the lake is accessible via automobile, if we really wanted to see it we'd do it another time. Our goal for that day was Timberline Lodge on Mount Hood. They have a restaurant, and cheeseburgers were again occupying our minds.

We kept up a good pace all day. Our knees were not causing any pain, and a couple of springs and a water cache kept us hydrated. When we stopped for lunch at the second spring we found two beers floating in the cold water. Talk about temptation. We overcame our desire for the cold beverage by guzzling down a liter of water flavored by drink mix.

Passing over Highway 26 the trail decides to climb over an eight hundred foot hill before going back down to Highway 35. While that little climb was annoying, it was only warming our legs up for the climb up the side of Mount Hood. Three miles into the 2000 foot climb up Mount Hood we exited the tree line. The wind was blowing strong from the west, and the sky was thick with smoke from a fire. We were hiking along a huge ravine, so we knew we were safe but still despised the heavy smoke as we needed all the oxygen we could get. The final climb into the wind was on a thick sandy trail, which only exacerbated the challenge.

It was about 8:00 p.m. when we made it to a grove of trees 200 yards above the lodge. Quickly setting up our tents, we stowed our packs and headed down to the lodge in search of food. We were directed to the bar upstairs which ended up being more of a restaurant than a bar. We sat there in the comforts of this luxury resort in our stinky hiker clothes and ordered eighteen dollar sandwiches and four dollar root beers. I felt I had definitely graduated into hiker trash as I looked around until I found an outlet to charge the phone. I could say it cost fifty bucks to charge the phone and the food came with it. It was after nine when we made our way back up the hill to our tents. We were fortunate to be in the trees, as the wind continued to howl around the side of this 11,000 foot mountain.

Descent into the Columbia Gorge – Mount Adams in the background

Chapter Thirty One – Timberline Lodge to Cascade Locks

August 15th
Day 131 –30.5 Miles
Total 2138 Miles

We were up at 5:30 a.m. and quietly put together our bags so as to not disturb our neighbors. As soon as we left the trees we descended into a ravine where water was coming off the snow packs above the ski resort. Crossing over the ravine we sat down and Family Man boiled some water for oatmeal and coffee.

We followed the tree line around Mount Hood until descending a couple of switchbacks to Zigzag River. Stone hopping across the river, the trail climbed a couple of long switchbacks back up to the tree line. It was a morning of ups and downs as we continued in and out of the ravines around to the northwest side of the mountain. After making our way around a basin where the Rushing Water Creek dumped over a rocky cliff we started a two thousand foot descent along a ridge. On the east side of the ridge was a ravine about 300 feet deep where the melting snow provided source to a windblown waterfall dropping deeper into the ravine on its way to Sandy River. At the bottom of the valley, Rushing River started living up to its name as we walked along it onto the Sandy River wash. The wash, some 100 plus yards across, showed evidence of erosion as the melting snow and ice made its way down from Reid Glacier. Someone was kind enough to throw a few small logs across the twenty foot wide river. It's always fun making your way across these not-so-stable logs as water rushes underneath. It looked like it could really be a dangerous river during the spring melt or after a big rain storm.

The trail followed the Sandy River wash down stream for about a mile. We considered taking a side trail up around Ramona Falls but decided to leave that for another day. Leaving the wash, we crossed over the Muddy Fork River foot bridge and found a place for lunch. Despite its name, the river was clear and a good place to fill up before we started climbing. While we were sitting there blocking the trail, some unexpected southbound day hikers showed up. We found out we were only a couple of miles from the Ramona Falls trail head where a parking lot, big enough to handle tour buses, let loose an unknown number of weekend wilderness warriors.

Leaving the river we climbed 1500 feet through a canopy of conifer trees to Bald Mountain before descending to Lolo Pass. We made our way up around Sentinel Peak and followed the ridge between Bull Run and Lost Lakes. As hard as we pushed it seemed the miles were just not adding up. It may be tunnel syndrome was working on our mental reasoning, and we had reduced comprehension of actual time and distance. By the time the sun was calling it a day, we had turned northeast along a well defined ridge and the wind had picked up. Looking back at Mount Hood, now some fifteen miles away as the bird flies, the snow packs reflected what little light still existed in another long day. We exited the canopy and were exposed to the cold wind. Cold enough to call for coats as we pushed further into the night. We had no idea how far we would go. All we knew was we didn't want to camp out on the exposed ridge in the wind. We did come to a partially protected spot, but it wasn't big enough for both tents. Looking at our maps we could see we were only 500 yards from Indian Springs Campground. A 150 foot descent took us down behind the ridge, out of the wind, and back into the trees.

The primitive campground had been abandoned and only a picnic table remained. We set up camp next to the table and away from the trees and brush which were already heavy with dew. Down a short path we found a piped spring to resupply our water. By the time we finished, a light rain had begun to fall. It was another day of over thirty miles, with only seventeen miles left to the Columbia River.

August 16th
Day 132 –17 Miles
Total 2155 Miles

At 4:00 a.m. I was awakened from my slumber by the rain hitting the rain fly. It was not a constant rain, but the drops sounded heavy. Fifteen minutes later it stopped, so I interrupted Family Man's sleep with the reminder it was a town day. If you haven't noticed, town days had become a major source of excitement and did wonders in motivating thru hikers. It didn't take long to pack up and head east along the ridge. We had not gone more than a quarter mile when the drizzle started. Walking through wet trees in the predawn hours, with headlamps lighting the soggy trail, we made good time descending the five hundred feet to Wahtum Lake.

The trail designers, for some reason, took us on a horseshoe route around the lake. By the time we arrived at the shoreline our lights were off and Family Man was somewhere out ahead. I really think his mind was on seeing Brittany at Cascade Locks. One of the few times we had cell service, we called the Bridge of the Gods Motel in Cascade Locks. The proprietor is hiker friendly and gave us the hiker special for two of their finest rooms. Then we called the girls and gave them the news, requesting they come prepared to spend the night with their hiker trash.

Coming to a trail that led up the hill I looked for a PCT sign and could not find one. I spotted what looked like Family Man's fresh foot prints on the trail, but my gut feeling was not good when I started up the hill side. There was the other trail that led around the lake, but I was thinking it must have been just a trail to campsites along the shore. About halfway up the hill my gut feeling won, and sure enough the GPS said the PCT was down by the lake. There I stood, torn between returning to the PCT or continuing the climb in hopes of finding Family Man. Not really caring to climb up a hill not needing to be climbed, I told myself the tracks could be that of another hiker. Back along the shoreline the GPS showed green and I was on a roll.

On the north side of the lake the trail started up the slope toward Chinidere Summit. The tread was wet from the rain, and there were no fresh tracks. I knew now that Family Man had not come this way. Coming to a trail junction, I decided this would be a good place to wait. I was there less than a minute when Family Man came down the trail from the ridge. Once he had gotten to the ridge around the lake, he felt something was wrong when he couldn't find any PCT signs. His maps showed he was at the right place, so he continued around the top of the ridge where the side trail started down, meeting the PCT coming up. We came to the conclusions the paper maps and the GPS app didn't match. Climbing around Chinidere Summit, we headed north on the ridge towards Benson Plateau. The rain started coming down and the ponchos came on. The ponchos were doing their job, but the dripping wet foliage caused our pants to become soaked along with our feet.

At 10:30 a.m. we had gone ten miles and stood at the north end of Benson Plateau looking at the cloud covered Columbia River 3,500 feet below. While the middle of the river was only three miles away, the trail snaked around the mountain for seven miles to the bridge. You would think it would be all

211

downhill from here, but no. The trail took us down 2,500 feet before making us climb 500 feet back up another hill before the final descent.

Descending below the clouds we had a good view of the river and the Bridge of the Gods which was our ticket to entering Washington State. We were exhilarated with the prospect of crossing over this legendary steel bridge. We met a few southbound hikers making the long climb up the mountain. Again the visions of cheeseburgers carried us through the rain and into the streets of Cascade Locks. At 1:45 p.m. I walked into the park and found Family Man sitting barefooted in the grass. Our first order of business was to check in at the motel and go get food.

When the motel clerk had no knowledge of our reservations we got a little nervous. A phone call later and things were straightened out. We dropped our packs, washed up, and headed down the street looking for a cheeseburger. Our destination was what used to be the legendary PCT Pub, but it had recently been sold and the name changed to Cascade Lock Ale House. We both ordered what was called the Screaming Eagle. The burger was topped with grilled onions, mushroom, bacon, fried egg, and provolone cheese. We also chose the optional beer battered fries to fill our relentless cravings. As a side note, I only recommend this incredible screeching bird to fellow hikers. If you drive there and eat like this, you may think about bringing a defibrillator with you.

The girls were expected to arrive at 6:00 p.m., so we headed back to the motel and took showers washing off most of the crud before soaking in a hot bath. Feeling clean, we washed our clothes and caught up on our journals as we waited for our trail angels. They showed up right on time and while Family Man and Brittany headed back down to the Ale House, Sharla and I rolled on over to Hood River for dinner and time alone to catch up on life. I don't think we heard anything out of them the rest of the night.

Goat Rock Wilderness Area

Chapter Thirty Two – Cascade Locks to White Pass

August 17th
Day 133 –11.5 Miles
Total 2166.5 Miles

We spent the morning with the girls. Needing to get supplies at Walmart and the grocery store, we all headed over to Hood River. A big, healthy brunch completed the buildup of fatty calories for this town stop. Back in Cascade Locks we sat in the grass at the park and finished packing all the groceries in our bags. With electrifying apprehension we faced the future on the other side of the river. We were down to the final state. Even though we only had 513 miles to the border, we were also faced with 115,000 feet of mountains to climb.

At ten minutes before one we walked up the ramp to the bridge. Looking back at the girls as they stood there waving definitely brought tears to our eyes. The plan, always subject to change, was for the girls to bring the boys to Snoqualmie Pass in ten days. Ten days may not seem like a big deal to those living in the civilian environment, but there on the trail it was an eternity. When you spend over fifteen hours a day trying to occupy your mind as your body is under stress, time moves at a crawl. We waved back and continued up the ramp, passing the flower boxes with their little American flags celebrating our crossing. At the toll booth the lady stopped the cars and hollered at us to come over to the other side, facing traffic. The driver at the window must have asked why we didn't have to pay because we heard her say, "If you walked all the way from Mexico, you would not have to pay either." It felt almost like rock star status stepping out onto the grated bridge. For us, it was better than walking any red carpet could ever be.

According to The Port of Cascade Locks, the Bridge of the Gods was first built back it the 1920's when the US War Department issued a construction permit to the Interstate Construction Corporation. This company sold their interest in the bridge, after only building one pier, to the Wauna Toll Bridge Company who completed the iron structure in 1926. The bridge was raised 44 feet in 1938 after the completion of the Bonneville Dam. Looking at the over one thousand foot cantilever I could only imagine the size of the jacks used to lift this thing.

There are a couple different stories as to how the bridge got its name. The one I like to use is more realistic and the other an Indian legend. I'll leave the Indian legend for another time. The Bonneville landslide happened sometime between 1060 and 1760 A.D. Now I know that may sound like a big time span, but no matter how much research I do on this story, I can't seem to find anyone willing to nail down an exact time. They seem to agree that a landslide did happen as a huge amount of debris from Table Mountain and Greenleaf Peak slid into the Columbia Gorge creating an approximate 200 foot natural dam. Eventually the river washed the dam out forming the Cascade Rapids. It is my understanding that this land bridge was called the Bridge of the Gods by the natives, and that name was carried over to the steel structure we were walking across. Looking up at the scars on Table Mountain and Greenleaf Peak, we could imagine the awfulness of that day when everything slid south. We have the same type of scar on our mountains above Wrightwood,

California, where in recent history a mountain slide took out a portion of the town.

Walking across the bridge that spans the Columbia River is not just a physical endeavor. It is also a symbolic achievement of passage. We laughed away our emotional tsunami, agreeing we were no longer novice hikers but had achieved the title of amateur backpackers. "When will we become professional hikers?" I asked Family Man. His humble response was, "Manning Park." The rock star status continued as we crossed over the middle of the river and people waved. Some rolled down their windows, giving us words of encouragement and wishing us well. We would have been walking on air if it wasn't for the thirty some odd pounds attached to our backs holding us down.

The sign said, "Welcome to Stevenson, Washington" and there we were. In just a few minutes we had walked the third of a mile. We took a little break, not because of physical exhaustion but because of the emotional upheaval. We met Kindergarten Cop and his son Thunder Song who had just crossed the bridge as well. Kindergarten Cop had hiked from Campo to Seiad Valley last year and was finishing the trail with his son this year. We spent about twenty minutes sharing stories before heading west along the road. A very classy Pacific Crest Trail sign directed us back onto the trail as it turned up into the mountain.

They call it a gorge. Webster says a gorge is a deep, narrow valley. And with all valleys there are mountains on each side. The Columbia Gorge is one deep valley. Climbing out was, as expected, long and difficult. We were moving kind of slowly but making progress never-the-less. By dinner time we had made it to a small creek where we filtered water. We were tanking up when a lady showed up leading a horse. She was just finishing her first day of a thru ride of Washington. She had set up camp just down the trail a hundred yards or so and had brought her horse up to the stream for water. The GPS showed we had hiked almost eight miles but were still only 1,500 feet above the Columbia River. Wanting to make it to the top we

215

pushed on. Climbing another 2,000 feet in three and a half miles, we finally topped out behind Table Mountain as the sun disappeared below the horizon. We were now up at 3,500 feet where the air was cooler. To the south, Mount Hood was standing tall and cloud free. Mount Adams, 42 miles to the east, was showing off its snow packs in the fading light. This was our first night in Washington and it looked like a dry one.

August 18th
Day 134 –29.5 Miles
Total 2196 Miles

We were up early and on the trail at 6:15 a.m. I used the "wake up, pack up" method to get Family Man going. Two miles down the trail I was fixing coffee when he showed up. A lot of ups and downs in the morning, but mostly downs as we made our way down to Rock Creek. It was only 9:30 a.m. when we arrived at the footbridge, but being hungry, we found a sand bar for an early lunch and filtered water. Descending another 500 feet we crossed Red Bluff Road and started climbing up a valley. A thousand feet higher we came to a seasonal creek where we found an older guy eating lunch. After introducing ourselves, we found out Greg was supporting Jessica, the lady with the horse. He assured us we still had a little climbing to do, and sure enough, 1,500 feet of climbing later we were back up at 3,000 feet ASL. Of course, there was no way the trail could just stay at altitude and meander across a ridge. We started back down 1,800 feet to the Trout Creek Bridge. By now we were getting pretty disgusted with the trail designers. This disenchantment of the trail design had been growing over the last two thousand miles, but here the design just didn't make sense. The only thing that helped us maintain any level of sanity was the fact that we had 115,000 feet to climb in order to reach Canada and every hill we climbed was clicking away at that astronomical number.

Descending further into the valley, we passed by the old Wind River Experimental Nursery and the Punk Whistle

Trailhead. Back up a hundred feet around Bunker Hill then back down to under a thousand feet ASL as we crossed the Wind River. The days were getting shorter even if it was by only 2-3 minutes a day. Over the month of August, in that part of the world, the days were shortened by an hour and a half. That is a reduction of about four miles a day.

Leaving Wind River we worked our way through the Warren Gap to Panther Creek. It was a quarter to six when we walked into the Panther Creek Campground, a primitive sort of place with pit toilets and a hand water pump. There were a few campers scattered throughout, so we found an empty site where we fixed dinner, got rid of our trash, and used the restroom. As we were leaving we stopped by the big green hand pump where we tanked up and filled up with fresh well water.

It was time to make our way back up to higher altitude. Our goal for the day still lay 2,200 feet above us and five miles farther along the trail. We started up the steep switchbacks, back and forth as we struggled for higher ground. Only a couple miles in we came to a cooler and got all excited about the chance of a carbonated beverage, only to have our hopes dashed when the cooler was empty. "You guys need water?" The voice startled us. Just a hundred feet away was a tent we hadn't even noticed. Mango, a section hiker from Tennessee had just settled in for the night and had heard us verbalize our disappointment with the empty cooler. We visited with him for a bit, explaining our addiction to carbonation and that we had plenty of water. He had hiked the trail from Campo to Sonora Pass in 2010 before an injury had terminated his thru hike attempt. He was back to complete the rest of the trail.

At 9:00 p.m., as it was getting dark, we crossed a fire road on the ridge and found a couple of spots suitable to set up our tents. It wasn't quite a thirty mile day but really close. For being only at 2,800 feet we sure did a lot of up and down that day, climbing 6,600 feet and descending 7,300 feet. Welcome to Washington.

August 19th
Day 135 –31.82 Miles
Total 2227.82 Miles

We were up at our normal time and on the trail fifteen minutes before the sunrise. As the sun joined us on the trail it reflected off the snow on Mount Hood 32 miles to the south. The day started with a four mile, 1,500 foot climb up to Big Huckleberry Mountain. In a solid overcast of pine trees the good trail condition made for easy hiking. An elderly hiker by the name of Birdman introduced us to huckleberries which were plentiful along the trail. This slowed us down while we enjoyed a few handfuls. Eight miles into the day we came to a spring where water was flowing out of a PVC pipe. Filling our bottles at a clean water spring was a lot quicker than filtering out of a mossy lake. Passing many lakes and going around the base of mountains like Gifford Peak, East Crater, and Bird Mountain, we put in a lot of miles, and I felt very little pain as the medication continued to minimize the swelling. A mother and her daughter doing some day hiking had a lot of questions. When they asked if we would like a bag of chocolates, I said, "No, thanks," at the same time Family Man interrupted me with an exuberant, "Yes!" They headed down the side trail to their car and we headed north along the ridge. Family Man shared some of his newly acquired chocolates with his introverted hiking partner.

By 6:00 p.m. we were going around Sawtooth Mountain and had a spectacular view of Mount Adams as we ate our dinner. The snow covered volcano towered almost 8,000 feet above our 4,500 foot altitude. We would only be climbing another 1,500 feet or so as we made our way around the west side the next day.

August 20th
Day 136 –30.18 Miles
Total 2258 Miles

We were late getting up the next morning and even later getting started. The first five miles were almost all canopy hiking with moderate ups and downs. As we were getting water from a spring, a southbound hiker by the name of Bing came by with a great attitude and visited for five minutes before heading on down the trail. After he left, Family Man said he thought it was Scott Williams. Later on we confirmed it was the hiking legend.

We talked about taking a side trip down to Trout Lake, but with little conviction. We had heard it is a great trail town with friendly locals. I think we may have decided we would go get a cheeseburger if someone was there waiting for us. The road was deserted, so we continued on down to Trout Lake Creek. Arriving at the bridge at 11:00 a.m. we sat down in the middle of the four foot wide wood structure to eat lunch.

Sitting there enjoying our noodles and hot chocolate, we were surprised to see a group of five hikers coming down the trail. We recognized Moses, Gnome God, and Operator. We were introduced to Godfather from Scotland and Wolfpack who had hiked with Moses in 2011 and had joined him for the state of Washington. They had all been down at Trout Lake and had confirmed the hospitality of the mountain town. The seven of us left the creek and started the long hard climb up to the tree line around Mount Adams. We started spreading out as the climb was steep and we all hiked at different speeds. A couple of miles before exiting the trees we made our way through a burn area. We came across Operator resting, as he was dealing with leg problems. It seemed like most hikers who had made it that far had either already had or were experiencing physical ailments of some sort.

Hitting the tree line, we turned north around the mountain and met Moses sitting at the exact spot where snow had caused him to turn around in 2011. It was an emotional time for Moses as he dealt with all the memories and now the anticipation of success. Moving around the dormant volcano we crossed a number of streams as the snow melted above us. The largest stream did not even have a name, yet was twenty feet wide and a couple feet deep. The depth was not as much of a

219

problem as the speed of the water. Melting off of the Adam Glacier the water was coming down the mountain rapidly. Someone had thrown a few logs between boulders over which we were able to navigate. Crossing over the Killen Creek Bridge just above the Killen Falls, we started on a gradual descent heading away from the mountain. As it was getting dark we could hear the sound of rushing water and were happy to find a footbridge at Muddy Fork. We came across Godfather's campsite and we hiked another 500 yards to the spring coming out of the base of the lava flow. It was dark by the time we made camp. I found a spot close to the spring, but Family Man had to climb 20 yards up the hill to find a good flat spot. The spring was so cold that when I washed my feet my lips turned blue.

August 21st
Day 137 –26.5 Miles
Total 2284.5 Miles

I was awake at 4:45 a.m. It was still dark and cold, but I had to get out of my sleeping bag to take care of business. Now wide awake I ate my breakfast of rehydrated cold oatmeal and a cup of cold instant coffee. Family Man did not respond to my wakeup call, so I hiked up the hill and roused him. Back on the trail in the predawn light we ran into a hunter in full camouflage carrying a compound bow. He was a little eerie with his quiet manner and warned us about cougars. He educated us on their behavior and how to look for their tracks. Sure enough just up the trail, we came to another trail crossing ours and there were cougar tracks on it.

Before the kitty cat returned, we headed on up the trail rounding Potato Hill. Potato Hill was more like a tater tot. Looking like a volcano that never made the big time, the rim of its crater was only six hundred feet above us.

We started a gradual climb towards Goat Rocks in heavy wooded forest. As we pushed higher into the mountains we met a few day and section hikers. One of the day hikers from

220

Washington told us we were in for good weather for the next two weeks. With nothing but wispy clouds floating overhead we assumed he knew what he was talking about. We climbed above the tree line and were rewarded with meadows full of lupine amongst the scattered red, white, and yellow wild flowers. The closer we got to Old Snowy Mountain in the Goat Rocks Wilderness Are, the more in awe we became. We had traveled through some of the most pristine wilderness in the country, and while I have scores of favorites, I would have to give Goat Rocks the trophy.

It was not quite dinner time when we arrived at Cispus River coming down off Ives Peak. Above the trail 500 yards or so was a herd of mountain goats. A hiker camping by the river told us a guy had been killed by 390 pound mountain goat in 2010 but not in this area. A half mile later we arrived at a tributary to Cispus River that was bigger than the river itself. A twenty-five foot waterfall tumbled over the cliff above us, spending just enough time to flood the trail before dropping into the basin below. Two boys and their dad were filtering water at the falls when we rock hopped across the stream. On up the hill we came across a big tent set up on the edge of a cliff. We gathered by the gear around the tent that it was for the trail workers. After making our way through Snow Grass Flats we started another strenuous climb and came across Godfather setting up his tent. We hollered a greeting and kept climbing. Getting close to the top of the mountain, we stopped halfway across a huge snow pack to take some pictures of the sunset. Once the sun dropped below the horizon, the sky turned to a canvas of orange, red, and yellow as it bounced off the thin wispy clouds.

All of a sudden a dog barked. Coming over the top of a hill, a big black dog came bounding across the snow as if we were trespassing. We took up the defense posture with trekking poles ready to put the hurt on this ravenous animal. It came within about eight feet before it realized we were not backing down. It had a collar on so we knew it had to have been domesticated at some time or another. From on top the hill we heard someone holler and the dog took one last look at us before running back up the mountain.

There was just a glimpse of daylight left when we came to the trail cutting across the slope under Old Snowy Mountain. Having not yet seen the sign that directed the PCT up over the mountain, we assumed it was our trail. As we were looking out across the slope, all of a sudden from high on the mountain, a two foot boulder came crashing down the slope across the trail. That stopped us in our tracks and changed our plans. Not wanting to be participants in a game of bowling for hikers, we retraced our steps down the trail about a hundred feet to a place we could make do with for the night. Moving rocks and sharp stones aside we set up to cowboy camp. It was getting chilly at 7,000 feet so we didn't take long at getting inside our sleeping bags. The moon had not come up yet, making the night sky glitter brightly with millions of stars. As we lay there waiting for our legs to cool down enough to let us sleep, we took in the mountains around us and the valley below. All this in contrast with the night sky gave tribute to God's creation.

August 22nd
Day 138 – 20.5 Miles
Total 2305 Miles

The full moon made its way over Old Snowy Mountain crossing over our meridian at about 3:00 a.m. Cowboy camping at this altitude on a clear night, the full moon had access to our optic awareness, and by 3:30 a.m. both of us were wide awake. As the moon reflected off the snow packs it revealed even the smallest of details. We contemplated getting up and hiking but considered the rocks we would most likely be encountering and decided against a nighttime start. Waking up again at 5:45 a.m. we lay there taking in the scene. The rock strewn mountains contrasted with the snow packs. The pastel sky stood out against the dark green valleys. It was all in constant change as the sun took over for the moon. The snow covered peak of Mount Rainier was the first to capture the sun's rays.

Climbing back up to the trail, we came to a couple of signs. One said, "Pacific Crest Trail Hiker Route" and pointed up the mountain. The other said, "Pacific Crest Trail Stock Route" and pointed out across the slope. We looked longingly at the fairly easy stock route and resigned ourselves to a four hundred foot rocky climb to the top. On top of Old Snowy looking north the trail descended a very steep knife edge. Switchbacks maybe ten feet long on loose shale tried to slip us up. Crossing over the top and following the two mile knife edge was slow and tedious. The view was worth the extra time. Once we were back on good solid trail we picked up our speed. At a seasonal stream where tributaries gathered the melting snow and the lupines returned with other wild flowers, I found Family Man sitting on the trail eating noodles. It was only 9:00 a.m., but there is never a wrong time to eat on the trail. We filled up with enough water to get us to White Pass a little over fifteen miles away. As we climbed and descended toward the pass, we were in and out of the canopy of trees. We came across Mr. Clean sitting on some rocks feeling somewhat discouraged. We gave him some food and encouraged him to keep going. It seemed like all of us were dealing with discouragement and mental roadblocks.

A couple of miles from the highway it started raining. Never trust day hikers, especially when they say you will have two weeks of good weather in Washington. At Highway 12 we walked a mile down to the Kracker Barrel. Passing log trucks helped the rain in making sure we were wet. As we arrived at the store, the rain stopped and the sun came out. Spitfire and a couple of others were occupying a bench out front. Retrieving our resupply box, we took over a table in the deli section. Plugging in the phone for a recharge, we drank our ice cold root beer and went through the box. It's surprising how excited you get when you fill up your almost empty food sack with all the stuff you like. First of all, the old dry food bar that you have been ignoring for the last three days gets thrown in the hiker box. We ended up having an excessive amount of food, and after giving Mr. Clean what he wanted, the rest went in the hiker box.

223

With cell service available we were able to talk to the girls. The boys were sick, and it was decided the support team would not be meeting us in Snoqualmie. We mutually agreed that exposing us to a cold virus was not a good idea. With our work complete, we ordered a couple of three inch thick deli sandwiches. They were kicking us out of the store at closing time when Godfather showed up. He came back out of the store with a handful of hot snacks. They were going to throw the stuff away anyway and figured hiker trash could always use food. We all sat on the bench and chewed the fat for a couple of hours before heading back to the trail. Spitfire offered to share a hotel room at the neighboring White Pass Village Inn. As tempting as it was, we really wanted to be on the trail when morning came. Finally, at 7:00 p.m. we headed back to the trail. At the trailhead we found a couple of cowboys sitting beside a horse trailer. They were operating a mule team supplying a trail crew fourteen miles north. We sat down and chatted with them for about 45 minutes before the oncoming darkness hurried us down the trail. Needless to say, we only made it a couple of miles before stopping for the night.

Chapter Thirty Three – White Pass to Snoqualmie

August 23rd
Day 139 –27 Miles
Total 2332 Miles

It was raining when we woke up, so we went back to sleep. We were on the trail at 8:45 with a goal to get to the parking lot at Chinook Pass. Five miles into the day we met a large group of Boy Scouts. All they were concerned about was the distance to White Pass. They were just completing a fifty mile backpacking trip and were anxious for it to be over. At lunch time we arrived at Snow Lake to resupply water and eat lunch. There we met a group of Mormon boys and their leaders. We shared a few stories of our adventure and they shared a big chunk of summer sausage.

An hour and a half later we arrived at Bumping River where Earth Corps was busy building the new footbridge across the river. With the law not allowing power tools in the wilderness, the team was only using hand tools. Cables and hand wenches were being used to position logs for retaining walls. We took a break and watched for awhile before making our way across a makeshift bridge. Climbing two thousand feet we made it to the ridge with a spectacular view down the valley to the east. By the middle of the afternoon dark clouds had surrounded us. Fifteen miles to the northwest Mount Rainier stuck out through a thickening layer of nimbostratus spreading east across the pass, which was our destination for the night.

Blueberries and huckleberries treated us to fresh fruit throughout the day but slowed us down. As nighttime came on we stopped picking berries and concentrated on walking. The trail crews do their best to keep the trail clear of brush with the goal of hitting every section of the trail at least once every three years. That is fine in dry climates, but in Washington the underbrush can take over a trail in that amount of time. I am by no means being critical of the volunteer trail crews. They are heroes in my book. Along with brush wanting to take over the trail, the rugged mountains and persistent rain storms make trail maintenance a constant battle. My constant complaining brought the familiar response from Family Man, "If you want easy, you should hike Interstate 5."

Darkness set in before we made it around Dewey Lake. Leaving the lake, the trail climbed seven hundred feet through heavy wooded canopy. Reaching the top of the climb we exited the trees onto the exposed slopes of Naches Peak. It was cold and windy as we walked through the moist, foggy air across Highway 410. Hiking down the dirt road turned trail, we arrived at the Chinook Pass parking lot at 10:30 p.m. The parking lot was filled with cars, but no one was around. We were pretty sure it was not an authorized campsite, but at that time of night and in dense fog we really didn't care. A couple of clean pit toilets made things even better. In the northeast corner what looked like a loading platform made for a good place to pitch our tents. Sure felt good to get inside the protection of a tent and in the warmth of our sleeping bag. We figured the worst case scenario would be that a ranger could wake us up and kick us out.

August 24th
Day 140 – 30.8 Miles

The sound of cars passing by on the highway disturbed our sleep. I wanted it not to be so, but sticking my head out of my sleeping bag confirmed my fears. It was morning. The clouds were still rolling through Chinook Pass and over Yakima Peak. It wasn't raining, but I still didn't want to get up. I lay there lamenting about the day ahead. I really was getting tired. Every night seemed to repeat itself. I'd get in my sleeping bag and try to keep my eyes open long enough to write in my journal, then immediately fall asleep. A short time later I'd wake up with my legs feeling like they were in a microwave as the muscles were still trying to cool down from hiking thirty miles. So I'd unzip my sleeping bag even if it was 35 degrees outside. Finally, I'd cool down and fall back to sleep. A little while later I'd wake up again freezing cold and zip back up. Sometime in the middle of the night I'd wake to excruciating pain in my hip. The half inch padding I was sleeping on did very little to protect me from whatever was below it. I'd spend the rest of the night tossing back and forth from one hip to the other just to make sure they both suffered equal pain.

The cloudy conditions were not really conducive to an early start. With every car door slamming we were sure a Ranger would kick us out of our flimsy shelters. Finally, we ate some cold oatmeal and packed up our camp. Leaving the parking lot at 7:30 a.m. we started a gradual climb paralleling the highway for a mile or so before we turned left and headed up to Sheep Lake. There was no water back at the parking lot, so we needed to stop at the lake and filter a couple liters. A number of tents were strewn about the fog enshrouded lake giving it the appearance of a popular weekend hiking destination. I would assume the short two miles from a parking lot was what made this lake popular. While sitting there squeezing water through the leaky Sawyer filter, a hiker arrived by the name of White. The name instantly rang a bell. White had asked Sharla for a ride down in southern California. She told him to ask me when we returned and we never saw him again.

Even though we were in and out of the fog, we did keep rather dry. After an hour and a half we had climbed a thousand feet and arrived at Sourdough Gap. A couple of surprises were waiting for us on the ridge. First, we found a cooler with fresh fruit. Second, and more importantly, we had cell service. Talking to the girls lifted our spirits even more than the apples. After dropping down a couple of switchbacks we followed the contour around the mountain to Bear Gap before going around Pickhandle Point and across Pickhandle Gap. There seemed to be a lot of gaps in that neck of the woods. After climbing Crown Point we sat down for a break and enjoyed the view of Crystal Mountain Ski Resort on the other side of the valley. From our vantage point high on the mountain we could see a lot of activity going on down at the ski lodge. We sat there that Saturday afternoon speculating about how some gourmet dining was probably happening far below at a millionaire's daughter's wedding. We didn't have the energy to hike down and find out, so we ate another bite of high protein packed dry food bar.

Moving on for three miles along the contour, we again crossed over the ridge at Scouts Pass and found a piped spring in the basin beyond. The half inch stream of fresh water filled our bottles in a hurry and we continued on our journey through these stunning mountains. We really weren't paying much of a price to see the beautiful landscape considering most of the time the trail was following the contour of the mountains. We had gotten used to the whole "into the valley and over the mountain approach" to trail design.

While the morning started slowly the afternoon pace picked up, and by 4:00 p.m. we were again getting water from a spring. Arch Rock Spring didn't look clean, so we filtered the water and ate a snack. We moved from a ridge in slightly rolling thick canopy, and a couple hours later we came to Government Meadows and the Urich Camp. A log cabin for public use was populated with numerous hikers and horseback riders. We could see Spitfire sitting around a fire with a few others. So, considering it was dinner time, we decided a half hour break wouldn't hurt. We were happy we stopped as Ice Axe, whom we had originally met back in southern California was there, and Mr. Clean arrived a short time behind us. Ice Axe had caught a ride up to Hart's Pass and was making her way back south from the border. Leaving the campfire we crossed the Naches trail, which looked more like a jeep road, and climbed around Pyramid Peak. It was late in the evening when we passed through about a mile of old burn area and came to a small spring. We hiked on into the dark watching what looked like a big camp fire in the valley to the southeast. There was a lot of gun fire going off in the same area, and we figured it was some hunters blowing off some steam. It was Saturday night and elk season was about to start. At 10:00 p.m. we moved over a ridge and out of sight of the campfire. Crossing a dirt road, we found a place in the undergrowth to set up our tents. Another thirty mile day was in the books.

August 25th
Day 141 –27.2 Miles
Total 2390 Miles

It was Sunday morning and I had no desire to get out of my sleeping bag. It was cold and any form of motivation had somehow left my body. At 6:30 a.m. we managed to get out of the tent to find the rain fly soaked with dew. Godfather was busy packing up his tent on the other side of the fire road a hundred yards away. Again we set our goal at thirty miles. A gradual climb along the ridge turned north and continued up over Blowout Mountain. A lot of dirt roads crisscross this area. It looked like they were used more for logging than for fighting fire. Family Man and Godfather were somewhere out ahead talking about food, while Stagecoach was all alone thinking about, well, food. We had a gradual thousand foot descent down to Tacoma Pass. When I arrived at the pass I found Family Man and Godfather sitting by a cooler, along with Oakdale and another hiker by the name of Voodoo Girl. The cooler, courtesy of a Class of 2012 thru hiker, was full of beer, soda, cookies, and a single Payday candy bar. My concern for all those behind us was somehow forgotten as I consumed the peanut coated chewy caramel candy bar. Drinking the cold root beer and helping the others polish off a package of cookies gave us energy to continue.

Climbing five hundred feet, we found ourselves back on the ridge and with minimal ups and downs we passed by Bear Paw and Snowshoe Buttes. It was the middle of the afternoon when I found Family Man right in the middle of a large group of trail workers. They were just finishing up their weekend trail maintenance and told us we could help ourselves to a spread they had laid out on a table. After eating a few brownies, some cherry tomatoes, and a couple of cinnamon rolls, we each drank down an ice cold soda. Not wanting to be rude by eating and running, we spent some time sharing stories with the trail crew.

I thanked the trail crew for their commitment to the PCT and headed up a freshly manicured trail. Coming around a corner just three hundred yards down the trial, I was treated to the south end of a north bound bear. I guess I had scared the caniform as it was moving fast. It left the trail and headed down into the brush. I did spot it down in the brush, but by the time Family Man arrived it was long gone. This ended up being the only live bear we would see in the five months we spent on the trail.

Down the trail we came across a pickup truck and three hunters sitting around a campfire. They said that elk season started the next day. That got me wondering why I didn't think to bring an orange hat.

Blueberries lined the trail on our way to our third and final trail angel encounter of the day. The map said, "Outhouse," so we had to check it out. Outhouse is a concrete pit toilet in the middle of nowhere. We were taking a break and watching the thunderstorms building when we heard what sounded like a big truck making its way up the hill. Eventually a fire truck arrived at the clearing and came to a stop. Three fire fighters jumped out and looked to the southeast. They were mobile fire spotters watching the big thunderstorm building a few miles away. They gave us a couple of Gatorades out of their cooler and wished us well. We thanked them as we put on our ponchos and the rain began to fall. Climbing and descending hills, we spent half the time in the trees and the other half in the blueberries. Family Man, being faster than Stagecoach, ate the most. As a side note, overconsumption of blueberries results in other fresh fruit emergencies.

With the rain coming down, we slopped our way forward with hopes of a dry camp spot. A quick stop at an easy spring next to the trail gave us enough water for the night. Two miles later, as we came out of a ravine, we had enough and decided it was time to stop. The rain had let up but there weren't any campsites available. Finally, we found a place where Family Man could put his tent on one side and I could squeeze mine in under a tree on the other. We had two feet between the tents. As soon as we started setting up our tents the rain returned. Family Man is a lot faster with this process and enjoyed laughing at me from inside his domain. I made it inside with minimal damage. The only problem was a rock under the middle of my tent that I had missed. Too tired to care I just left it there.

I don't know how long it was before the sound of approaching footsteps brought my consciousness to full alert. The footsteps didn't slow down as they rushed on by. Five seconds later another hiker passed by. By the sounds of hushed voices we could tell it was Oakdale and Voodoo Girl. They must be crazy hiking through the night in the rain. Guess we are all crazy in some aspect.

August 26th
Day 142 –12 Miles
Total 2402 Miles

When we woke up in the morning the rain had stopped, but the pain from sleeping on hard ground was still there. The rain fly was still soaking wet when we finally crawled out of the tent. Shaking off what we could, we packed everything up so we could get headed down the trail. With only twelve miles to

Snoqualmie we knew it was going to be a good evening. Right out of the gate we walked through undergrowth encroaching on the trail. This wet foliage soaked our pants by the time we were a hundred yards down the trail. By 9:30 a.m. we were three miles into the day and had just completed a five hundred foot climb. We took a break by a stream where the runoff from Mirror Lake tumbled over the edge of the mountain. It was a great place to sit down for a break and filter water. Looking out over the valley we could see past Lost and Keechelus Lakes to Interstate 90 only six miles away.

With visions of cheeseburgers interrupting our tranquil view, we loaded up and hiked past Mirror Lake, climbing another four hundred feet to a ridge before starting a long and gradual descent. By 11:30 we were coming around Silver Peak and paralleled Interstate 90 for six miles continuing a gradual descent as the highway climbed towards the pass. Three miles out we climbed over a hill and passed a couple of lakes before descending across the wild flower covered ski slopes to the resort village of Snoqualmie.

Arriving at the hotel we found Oakdale and a few other hikers hanging around outside. Shortly Voodoo Girl showed up with wet hair. One of the hikers had let her use his shower, and she was happy. Checking in we dropped our packs and walked back over to a food truck called The Aardvark for lunch. Washing our clothes and taking showers revitalized our spirits. Once we were done we hung our tents and rain flies in the shower to dry. That poor bathroom looked like a war zone.

The girls not being able to meet us was the downside to our night in civilization. We were able to do some Face Time and work out the end game. As much as we would have liked the girls to be at Manning Park when we completed this expedition, it was becoming evident that was going to be a logistical nightmare. At one time we even had visions of them hiking in from Manning Park to the border to be part of the celebration. After all, it was only 9.5 miles each way. Finally, reality won over and we agreed that public transportation back to the states was the best choice.

Without the girls, we did not have our resupply totes to fill our food sacks. With 172 miles to our next resupply we needed a lot of food. Our first stop was a small grocery store where we bought over a hundred dollars worth of trail food. They sure know how to skin the wildlife. We then hit the gas station picking up a few more items.

For dinner we headed down to the restaurant attached to the hotel and found it completely inept. We sat at a table for ten minutes before the single waiter told us this dining area was closed and to go sit in the bar. In the bar there wasn't an empty table available. So we left that dump with a bad attitude and went back over to the food truck. They were happy to take care of our culinary cravings. The lady working at the food truck was extremely hiker friendly and stayed late just to make sure the hikers got their fill.

August 27th
Day 143 –11.5 Miles
Total 2413.5 Miles

After many days in the wilderness even an old second hand mattress brings bliss. So, in the morning as I rolled over and went back to sleep, I blamed the clean sheets and the soft mattress for my sluggishness. Waking up again at 7:00 a.m., I started messing with Family Man, telling him to wake up and get out of his tent. He didn't buy off on it. He only moaned a couple of times and was sucked back into the luxurious mattress. Finally, when I mentioned a big healthy breakfast with bacon he was wide awake. The Pancake House that had bad service the night before redeemed themselves by having better help, good food, and playing Christian worship music on the speakers.

Back in the room I took another shower while Family Man made use of the Jacuzzi. With full packs we checked out at the required 11:00 a.m. time. Walking back towards the trail we had to pass by the food truck which translated into lunch. We had to try the Avalanche Pancake, which is a bacon filled, ice cream enveloped pancake. You add your hot sauce from their selection of about twenty-five different choices. The cook told us we also had to try the tacos. We counted our cash and told her we could pay for the tacos but did not have any extra for tip. Considering we had already tipped her five bucks, she didn't seem to care and fixed the tacos.

Chapter Thirty Four – Snoqualmie to Steven's Pass

With full stomachs and heavy packs we crossed under the Interstate and headed up the mountain. The sign at the trailhead explained the trail ahead was "Most Difficult." The next six miles consisted of a three hour, 3,000 foot climb up into the Alpine Lakes Wilderness Area. By 4:00 p.m. we found ourselves sitting by Ridge Lake looking out over some spectacular landscape. Walking across the slope high above Alaska Lake, a rain shower lasted just long enough for us to put on our ponchos. The trail almost made it to the top of Alaska Mountain before switchbacks took us down to a ridge separating Edds and Joe Lakes. The rain stopped, so we took a dinner break around 6:00 p.m. Godfather had taught Family Man how to adjust the flame on the Jetboil which allowed him to fix macaroni and cheese for dinner. We threw in a handful of chili flavored Fritos and called it Chili Mac. The view was amazing. The ragged peaks stuck out of heavily wooded mountains, and the turquoise blue lakes contrasted with the dark green pine trees. It was a landscape that came close to pushing out Goat Rocks in the most spectacular category.

We didn't go far after dinner before we ran into a handful of mountain goats. These were smaller ones that just watched us intently as we made our way up to the ridge on the north side of Huckleberry Mountain. We were about to go out on the south slope of Chikamin Peak. The three mile stretch was exposed and a rain storm was rapidly approaching. We tossed it back and forth before deciding to kick the goats out of the little patch of grass and set up camp. It was a difficult decision as it was nowhere near dark, but we did not want to be caught on an exposed trail in a thunderstorm. It began to sprinkle while we put up our tents, and by the time we crawled inside the storm hit with full force. All I could do was thank God for a dry home for the night.

August 28th
Day 144 –24.5 Miles
Total 2438 Miles

During the course of the night, our sleep was interrupted a number of times by goats running by the tent. When daylight came, we woke to the sound of rain hitting the tent. With no desire to get out into the rain, I went back to sleep. It wasn't until 9:50 a.m. that the rain stopped and we crawled out of the tents. We were packing up our stuff when Number Two and Godfather walked by. We climbed a little higher onto Chikamin Mountain and followed the contour east along its rocky face. We stopped once to get water that was dripping out from under a rock. It took awhile with the eighth inch stream but it was cold and fresh. Leaving Chikamin, the trail descended 3,000 feet into the Lemah Valley.

On the way down we met a lady hiking southbound. Her demeanor was one of anguish. She had left Snoqualmie the morning before, and after spending a night in the rain, she had had enough and was heading back home. She looked like she belonged in an office cubicle in Seattle, not on the PCT. She'd be happier there. I do give her credit for trying though. Maybe she can come back out some day when it's not raining.   In Washington that is highly unlikely.

We came to the bridge where a spectacular waterfall cascaded over a cliff and tumbled under the bridge. It was a great place to sit down for a second lunch and fill up with water. Reaching the valley, we came to the Lemah Creek where we found Number Two and a washed out bridge. Guess we can't win them all. Forging rivers takes time and slowed us down but was part of the overall experience.   Another part of the experience was the 2,400 foot climb out of the valley.   The twenty switchbacks late in the afternoon literally took my breath away. Halfway up the mountain we found a little stream where we filled up with water and ate dinner. It was getting late and the clouds were threatening. Not wanting to get soaked, we put on our ponchos and headlamps and moved on. The rain only lasted for a short time. Crossing over the top of the mountain in the dark, we descended 2300 feet into the Waptus Valley. We stopped for the night when we reached the river at 11:00 p.m.

August 29th
Day 145 –25.5 Miles
Total 2463.5 Miles

Does it always rain in Washington? I'm still questioning the integrity of the local hikers who told us about the two weeks of good weather. Can we stay in our tent forever? It's dry in here. These were the thoughts bouncing around in my head as I heard the splatter of raindrops hitting the rain fly. But morning has come and we must move on. I know it's only a matter of time before Family Man spews out his favorite comment of resignation, "I guess we'll get to Canada next year." I put him off until 7:00 a.m. when we finally packed things up in the rain and headed down the trail. The first three miles were fairly flat as we passed Waptus Lake and turned up the valley along Spinola Creek. After hiking upstream for four miles in the rain we finally came to Deep Lake.

In the rain we couldn't get the phone out to check the GPS, and the maps are made of paper, so Family Man had left them buried deep within his pack. Cathedral Rock stood high above Deep Lake as we slopped through the water two inches deep on the trail. There's no need to mention how wet and cold we were, that is a given. At some point we missed a sign where someone had put an arrow with "PCT" written in black. The trail went from one campsite to another and got narrower with every step. Finally, we decided we were no longer on the right trail and turned around. Sure enough, after wading back through the waterlogged trail, we saw a PCT sign on a tree off to our left.

Back on the PCT we came to a thirty foot wide stream. It was a shallow runoff from Deep Lake, and the trail workers had placed large stones about every three feet all the way across. We went across on the stones even though it wouldn't have made our feet any wetter walking through the water. Crossing the stream, we climbed 1,200 feet of switchbacks and passed around the east side of Cathedral Rock. High above Deep Lake we had a great view of the mountains on the far side of the lake and a spectacular waterfall that cascaded a thousand feet down from Circle Lake. The clouds were swirling down over the mountains briefly hiding our view. Soon they would blow on and we would have another magnificent image forever imprinted on our memory. It was raining at lunch time, and we were cold and hungry.

Family Man talked me into stopping for lunch under a big pine tree. We sat there in the damp, cold mountain air as water dripped down through the branches and down our backs. Watching the torrential rain fall around us, we ate our warm noodle soup. At least it warmed our insides. Soon we were back out in the rain, forever moving north.

With every climb there is a descent, and so we descended 1,900 feet to cross a stream. A number of times I found myself on my bottom as my feet slid on the muddy trail. We arrived at the stream not worthy of a name on the map, but which also had a note that it could be dangerous. Rushing down a steep mountain valley between Mount Daniels and Blue Ridge, the three pronged river looked intimidating. Looking up and down the valley, it was evident that at times this river had been strong enough to take boulders off the mountain. We worked our way across the first two streams on limbs that someone had laid across the stream. On the last stream we had to step across on boulders. With the deafening roar of water, I froze standing on a stone in the middle of the stream only eight feet wide. Looking up, all I could see was water cascading over the rocks twenty feet upstream. It rushed past the rock I was standing on and disappeared over the ledge to my right. I knew that one wrong step and I'd be somewhere below the trail. How far I would go was unknown, and I didn't plan on finding out.

After crossing this unnamed stream, we crossed Deception Pass. The name Deception must come from the fact that we were deceived into thinking we were done climbing. We continued the 2,500 foot climb up to Surprise Mountain. I guess the name comes from the surprise that you made it. The rain stopped and we needed water, so we took a break at a small stream and campsite about half way up the mountain. Family Man fixed a dinner of rice with chicken which we wrapped up in tortillas to make burritos. While he cooked, I filtered water. After eating, we lay there on our mats looking high up in the trees. We were mesmerized by the water droplets coming off the pine needles and dropping some forty to fifty feet before splattering us in the face. Entertainment is hard to come by on rainy days in the wilderness.

Surprise Mountain was more dreamlike than a surprise. While the mountain itself is as beautiful as any other we had seen, the clouds that swirled over and around it gave it its enchantment. The mountains, the rocks, the clouds, and the trail all worked in unison to create a whimsical environment. Descending below one layer of clouds, we came to an open wash where years of erosion had brought stones and gravel from the mountain down to the shores of Glacier Lake.

When the clouds below us briefly blew out of the way, it gave us a view of Surprise Lake and the darkening valley beyond. Four miles down that valley, Highway 2 sped up the mountains towards Stevens Pass and civilization. As we walked along into the darkness the clouds again closed in around us. With headlamps on we started up another mountain. The trail was overgrown and the foliage was wet. Back and forth on the short switchbacks we climbed. A thousand feet later, with a really bad attitude, we arrived at the top with cold, soaking wet legs. We were above the clouds where the stars shined bright. The ridge was only about twenty feet wide, but that was plenty of space for a couple of tents. The cold wind that was driving the clouds which blew around us also drove us into our tents in search of warmth. Tired and sore, we crawled into our sleeping bags at 9:30 p.m., ready for a good night's sleep.

August 30th
Day 146 –16 Miles
Total 2479.5 Miles

The rain woke me up at 1:00 a.m. and continued to do so throughout the rest of the night. The rain, along with the strong winds, made an early start unlikely. Around 10:00 a.m. Number Two came by and a short time later an unnamed northbound section hiker came over the hill. With this kind of traffic, we decided to get up. While packing, three southbound hikers arrived at the summit and told us that the restaurant at Stevens Pass was open until 6:00 p.m. The vision of a big fat cheeseburger popped into our minds and we were in gear. As we finished packing our bags, Godfather topped the hill. We all headed down the mountains with food on our minds.

Family Man was out ahead with Godfather, and they were moving fast. I did my best to keep up, but they disappeared down the trail. Five miles from Stevens Pass, at the Icicle Creek Trail Junction, I found Family Man and Godfather taking a break. I had no more than sat down when Oakdale came flying down the trail. I was sitting there verbally dreaming about a root beer when Oakdale pulled out an A&W root beer barrel and handed it to me. Sweet! I was happy now. With this taste of what's to come, we all headed for the pass. We had one more ridge to go over. At the top was a big structure housing the top end of a ski lift.

By the time I got to the restaurant, Family Man had already ordered our food. He was concerned that I might not make it before the restaurant closed. We were sitting on the deck overlooking the ski slopes when Godfather came out of the restaurant carrying his food. He said, "Stagecoach, this may look like a cheeseburger and waffle fries to you, but to me it looks like a little bit of heaven." An outside outlet allowed us to charge our phones and call the girls while we ate our fatty foods. The root beer was flowing freely as the "No free refills" sign at the soft drink dispenser did not apply to thru hikers. That was what the cashier told us anyhow.

I found an ATM in the lobby where I could get some cash. We had spent all our cash at the Aardvark forgetting about the bus ride down to Stehekin. I had seen online that they only accepted cash.

Chapter Thirty Five – Stevens Pass to Stehekin

The resort was pretty much deserted as we walked across Highway 2 on a footbridge built to keep pedestrians from certain death on the four lane road. For the next four miles the trail was fairly level and followed an old fire road. About a mile in we met a southbound section hiker who had hiked down from Hart's Pass. He had been on the trail for about a week and was meeting his wife at Steven's Pass. Even though he was anxious to meet up with his wife, he had all kinds of questions about our journey. All of a sudden he hollered and took off running. Looking behind us we could see why. His wife was running up the trail to meet him. What a picture that painted. We turned and continued on. That would be us some day. After the light was gone we found a place to camp for the night. Only one more encounter with civilization before trail's end. And that would be Stehekin, a town with minimal connection with the outside world.

August 31st
Day 147 –26.8 Miles
Total 2506.3 Miles

It was another morning without motivation as we tossed, "You out of your bag yet?" back and forth. Finally out of our tents and on the trail at 8:00 a.m. we started the climb up to Lake Valhalla. Family Man was somewhere out ahead and I was feeling somewhat depressed. Most likely it was the knowledge that this journey of a lifetime was in its final week. Coming to an open spot, I stopped and called Sharla and she cheered me up. Another call to my parents also helped get me out of the emotional funk as well. We were starting to realize that life after the trail would definitely be emotionally difficult.

I had just got off the phone when Dave, a day hiker we had met earlier, came back down the trail. He stopped for about ten minutes before heading on down the mountain. Getting to the top of the mountain I found Family Man a little concerned about my absence, but he soon got over it. He had fixed hot chocolate and a couple of bags of oatmeal, and was considering coming back down the trail in search of a broken down Stagecoach.

At Janus Lake we found a vacant trail workers' camp. The coolers sitting under a big open tent were about as tempting as it gets. If the trail cook was there, he would offer us a drink, but even being in the wild this long we still had a conscience, so we walked on. Coming to a sign that said "Toilet" with an arrow pointing into the underbrush was even more tempting than the coolers. Family Man took off down the side trail. Returning after a few minutes with a big smile he told me I had to check it out. Finding this "place of business" was difficult as I pushed my way through the brush and over the logs. The throne was a two foot square box sitting up on small wooden platform topped off with a wooden lid. The custodian of this throne in the wilderness moves the facility whenever the hole fills up. Not one of the most desirable job descriptions in the forest ranger's handbook, I'm sure.

Climbing out of the canopy of trees, we followed a ridge for about three miles coming to Grizzly Peak. Without a cloud in the sky we hung our stuff on the bushes in the sun to dry and found shade in a small grove of trees to take a nap and eat lunch. Godfather joined us for a brief spell before he and Family Man took off for the next water source at Pear Lake about four miles away. The turquoise blue water of Pear Lake transitioned into an eight hundred foot climb up a rocky mountain where we followed the ridge. There was no such thing as following the contour in these parts. Even the shorter climbs are getting tiresome. After crossing over Pass Creek in the early evening we still had 2,100 feet to climb before we reached our goal for the day. Putting in a late night we pushed our way up toward Skykomish Peak. Hiking along the steep and rocky eastern slope of the mountain, we could tell that the mountain dropped off into a deep valley below us. The problem with hiking at night is that all you can see is the twenty to thirty feet illuminated by your light. Before midnight we made it to Dishpan Gap where we spotted a medium sized tent set up in the grass. Not wanting to disturb the weekend hikers, we climbed a small hill into a group of trees. The stars were shining bright so we rolled out our sleeping bags and cowboy camped under the stars amongst the pine trees.

September 1st
Day 148 – 25.45 Miles
Total 2531.75 Miles

Waking up from a night of cowboy camping is a lot easier than trying to get out of a tent. You still have to get out of your bag though. Sticking my face outside I could sense the moisture before I felt it on my sleeping bag. While the sky was clear, the dew was extremely heavy leaving moderate moisture on our bags. Looking over to my left I spotted a bunch of blueberries within arm's reach. For the next few minutes I lay there eating berries. Looking up I spotted a couple of stuff sacks hanging over our head. We found humor in the twenty pounds of food above our heads (to keep the bears out). We slept with ours. We were packed up and heading down the hill towards the trail when we met a lady coming up to retrieve their supplies. I can't really blame them. It is the right thing to do.

We have been on the trail so long that our food has become extremely important to us. We weren't about to let a one eyed bear get it. One eyed bear? Yeah, because the other eye was going to be poked out by a trekking pole if that carnivore tried anything fancy. If you are reading this as a how to book, don't sleep with your food. Hang it from a tree properly or take a bear canister and keep it away from your tent.

We made our way around Kodak Peak and down to the Indian Creek Trail before making our way around the steep west slope of Indian Head Peak. Every mountain up there has a name. Some of them we named ourselves; most of those names are not real positive. North of Indian Head Peak we followed along the east side of a ridge with Glacier Peak directly ahead. We had good trail as we crossed over White Pass and along the west side of the ridge under White Mountain. Approaching Portal Peak we made a turn over the ridge and descended 3,000 feet down close to Chuck River at the base of Glacier Peak. We are still puzzled by the descent, because once we got to the bottom we started climbing again. The melting snow off the mountain created numerous streams flowing down its ravines. Each one was unique and beautiful.

The spectacular streams were not without challenges as each one needed to be crossed. Kennedy Creek had a log with handrails, but sometime in the past it had broken in the middle. Sketchy, but still usable we kept our feet dry. The one creek I liked the best was Pumice Creek. The fifteen foot wide stream came cascading through the ravine dropping twenty feet into a boiling whitewater before tumbling the hundred yards in and around the boulders down to the trail. Someone had put a couple of eight inch logs across the stream just above the trail to help keep the hikers' feet dry. Over time erosion filled in behind the logs creating a two foot water fall coming over the logs dumping onto the trail. After pausing just long enough to become crystal clear, it returned to a boiling white rage as it dumped into the ravine below us, disappearing into the trees. Looking up the mountain at the glaciers, I was quite confident this was some of the cleanest water we would ever find. Tanking up and filling up we moved on up the mountain.

By the time we made it to the top of the ridge we had climbed another 4,000 feet. Hiking late into the night, we finally made it to Mica Lake located on the ridge northwest of Glacier Peak. Godfather was already there along with weekend warriors scattered around the lake. We moved down from the ridge past some cascading waterfalls. About 10:00 p.m. and a half mile beyond the lake we forged a stream and found a place to camp. We had climbed 7,500 feet and descended about the same. Tucked away in our tents amongst the trees we were tired.

September 2nd
Day 149 – 33.75 Miles
Total 2565.5 Miles

In the civilized world it was Labor Day. In the wilderness it was a day to descend through two deep valleys and climb two high mountain ranges. We were on the trail at 7:15 and descended 2,500 feet to Milk Creek. On the way down we came to a detour around a recent landslide that had taken out part of the PCT. It wasn't so much of a detour as it was a short cut. The problem with shortcuts on switchbacks is the ratio of altitude to distance. We just slid the twenty yards down the mountain to rejoin the trail.

A recently built bridge made for easy crossing but added a half mile and was 100 feet lower in altitude. The melting snow packs from the Ptarmigan Glacier on Kennedy Peak created milky water, giving this river its name. Crossing the bridge we started a long 3,000 foot climb up to the headwaters of the East Fork Milk Creek. After climbing a couple hundred feet we came to a trail junction and found Godfather. He had taken the old unmaintained trail cutting off the half mile. We told him we were "doing the log" across Suiattle River and he wanted to join us. Because of the calculated risk of falling in the river he didn't want to do it alone.

Halfway up the switchbacks we stopped for a break, and the boys talked me into eating some energy gel we had acquired from the hiker box in Snoqualmie. I don't know if it did any good, but its texture was weird and it tasted strange. It was sort of like eating a sweet tasting raw egg.

By the time I got to the top of the switchbacks Family Man and Godfather were out of sight. Winding on up the hill I spotted Keymaster sitting on a rock. We hadn't seen Keymaster since the Mount Whitney turnoff south of Yosemite. At close to 6,000 feet we made our way around a grassy flower strewn basin where many small streams were coming together to create the East Fork of Milk Creek. The sun was shining brightly when I found Family Man and Godfather sitting by a nice stream eating lunch. It was a good place to dry out the sleeping bags and rain flies.

With over 3,000 feet to descend we started down the switchbacks to Vista Creek. Following the creek down the valley for three miles we came to the old PCT trail. In 2003 an epic flood wiped out almost all foot bridges on the Suiattle, closing the trail. For the next eight years the PCT hikers continued to use the trail, crossing on a log that was lying across the river. At the cost of approximately 1.2 million dollars a new bridge was built downstream adding 5.5 miles to the trail. The log crossing is such a legendary part of the trail that the more adventurous thru hikers still use it. Heading down the unmaintained trail we had to bushwhack our way through the downed trees and overgrown path. The old footbridge at Vista Creek was washed out but we found a twelve inch log crossing the creek. The water was probably only about three feet deep and about fifteen feet across but the fast moving water was intimidating. Family Man had no problem crossing. It took me awhile, which scared Godfather who ended up going on upstream to a better place to cross.

After another two miles of crawling over logs and shoving brush out of the way, we came to the Suiattle River. Even though the wash was almost five hundred feet across, the river was only about forty feet wide the day we arrived. The wash was littered with downed trees that had been ripped from the sides of the wash during floods, rain storms, or even normal erosion. The log we found had at one time been flowing down the river and somehow got wedged from one shore to the other. It was 16 to 18 inches at the big end and got smaller as you crossed the river. Starting at the water's edge, the log sloped up to ten feet above the water on the far side.

Godfather, on his hands and knees, was the first to make it across. Next I watched Family Man pack up his poles thinking he was going to do the same. Then, with little hesitation, he stepped out onto the log and walked across the raging river. Great, now he showed up Stagecoach. There was no way I was going to walk across this log. I had already climbed 6,500 feet and my knees were shaky at best. Down on all fours I inched along with my eyes focused on the log. Fear arose within me as the raging current entered my peripheral vision. All I could do to ease the panic was to start softly singing, *"When peace, like a river, attendeth my way, When sorrows like sea billows roll. Whatever my lot, Thou hast taught me to say, It is well, it is well with my soul."* Arriving at the other side of the river I noticed Family Man hoisting his backpack on his shoulders. He had dropped it soon after I had started across. He was ready to go for a swim if I had fallen from the bridge of pride. I am still not sure today if the glory was worth the fear.

We still had a half mile of bushwhacking to get back up to the groomed trail. After a handful of switchbacks we started a long climb up along Miner Creek. Crossing the creek three miles later we continued the 3,500 foot climb up to Suiattle Pass. At 8:00 p.m. as daylight was disappearing, we stopped for dinner along a small stream. It was totally dark by the time we made the pass. From the looks of things it would have been a great place to spend the night. With twenty miles still to High Bridge, where the bus service hauled hikers down the river to Stehekin, we continued on. We badly wanted to make the 3:00 p.m. shuttle into town the next day in order to retrieve the resupply package before the post office closed.

We left the pass in the dark and headed down the eastern slope of Plummer Mountain across the headwaters of Agnes Creek. We stopped for a break at a big rocky landslide between Plummer and Sitting Bull Mountains. Three miles later we finally found a campsite on a small knoll next to the trail. We had experienced a rugged day, climbing over 9,700 feet and over 28 miles. Family Man and Godfather were manly about their decision to cowboy camp under the cloudless sky. I wasn't as concerned about rain as I was the critters, so I set up my tent. Around 2:00 a.m. the sound of raindrops hitting my rainfly brought me to full attention. I hollered at the guys and they were stirring around immediately. I heard Godfather mutter in his Scottish accent, "The irony!" All I did was lie there in my warm and dry sleeping bag chuckling. Guess I was the lucky one.

September 3rd
Day 150 – 14.5 Miles
Total 2580 Miles

I was up at 6:00 a.m. and got things together while Family Man was waking up. He said he would catch up, so I took off down the valley. With fifteen miles to the bridge we didn't want to waste time. Three miles into the day we came to the South Fork of Agnes Creek which needed to be forged. We looked up and down the thirty foot wide creek for a log and finally took our shoes off and waded across the icy creek. It was only about knee deep, but it was cold. On the other side we dried off and headed on down the trail to find a large hewn log across the creek we had just waded across. Now we know!

The GPS said we had 4,000 feet to descend, but it also said we had a thousand feet to climb. I hate climbing. We did climb periodically, but overall the thousand feet was dissipating climb. We were eating our lunch at Six Mile Camp when Oakdale came high tailing it up the trail. After crossing Swamp Creek on a gnarly log, Family Man and Oakdale left me in the dust with the understanding they would be at the bus stop. Coming down the switchbacks into Agnes Gorge I came face to face with a seasoned hiker who had the biggest grin on his face and knew me. At first I didn't recognize Sea King, but as soon as he started talking it clicked. Our last meeting was four months earlier at Ziggy and the Bears in southern California. He was section hiking the trail and decided to flip flop by going to the northern border and heading south.

I walked into High Bridge at 2:00 p.m. where I found Family Man with his tent and sleeping bag spread out on some benches to dry. I spread mine out as well even though they weren't as wet as his. We had plenty of time as the bus wasn't scheduled to arrive for an hour. Two older guys, doing some section hiking, gave us a couple bags of candy bars and trail mix for sharing our stories with them. We were all over the high sugar confections like a hippy on crack. When Family Man was throwing his trash away he found a pair of handmade flip flops that someone had tossed. He considered the new footwear as a prize and happily replaced his hiking shoes.

The 3:00 p.m. bus arrived dropping off a large number of hikers, among them was Zen, the guy who had tossed Family Man's new taped up flip flops. They had a good laugh as he told Family Man he had made them in Wrightwood. Some of the others we knew were Hakuna Matata, Texas Grit, Bow, and Siesta. Siesta was the girl who had passed me north of Crater Lake when I was hobbling with bad knees. The 11 mile bus ride down to town took almost an hour.

Stehekin is a remote village where modern technology has been ignored. No ATM machine, cell service, or internet. There is a satellite phone that you can use with a calling card. Fortunately they sell the cards at the grocery store where they will also take a credit card. The only way in and out of Stehekin is to fly in or bring the boat. We made it to the post office before they closed. It was just a small hole in the wall place with hiker resupply boxes stacked everywhere. The post master had to lock up so he could go to the basement and find our package. He also had my Canadian entrance permit that Sharla had sent overnight.

With box in hand we made our way up to the campground and set up our tent. Oakdale offered to share a hotel room, but the rooms were way too expensive in my book. We made our way back down to the restaurant and ordered a ribeye dinner. We figured all the money saved by sleeping in a tent would more than cover a good dinner. It was dark by the time we headed back to the campground. Stopping by the phone booth we called the girls. We were happy to find out they had already moved Family Man's possessions back into their house and had the RV in the drive. We had expected to have that job to do as soon as we return to civilization. What a support team. We owe them forever!

An elderly gentleman was waiting for the phone when we got through. He inquired how it worked and looked heartbroken when we explained the need for a phone card. He needed to call his wife and would have to wait for the store to open in the morning. We had plenty of time left on our card so we gave it to him. It totally slipped our minds that we had just told the girls we would call again in the morning.

Back in the tent we are hearing voices, not the ones I normally hear in my head. These were groups of hikers throughout the campground. In the wilderness after 9:00 p.m., which is hiker midnight, you hardly hear anything from other hikers. Maybe it was the availability of alcohol. We were starting to wrap our thoughts around a journey that was not yet complete, yet so near its end. The days were getting noticeably shorter and the air was starting to feel like fall. We tried to stay focused on the goal, yet we were scared of the future. *What would the transition back into civilization be like? Did we want to return to civilization or just move deeper into seclusion?*

Chapter Thirty Six – Stehekin to Manning Park

September 4th
Day 151 – 20 Miles
Total 2600 Miles

We woke up at 6:00 a.m. with the goal of making it to Rainy Pass by nightfall. The twenty mile hike would require we leave on the noon bus for our return to High Bridge. There was an earlier bus, but we needed to eat breakfast and wash our clothes. I grabbed our clothes and got them down to the laundry room before any other hikers woke up and took over the machines. Once we had consumed a big breakfast at the restaurant we hung out on the patio watching as the ferry arrived, bringing civilization to the small mountain resort. The air taxi, a bright yellow 1958 DeHavilland DHC-2 Beaver, landed on the lake and taxied up to the dock. This service from Chelan to Stehekin makes a handful of trips each day providing a thirty minute alternative to the four hour boat ride.

A mid-morning rain shower dampened our utopia, but we got everything dried off and packed up, returning to the patio to wait for the bus. At 11:15 the big red bus arrived with a few hikers, White was among them. He had taken the earlier bus up to the trailhead only to find out he had left his trekking poles in town.

The driver stopped a mile up the road at the bakery where we picked up a pizza, ice cream, bacon & cheese stuffed rolls, and two bottles of root beer. The smell of fresh baked bread and pizza was overwhelming. Oakdale bought a whole blackberry pie which he dumped into a Ziploc bag to save weight. We tipped our driver by buying his lunch which really made him happy. He had said it would only be a ten minute stop, but I figured if he was getting food out of the deal he would be more willing to wait for us.

We were back on the trail at 1:00 p.m. following the Stehekin River upstream for five miles. Godfather started out with us but fell behind which was unusual for him. Coming to a dirt road we walked by Bridge Creek Campground before rejoining the trail a quarter mile later. We followed Bridge Creek for three miles before crossing a foot bridge taking us to the west side under the shadow of the 7,700 foot Mount Banzarino. Might not be the highest mountain, but down along the river we were only at 2,600 feet. Climbing up along the slope we came to White sitting beside the trail. He had slipped and twisted his knee. After he assured us he would be all right we moved on. A short time later we came to a swinging bridge crossing Maple Creek. On the far side of the bridge we sat down to fill our water bottles and eat dinner. While we were sitting there eating bacon & cheddar filled rolls, Godfather came up the trail along with White who was now on the move even though he had a bad limp. It was almost painful watching him cross Maple Creek. He had chosen to cross on the rocks instead of going up over the swinging bridge.

Family Man was trying a new thing where he would tank up at the water source and not carry water with him. It worked fine until late in the day. When I had last seen him he said he would be at the next watering hole so we could filter water before dark. I was concerned when I arrived at the creek bed and found neither Family Man nor water. We never hiked alone after dark, so I assumed he was thirsty and had moved on in hopes the next water source actually had water.

I walked on into the twilight keeping the light off as long as night vision allowed it. When my toes started complaining about kicking too many roots, I turned on the dim lights and started following Family Man's foot prints. It wasn't only Family Man's footprints on the trail. Blueberry laced purple bear scat made me think the bears in this neck of the woods were eating too many blueberries. I really wasn't concerned about bears sharing the trail as we had seen a lot of bear scat over the last few hundred miles. It wasn't until I came across a pile of the bear droppings on top of Family Man's footprint, which told me this bear was between Stagecoach and Family Man, that I became concerned.

About an hour after dark, climbing a pretty long grade, I found Family Man sitting by a small spring. He shared how he had been sitting there waiting when a flying squirrel buzzed over his head. Filling up with water we pushed on up the hill to Highway 20. Paralleling the highway for a couple of miles, the trail crossed over at the road leading up to the trailhead parking lot. We had made it to Rainey Pass after climbing 5,400 feet this afternoon. It was damp and foggy when we arrived at the parking lot. We sat down by a block wall and congratulated ourselves for the accomplishment of reaching 2,600 miles. Eating pizza and drinking root beer at 11:00 p.m. in the wilderness on a foggy night was epic.

We sat there looking at the pit toilets thinking about how dry it would be inside for the night. We were never serious about becoming toilet campers, but it was a temptation. We hiked up the trail five hundred feet to a place under the trees where we set up camp. While putting up our tents we noticed another tent not more than fifty feet away. This quieted us down so as to not disturb the occupants.

September 5th
Day 152 – 25.6 Miles
Total 2625.6 Miles

I lie here in my tent, as the thunderstorms rage around us. The splattering of rain on the rain fly was the tool God used to bring me out of my normal dream and into reality. The *normal dream* I'm talking about had been haunting us for the last two weeks. It was a simple dream; I'm sleeping peacefully in a soft warm bed only to wake up to a cold damp morning with sore ankles and aching hips. How a person can have the same dream over and over for this long is still a mystery. Awake, yet in a stupor, I was aware of someone walking by. As he passed I heard him say, "Good morning headlamp hikers." I don't know if that was a compliment or a chastisement for waking him up late last night.

Once the rain stopped, we started out with a 2,000 foot climb up around Cutthroat Peak along the Porcupine Creek. Soon after we got on the trail we came to a tributary only a couple feet wide but cascading across the trail. It was a great place to fill up our water bottles. The broken clouds moved rapidly at higher altitude as wispy clouds moved in and out of valley we ascended. We met Godfather taking a break. You would think that after 2,600 miles and close to a half a million feet of climbing it would get easier. It doesn't. About a mile from the top I came across Family Man lying in the grass on his mat with his arm over his eyes. This surprised me as we had just taken a short break a mile before. He had all of a sudden gotten a migraine which stopped him in a hurry. By the time we were back on the trail Godfather and White were in the lead. The migraine didn't last long, and soon after noon we crossed over Cutthroat Pass. Again we passed White who was struggling with the injury but still pushing forward.

A mile farther we crossed a ridge and started down a rocky handful of switchbacks to Granite Pass. We could see the trail run along the contour below Tower Mountain. We caught up with Godfather getting water. Family Man stayed with him while I moved on ahead. As I got close to a campsite just below Lower Snowy Lake, I saw smoke coming from a fire ring. No one was around and for a quarter of a mile I grumbled about some hiker not making sure his fire was out. Getting closer I did see a sleeping bag and other items laid out around the fire. It wasn't until I crossed the creek that someone climbed up over the hill below the camp. I didn't give him a hard time as it looked like his wet gear was punishment enough.

I was taking a break at Methow Pass when Family Man and Godfather caught up. We headed down switchbacks for the initial 1,000 feet passing through the headwaters of Methow River. The rest of the seven mile descent was along the river around two eight thousand foot peaks. The cumulus clouds grew darker as their tops were building. We knew what it meant and could do nothing about it but walk on. At the bottom of the descent we crossed a footbridge over Brush Creek and started the climb up the valley towards Glacier Pass. By 8:00 p.m. we were closing in on the pass and it was raining. Sitting there on the trail under a soppy poncho I declared my disdain for the state of Washington. Just like the constant hammering of the rain erodes these spectacular mountains, it eroded my spirit as well.

At Glacier Pass we put on our headlamps and started up the 21 switchbacks. We had 1,200 feet to climb to the ridge and the thunder was only dulled by the strong wind out of the north. We could see Godfather's headlamp cutting through the darkness high on the mountain. The rain hit about halfway up, and with each turn to the north it felt like frozen ice hitting our face. There would be no comfort in taking a break in this torrential downpour. I did not keep track of the switchbacks. I had no idea how many times we had turned into the wind, but the two miles up the mountain seemed to go on forever. Finally we crossed over Grasshopper Pass and walked north along the top of the ridge for a quarter of a mile before the ridge rose and we moved off to the east side.

The thunderstorm had dissipated and the ridge protected us from the wind. We were exhausted and anxious to find a place to camp. As we looked down the mountain, the beam of our light reflected the penetrating eyes of a large mammal. Its eyes moved slowly as it was obviously watching us.

I would assume its night vision was better than ours. Continuing on, looking for the spring, I kept a watch on our back. Not scared, just cautious. We passed Godfather already tucked away in his tent. His light was still burning so we knew he was awake. A quarter mile further we realized we had missed the spring. I was down to an inch of water in my last bottle. Family Man said he would go get the water. Dropping his pack he took off back down the trail. I covered his backpack with his poncho and sat down on a rock on the downhill side of the trail.

Lightning flashed, and for a brief moment it illuminated the jagged mountain above the trail. I sat there on a cold rock looking around with each flash not knowing when I might spot the cougar we were sure we had seen about a half mile back. Another flash and thunder rolled up the valley. *Where is Family Man?* We had missed the spring and the next reliable water was 21 miles away. Family Man had left me with the backpacks twenty minutes earlier and returned the estimated 300 yards back down the trail to find the water.

"Where is Family Man?" I muttered again. It could have been a deer, but the methodical movements of the eyes were different from the many deer we had seen over the last 2619 miles. My thoughts returned to the beginning of the trail where our journey had started five months before. As I thought about what had transpired since we had left the Mexican border, I started softly singing, "O Lord my God/ When I in awesome wonder/ Consider all the worlds Thy Hands have made." The lightning strikes were getting closer now and all I could do was turn to the One who had seen us safely through this far and with much greater volume sing out, "I see the stars, I hear the rolling thunder/ Thy power throughout the universe displayed."

The flicker of light coming up the trail eased my apprehension. With a full liter of water we continued up the trail towards a saddle about a half mile away. The climb was worth it as we found the saddle flat and grassy. Quickly we set up our tents as all the thunderstorms in northern Washington converged on Stagecoach and Family Man. For the next six hours the torrential rain pounded our ridge.

We got very little sleep as the storms raged around us. Finally, at 5:00 a.m. the rain ceased. Falling into a fitful sleep we woke up at 6:30 to find our tents full of water. Here we were after 152 days on the trail and we just learned a new lesson. Don't place your tent on flat ground when it's going to rain. I guess all the other times we couldn't find flat spots to camp. Shivering, I crawled out of my tent to find we were in a two inch deep lake.

We were miserable, packing up our backpacks as the overcast sky let loose with a periodic drizzle. Family Man's soaking wet tent was in a garbage bag hanging low on his back. We had heard rumors that there would be some trail magic at Hart's Pass. With only five miles of moderate trail between us and the pass we headed down the trail. We hadn't gone a half mile when we came to a stream of water coming down across the trail. It looked like just run off from the recent rain, but we had to laugh about the 21 mile water warning. Why were we so concerned last night? We walked past the burnt out Meadows Campground and over a small ridge as the sun broke through the clouds, giving us some hope of a drier day. Coming around a mountain and seeing a van sitting next to a couple of canopy tents brought enthusiasm to a lethargic morning.

Meander greeted us as we walked into the makeshift paradise with its wood burning stove. Pulling up chairs, he invited us to warm ourselves by the fire. The warm apple pastries taken off the top of the stove melted us into the vortex. We spread our sleeping bags on top of his van to dry in the sun, which was doing its best not to disappear behind the building clouds. Godfather showed up and we all sat around the stove drying out our feet, listening to and telling stories of the trail. Meander, a trail angel of the purist form, and a legendary backpacker, had just taken a trek up to the border and had helpful advice for our next thirty miles. As if the vortex was not strong enough, he showed us the steaks he was preparing for dinner. He had seen enough hikers to know his enticement was not going to work, as we had our eyes on the goal just two days away. As we were getting ready to leave, Meander took us to the back of the van where he gave us Snickers bars, M&Ms, and food bars to help us make it to the end. What a great trail angel.

We spun out of our final vortex soon after noon as the rain returned. Hiking up the mountain with ponchos on, even in the rain our spirits were high; we knew the end of this journey was near. Climbing 800 feet to a ridge, we passed under the fire lookout on Slate Peak. Moving north we crossed over numerous ridges with names like Buffalo Pass, Windy Pass, Jim's Pass and Foggy Pass. None of them changed much in altitude. Going around the Devil's Backbone we descended into the trees. We passed through a valley before starting up towards Rock Pass. For most of the afternoon we walked in the rain, some heavy at times.

It was hard to stop for even a short break as the cold rain tried to demoralize our very being. Godfather went on ahead and Family Man stayed with me. I don't know if it was for my safety or the solemnity of the occasion. The atmosphere around our adventure was so surreal. We knew tomorrow would be the final day. It would be a day of rejoicing and celebration. Yet today was not that day. Today was a day we spent thinking back on the long walk that brought us here. Today we were thinking about how close we had come to our God who had revealed Himself in so many ways.

It was still raining when we arrived at the grove of trees a mile or so below the pass. Here we found Godfather, Oakdale, Gourmet and Cool Ranch. The last two had joined Oakdale at Hart's Pass to finish out the trail with him. With only fourteen miles to the border we put our tents up for the last time. As I vegetated in my tent Family Man prepared a dinner of salmon on a bed of couscous. Gourmet had invited Family Man to cook under a tarp he had stretched between the trees.

Tonight I lie here, my mind numb from the past five months. Is it real? Have we really accomplished the goal we had set out to do? It is impossible to explain all the emotions bombarding our every thought. The dripping of the rain on the tent only added to the surreal cloud that hangs over this grove. Knowing that we had been the recipients of thousands of blessings over the last five months, I thanked God for all the people He had brought into our lives during the journey. I thanked Him for the protection from all the unseen dangers. I thanked Him for providing us not only the physical necessities but also the emotional strength to make it through. It did stop raining shortly after midnight and I was able to go to sleep. At 3:00 a.m. the rain returned and was still coming down when daylight arrived.

September 7th
Day 154 – 23.5 Miles
Total 2669.5 Miles

It would have been nice to have a sunrise on our final day, but that was not to be as the solid cloud cover showed no sign of breaking up. Finally, at 7:00 a.m., for the last time we got out of our tents and packed our bags. Godfather had left about the time we got up and the other three were stirring when we took off up the trail for Rock Pass. Crossing over the pass we descended four switchbacks to a contour below the rock face of Powder Mountain. Meander had told us about the washouts through this area and he was accurate with his description. Recent storms had washed huge ravines down the mountain, taking out the trail. From past reports seen on social media some hikers had descended to the valley crossing to get across. The challenge with that is you had to climb back up the other side.

The first few washes were not difficult at all; some, while deep, could be jumped across. Thinking we had it made, we came to the big ones. Fifty feet across and twenty feet deep, we slid our way down into the wash through loose gravel. Getting up the other side was a whole different ball game. By the time we got to the last wash, Oakdale and his two friends passed us up. They had left their gear in camp and were just pushing to the border to return back to camp before nightfall. They were crossing the last and deepest wash a hundred feet below us when Family Man stepped on a loose boulder that took off down the mountain, scaring the hikers below us. Through a lot of struggle, we made it up the north bank of the last wash. Now, clear of the washed out trail, we still had to climb three hundred yards straight up the mountain to rejoin the trail.

Back on the trail we climbed eight hundred feet over Woody Pass. Remember the 115,000 feet we had to climb when we crossed into Washington twenty-two days prior? We were now down to less than a thousand. A couple more small passes to cross and it would be downhill to Canada. On the north side of Three Fools Peak we sat down for our final lunch break. We sat there on boulders drinking our cold double shots of coffee laced with hot chocolate mix. I knew Family Man was out of anything good to eat, so I handed him my last bag of peanut M&Ms. The look he gave me was priceless.

We crossed over Lakeview Ridge before descending down the Devil's Staircase to Hopkins Pass. The broken clouds to the north showed signs of blue. It was if Canada was sending out a welcome sign. Our stop at Castle Pass at 1:00 p.m. was brief. The GPS said we had climbed 486,721 feet since we had left Mexico and only had 35 more feet to climb. It was time for a little premature celebration as the last mountain had been conquered. It was finally all downhill to Canada. Less than a mile from the border we met Godfather on his way back south. He had decided not to cross into Canada but return to Hart's Pass. It was an emotional goodbye as he had already reached his goal and we were almost to ours. A half mile out Family Man turned around and motioned for me to hurry. With the biggest grin on his face he again motioned, "Come on, Dad, come on, Dad, let's go, come on!" This was his dream coming to fruition. He had worked so hard to make it happen. It was at this moment the transformation happened. Stagecoach had served his purpose and returned to being Dad.

I waved him on and told him I would meet him at the border. Family Man ran. Ten minutes later I heard the sounds of shouting in the valley and tears rolled down my cheeks. I knew that Quentin had just completed the most life changing endeavor of his lifetime. Coming around the bend I could see the line in the trees which was a symbolic separation between my homeland and our neighbors to the north. There was not a wall or a fence or guards. There was just a scar in the woods where sometime in the past the trees had been chopped down. A simple monument had been erected to mark the border where Family Man, Oakdale, Gourmet and Cool Ranch sat taking in the moment. As I exited the trees they loudly cheered me on. Stumbling past the monument I threw down my trekking poles and backpack. For good measure and theatrical effect, I kicked them a couple of times.

Walking over to the monument that had been our vision for the last two years, I kissed it as the emotions of pain, hunger, thirst, excitement, fear, loneliness, exhaustion, the freezing cold, and searing heat, all swept through my soul.

It was time to tell those who had supported us that success had been achieved. Once the SPOT confirmed it had successfully transmitted the message, we sent out a second message to social media so the naysayers could change their tune. What we didn't realize was the first message was an answer to many prayers. From the time we had left Stehekin three days earlier, none of the messages sent out was received. We suspect it was electromagnetic interference from the numerous thunderstorms. This, along with not calling the girls before we left Stehekin, had caused a little concern amongst our family and friends.

After a half hour of song and dance, Oakdale and his friends had to head back south wanting to at least cross the washed out trail before dark. I surprised Quentin by pulling a root beer out of my backpack, and he pulled out a package of sugar wafer cookies he had been saving. I don't know how either one lasted this long. We were sitting there basking in the glory of the moment when it started raining. Considering we didn't have a limo pull up to whisk us away to a five star resort, we pulled on our backpacks for the nine and a half mile hike to Manning Park.

It would have been great if it was downhill to the park, but that would be too easy. We still had 2,500 feet of climbing and 2,800 feet to descend. After stopping by the PCT Camp for a restroom break, we crossed over Windy Joe Mountain. Crossing over the top the trail widened out, so most of the way down the fifteen hundred foot descent we walked side by side filled with a happy sadness that cannot be explained in words.

Reaching the paved road at 6:30 p.m. we walked the mile down to the resort. Along the way we met a whole slew of teenagers running at us. I think we may have been more scared of them than a mountain lion. They ran right past us. After asking one if they were running a marathon, we found out they were all part of a youth group involved in a scavenger hunt. Arriving at the lodge, Family Man wouldn't let me go in until I had taken off the bottoms of my hiking pants. They had become all frayed, so I had cut about five inches off the bottom. Now they looked really bad, even for hiker trash. At the front desk we found the place filled to capacity. I don't know if it was the sad puppy look on my face, or the smell of hiker trash, that made the lady hesitate. She went on to explain they just happened to have a cabin available for $200.00. I gulped a couple of times and slid the credit card across the counter. We were not sleeping in our tents tonight.

Chapter Thirty Seven – Manning Park

We dropped our backpacks and headed back up to the restaurant for dinner. They were kind to us even in our post hiking state. While we were eating, another hiker by the name of Waterman came in and we waved him over to our table. He had been looking for us. We had left it with the front desk that we could house any additional hikers who might stagger in tonight. Waterman was from New Zealand and happy to know he had a place to sleep and willingly shared the cost.

After we finished eating our dinner, the waiter told us our bill had been paid. Wow! Now we really felt like celebrities. Looking around the restaurant we spotted a couple we had met in the parking lot. We figured they were the guilty party and stopped by their table on the way out. They were leaving in the morning to hike up to the border to meet their son who was finishing his thru hike. It was dark and we were walking through the parking lot when a couple of girls jumped out of a car and hollered, "Hiker trash!" They had been sitting up at the trailhead all afternoon with cold beer fishing for hikers. They were from the area and loved to hang out with hikers. We chatted with them for a couple of minutes before excusing ourselves as we were tired and needed to take showers. The long hot showers and clean clothes were followed by the ceremonial burial of our stinking, half rotten, hiking clothes in the kitchen trash can.

Chapter Thirty Eight – Going Home

It was Sunday morning and we were speeding along the highway in a Greyhound bus. The mountains along each side of the valley were drawing us in like a spirit calling us home. We could feel the grip on our hearts as it tore our emotions to shreds. So desperately we wanted to be home with our family, yet we agonized over the reality of a journey's end. The uncertainty of tomorrow was beginning to fog our consciousness. We wondered why we had to return to a world so complex it clouded our view of God. Could we not find existence in a simplistic world where we could be surrounded by our family and friends, yet be removed from these layers of uncertainty?

The bus was getting louder now as more and more passengers boarded the bus at each stop we made. The world was closing in around us as the tree covered mountains gave way to big buildings and concrete sidewalks. Humanity everywhere, scurrying about with little interaction with each other. They had neither the time, nor most likely the desire, to stop and chat with others on these concrete trails. I looked down at the bottle of root beer I was holding. This beverage, which just yesterday was the subject of excitement, was rapidly losing its appeal. How much longer could we hold on to the zeal we found in trusting God to provide our basic needs? Would this simple faith lose its appeal as well?

The train station in Vancouver was full of Sunday afternoon travelers. They only briefly glanced at the hiker trash sitting on the hard wooden benches. Was it their fear of grubby looking guys with dirty backpacks that caused them to quickly look away? I wondered if they could see past the facade to the reality of two souls being brought back into civilized captivity after five months of freedom. We walked across the street to a Subway for a sandwich. Quentin got chastised for refilling his cup. The employee's, "No free refills!" while shaking her finger at him was more than he really cared to experience. Back at the train station we sat down next to the building waiting on our bus that would take us to Seattle. There were trains heading south as well, but the bus would get us there sooner. The customs agent must have seen our type before as he took little notice of our backpacks and welcomed us home.

It was dark when we arrived at the Seattle train station. Somewhere inside that big stone building our support team awaited our arrival. It had been twenty-two days and over five hundred miles since we had left them at the Columbia River. Like two lost puppies finding their master was our excitement in finding our best friends. We soon realized that their work as our support team lasted long after we finished the trail. Our dependence on them to help us live in a civilized world again became quite evident. After stopping at a Denny's for a late night dinner we arrived back in Salem, Oregon well after midnight.

The second and frequently skipped verse of "How Great Thou Art" rings with clarity as we enter a new phase in our lives and we pray these words will remain with us for eternity.

When through the woods, and forest glades I wander,
And hear the birds sing sweetly in the trees.
When I look down, from lofty mountain grandeur
And see the brook, and feel the gentle breeze.

Then sings my soul, My Savior God, to Thee,
How great Thou art, How great Thou art.

Epilogue

Around 2:00 p.m. we left the Olallie Lake store and climbed south with heavy packs. A year has gone by and we have found it difficult adjusting to post trail life. Family Man has returned to his job at the Willamette Valley Winery and is living up to his trail name with his wife and sons. Stagecoach, being retired, just tries to keep busy working with his wife and playing a lot of golf. The solitude of walking the golf course seems to bring some kind of sanity to a world gone crazy.

The trail has not changed as we work our way higher onto a ridge overlooking the lake. The winter spent in Indiana had done its job of returning the weight lost on the trail. With the added weight the climb seems harder than it did a year ago. Three miles in, after passing Upper Lake, we arrived at a small meadow where we took a break.

The scars from an aging fire still stood amongst the new growth as Family Man and I sat there reminding each other of things that had happened on the trail. It really amazes us how something so taxing, both physically and mentally, can continue to have such a grip on our lives. Was it the way the adrenaline rushed through our bodies as we topped a mountain? Was it the drive we felt when we knew that that day we would be eating a cheeseburger? Could it have been the possibility of finding a flat soft place to sleep? While these things all added to the overall trail experience, what we miss the most about the trail is the security we felt in communing with God for hours each day as we walked along in solitude.

We got excited as we spotted a hiker making his way down the mountain. We would get to hear some stories of the trail as we shared our food and soda. All of a sudden Family Man burst into laughter as the hiker exited the trees and he recognized our old friend Slim. It is just another confirmation as to the power of the Almighty. Slim had not changed and continuously cursed the trail and the trail angels as he scraped some rocks and twigs away. Plopping down in the dirt he rapidly consumed the loaf of cheese bread and soda we gave him. He wanted more and we gave him another soda but saved the bread for others. When he got done ranting about his glorified hike, he asked what we were doing. When we told him we were just out doing some trail angel work, he wanted to know where the coolers were. It's really hard for a zebra to changes its stripes.

After feeding another hiker we moved on up the mountain meeting a few more. As evening approached we decided to do something different and not hike into the night. Stopping at a spot overlooking the valley we rolled out our sleeping bags for a night of cowboy camping. We had left our tents at home because the weatherman had assured us it was going to stay dry. From the comfort of our bags we watched the hazy shadows in the valley darken as the stars revealed themselves in the clear night sky. Somehow we finally drifted off with a very light heart.

Morning brought with it a cold wind blowing a cloudy mist over the ridge and damping our sleeping bags. The humor of this miserable weather stuck with us as we packed up for our return to Olallie Lake. Moving away from Mount Jefferson, the sky cleared making for an enjoyable hike back to the car. Will we ever return to life on the trail? We have discussed doing the Colorado Trail which is around five hundred miles and there is always the AT (Appalachian Trail) haunting the back of our minds. In the meantime we will just look for shorter trails to satisfy our need for aching knees and blistered feet.

As time continues to move forward at an ever increasing speed, we anticipate the future while clinging to the memories of that summer that changed us forever.

~Stagecoach & Family Man

Appendix

Trail Food (Partial List)

Instant mashed potatoes	Beef Jerky
Spam	Tuna
Noodles	Couscous
Food bars	Dried Fruit
Trail Mix	Nuts
Jolly Ranchers	M&M's
Snickers Bars	Skittles
Smarties	Jelly Bellies
Starburst	Freeze dried meals
Instant Coffee	Hot Chocolate mix
Other candy	Gatorade
Misc drink mixes	Oatmeal

Equipment

Stagecoach	**Family Man**
Backpack	Backpack
Trekking poles	Trekking poles
Tent	Tent
Sleeping bag	Sleeping bag
Sleeping pad	Sleeping pad
1st aid kit	Water filter
LED Headlamp	LED Headlamp
Ice Axe	Ice Axe
Knife	Knife
Spork (Spoon /Fork)	Spork (Spoon/Fork)
Toilet Paper	Jetboil
Hydration System	Hydration System
Smart Phone (GPS/Camera)	Paper Maps
Goal Zero Solar Charger	Kodak Sports Camera
Poncho	Poncho
Wash Cloth	Wash Cloth
Duct Tape	Duct Tape

Clothing (Varied from section to section based on individual preference)

Convertible hiking pants
Lightweight fast drying shirt (the second half we just got cheap shirts at thrift stores)
Two pair of boxers
Three pair of wool socks
Lightweight shorts
T-Shirt
Frogg Toggs rain gear (switched with ponchos based on forecast weather)
Hanky

Maps

PCT Half-miler paper   PCT Half-miler iPhone
Guthook iPhone

Data

Total Days – 154
Zero Days – 26
Nero Days (Less than 10 Miles) – 12
10 – Less than 20 Mile Days – 42
20 – Less than 30 Mile Days – 56
30 – Less than 40 Mile Days – 17
One 40 Mile Day on July 31st

Average miles per day overall – 17.33
Average miles per day hiking – 20.86

Total feet of climb – 489,417
Highest climb for one day – 9700 feet (September 2nd)
Total feet of descent – 488,409
Highest amount of descent in one day – 10,090 feet (September 2nd)

Nights in the RV – 37
Nights in Hotels - 6
Nights with Trail Angels – 2
Nights in tent – 77
Nights at home – 16
Nights Cowboy Camping – 16

CPSIA information can be obtained
at www.ICGtesting.com
Printed in the USA
BVOW11s1755050517

483061BV00006B/67/P